Droid™ X2

FOR DUMMIES®

Droid™ X2 FOR DUMMIES®

by Dan Gookin

WILEY
John Wiley & Sons, Inc.

Droid™ X2 For Dummies®

Published by
John Wiley & Sons, Inc.
111 River Street
Hoboken, NJ 07030-5774

www.wiley.com

Published by John Wiley & Sons, Inc., Indianapolis, Indiana

Published simultaneously in Canada

For general information on our other products and services, please contact our Customer Care Department within the U.S. at 877-762-2974, outside the U.S. at 317-572-3993, or fax 317-572-4002.

For technical support, please visit www.wiley.com/techsupport.

Wiley also publishes its books in a variety of electronic formats and by print-on-demand. Not all content that is available in standard print versions of this book may appear or be packaged in all book formats. If you have purchased a version of this book that did not include media that is referenced by or accompanies a standard print version, you may request this media by visiting http://booksupport.wiley.com. For more information about Wiley products, visit us at www.wiley.com.

Library of Congress Control Number is available from the Publisher.

ISBN 978-1-118-14864-8 (pbk); ISBN 978-1-118-16470-9 (ebk); ISBN 978-1-118-16471-6 (ebk); ISBN 978-1-118-16472-3 (ebk)

Manufactured in the United States of America

10 9 8 7 6 5 4 3 2 1

About the Author

Dan Gookin has been writing about technology for over 20 years. He combines his love of writing with his gizmo fascination to create books that are informative, entertaining, and not boring. Having written more than 120 titles, with 12 million copies in print translated into over 30 languages, Dan can attest that his method of crafting computer tomes seems to work.

Perhaps his most famous title is the original *DOS For Dummies,* published in 1991. It became the world's fastest-selling computer book, at one time moving more copies per week than the *New York Times* #1 bestseller (though as a reference, it could not be listed on the NYT Bestseller list). From that book spawned the entire line of *For Dummies* books, which remains a publishing phenomenon to this day.

Dan's most popular titles include *PCs For Dummies, Word For Dummies*, *Laptops For Dummies*, and *Droid X For Dummies.* He also maintains the vast and helpful web site, `www.wambooli.com`.

Dan holds a degree in Communications/Visual Arts from the University of California, San Diego. Presently, he lives in the Pacific Northwest, where he enjoys spending time with his sons playing video games inside while they watch the gentle woods of Idaho.

Publisher's Acknowledgments

We're proud of this book; please send us your comments at http://dummies.custhelp.com. For other comments, please contact our Customer Care Department within the U.S. at 877-762-2974, outside the U.S. at 317-572-3993, or fax 317-572-4002.

Some of the people who helped bring this book to market include the following:

Acquisitions and Editorial

Project Editor: Susan Pink

Acquisitions Editor: Katie Mohr

Copy Editor: Susan Pink

Technical Editor: Stephen Worden

Editorial Manager: Jodi Jensen

Editorial Assistant: Amanda Graham

Sr. Editorial Assistant: Cherie Case

Cover Photo: ©istockphoto.com / 4x6; ©istockphoto.com/Konstantin Inozemtsev

Cartoons: Rich Tennant (www.the5thwave.com)

Composition Services

Project Coordinator: Kristie Rees

Layout and Graphics: Samantha K. Cherolis, Lavonne Roberts

Proofreader: Linda Seifert

Indexer: Steve Rath

Publishing and Editorial for Technology Dummies

Richard Swadley, Vice President and Executive Group Publisher

Andy Cummings, Vice President and Publisher

Mary Bednarek, Executive Acquisitions Director

Mary C. Corder, Editorial Director

Publishing for Consumer Dummies

Kathy Nebenhaus, Vice President and Executive Publisher

Composition Services

Debbie Stailey, Director of Composition Services

Contents at a Glance

Table of Contents

Introduction

To call the Motorola Droid X2 *another* cell phone is to do the gizmo a disservice. Sure, it can make phone calls. More than that, though, it's a portable technology marvel. As such, the Droid X2 can be a daunting device. In fact, I know a lot of people who shy away from using their cell phones beyond using its basic phone features simply because of the complexity. That's sad.

The factor that's probably most intimidating about the Droid X2 is that it's a *smart*phone. People don't like using devices that they believe are smarter than they are. But — trust me on this one — it isn't the phone that's smart.

Nope, even though the Droid X2 is an amazing piece of technology, it harbors no native intelligence. The only way to prove it to you is to write a book explaining how the Droid X2 works and do it in an informative, relaxing, and often humorous manner, which is exactly what this book does.

About This Book

This book is a reference. I don't intend for you to read it from cover to cover. In fact, I forbid you to do so.

Each chapter is written as its own, self-contained unit, covering a specific topic about using the Droid X2 phone. The chapters are further divided into sections representing a task you perform with the phone or explaining how to get something done. Sample sections in this book include

- Typing on the Droid X2
- Receiving a new call when you're on the phone
- Setting up a Google Voice account
- Uploading a picture to Facebook
- Listening to FM radio
- Dialing an international number
- Saving battery life

You have nothing to memorize, no mysterious utterances, no animal sacrifices, and definitely no PowerPoint presentations. Instead, every section explains a topic as though it's the first thing you read in this book. Nothing is assumed, and everything is cross-referenced. Technical terms and topics, when they come up, are neatly shoved to the side, where they're easily avoided. The idea here isn't to learn anything. This book's philosophy is to help you look it up, figure it out, and get back to your life.

How to Use This Book

This book follows a few conventions for using your phone, so pay attention!

The main way you interact with your phone is by using its *touchscreen,* which is the glassy part of the phone as it's facing you. Buttons also adorn the Droid X2, all of which are explained in Part I.

The various ways you can touch the screen are described in Chapter 3.

Chapter 4 discusses text input on the Droid X2, which involves using an onscreen keyboard. New to many smartphones in addition to the Droid X2, the Swype keyboard is featured for superfast text entry. And, when you tire of typing, you can always input text on your Droid X2 by dictation.

This book directs you to do things on your phone by following numbered steps. Each step involves a specific activity, such as touching something on the screen. For example:

3. Choose Downloads.

This step directs you to touch the text or item on the screen labeled Downloads. You might also be told to do this:

3. Touch Downloads.

Some phone options can be turned off or on, as indicated by a gray box with a green check mark in it, as shown in the margin. By touching the box on the screen, you add or remove the green check mark. When the green check mark appears, the option is on; otherwise, it's off.

You can use the barcodes, known as QR codes, in the margins to install recommended apps. To install an app, scan its barcode using special software you install on the Droid X2. Chapter 18 discusses how to add software to your phone, and in Chapter 26 you'll find information on how to use the Barcode Scanner app. You can use the app to read the barcodes.

Foolish Assumptions

Even though this book is written with the gentle handholding required by anyone who is just starting out, or who is easily intimidated, or who may be sick of constantly asking younger people how technology works, I have made a few assumptions. For example, I assume that you're a human being and not merely a cleverly disguised owl.

This book covers the Motorola Droid X2 phone. That's a big assumption. You can have other Android phones and still use this book, though the text and illustrations are specific to the Droid X2.

This book also covers the original Droid X phone, providing that the phone has been updated to the Gingerbread version of the Android operating system. To confirm that upgrade, at the Home screen press the Menu soft button and choose Settings. Then choose About Phone. Beneath the heading Android version, you should see the number 2.2.2. If you see 2.2.1, your Droid X has not yet been updated.

Any differences between the Droid X2 and original Droid X are noted in the text. Otherwise, you can assume that any time I refer to the Droid X2 I'm also referring to the original Droid X phone as well.

Cellular service for the Droid X2 is provided by Verizon in the United States, and some of the information in this book is specific to that carrier.

I also assume that you have a computer, either a desktop or laptop. The computer can be a PC or Windows computer or a Macintosh. Oh, I suppose it could also be a Linux computer. In any event, I refer to your computer as "your computer" throughout this book. When directions are specific to a PC or Mac, the book says so.

Programs that run on the Droid X are *apps*, which is short for *applications.* A single program is an *app*.

Finally, this book doesn't assume that you have a Google account, but already having one helps. Information is provided in Chapter 2 about setting up a Google account — an extremely important part of using the Droid X2. Having a Google account opens up a slew of useful features, information, and programs that make using your Droid X2 phone more productive.

How This Book Is Organized

This book has been sliced into six parts, each of which describes a certain aspect of the Droid X2 or how it's used.

Part I: More Droid, More X

Part I serves as your introduction to the Droid X2. Chapters cover setup and orientation and familiarizing you with how the phone works. Part I is a good place to start, plus you discover things in this part that aren't obvious from just guessing how the phone works.

Part II: It's the Phone!

Nothing is more basic for a phone to do than make calls, which is the topic of the chapters in Part II. The Droid X2 can make calls, receive calls, and serve as an answering service for calls you miss. It also manages the names of all the people you know and even those you don't want to know but have to know anyway.

Part III: Other Ways to Stay in Touch

The Droid X2 is about more than just telephone communications. Part III explores other ways you can use your phone to stay in touch with people, browse the Internet, check your email, do your social networking, exchange text messages, and more.

Part IV: O What Your Phone Can Do!

Part IV explores those non-phone things that your phone can do. For example, your phone can find things on a map, give you verbal driving directions, take pictures, shoot videos, play music, play games, and do all sorts of wonderful things that no sane person would ever think that a phone could do. The chapters in this part of the book get you up to speed on those activities.

Part V: Specifics and Particulars

The chapters in Part V discuss a slate of interesting topics, from taking the phone overseas and making international calls to customizing and personalizing your Droid X2, to the necessary chores of maintenance and troubleshooting.

Part VI: The Part of Tens

Finally, this book ends with the traditional *For Dummies* Part of Tens, where each chapter lists ten items or topics. For the Droid X2, the chapters include tips, tricks, shortcuts, things to remember, plus a list of some of my favorite Droid X2 phone apps.

Icons Used in This Book

This icon flags useful, helpful tips or shortcuts.

This icon marks a friendly reminder to do something.

This icon marks a friendly reminder *not* to do something.

This icon alerts you to overly nerdy information and technical discussions of the topic at hand. Reading the information is optional, though it opens up a random yet prestigious talking point at the water cooler.

Where to Go from Here

Start reading! Observe the Table of Contents and find something that interests you. Or look up what puzzles you in the index. When those suggestions don't cut it, just start reading Chapter 1.

My email address is dgookin@wambooli.com. Yes, that's my real address. I reply to all the email I get, and you'll get a quick reply if you keep your question short and specific to this book. Although I do enjoy saying Hi, I cannot answer technical support questions, resolve billing issues, or help you troubleshoot your phone. Thanks for understanding.

You can also visit my web page for more information or as a diversion: www.wambooli.com.

Enjoy the book and your Droid X2!

Part I

More Droid, More X

"Okay antidote, antidote, what would an antidote app look like? You know, I still haven't got this Home screen the way I'd like it."

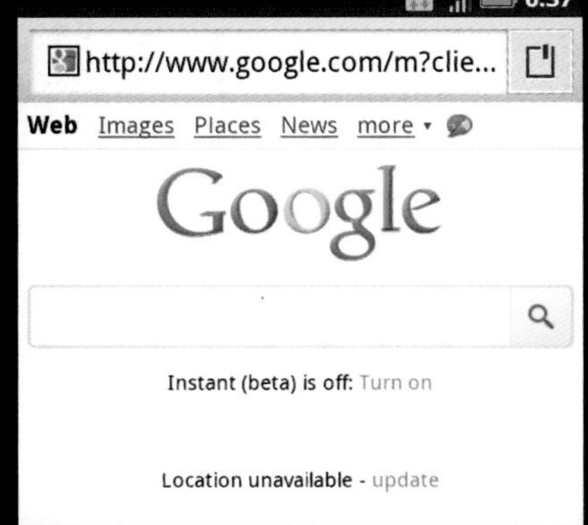

In this part . . .

Believe it or not, a stigma is attached to various letters of the alphabet. The best letter, by far, is A. It's the first letter, the number-one, the top-of-the-list. After all, they don't call it C1 Steak Sauce. The letter Z is reserved for use by aliens and bad guys in science fiction. But the letter X? It's cool. X-things are spiffy, wildly unknown, not too risky to be unsafe.

Obviously Motorola upped the ante by naming the latest version of their popular Droid phone the Droid X2. That's much better than the Droid Y, and definitely cooler than the Droid K. No, when it comes to names, the Droid X2 has a lot going for it. The only thing you need is a friendly, handholding introduction to the device, which is what you'll find in this part of the book.

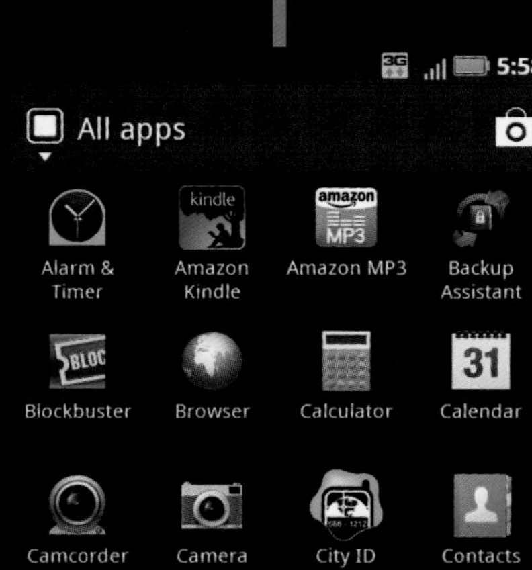

1

Twice the Droid X for You

In This Chapter

- Putting your phone together
- Charging the battery
- Identifying the phone's pieces and parts
- Taking the phone with you
- Keeping the phone in one place

The word *droid* comes from *android*, which is used in science fiction literature to refer to a robot in human form. That can be a scary thought, because such science fiction literature typically has the theme of those androids turning on their human masters, enslaving us all for our own good. That's not a happy thing.

You don't have to worry about your Droid X2 phone enslaving you. Truly, it's not evil, and it can be your favorite pal once you get over that whole "The androids are trying to kill us" thing. Your high-spirited adventure begins by freeing the phone from the confines of its box and doing some basic product orientation and identification.

Initial Droid X2 Setup

The cheerful folks at the Verizon Store most likely set up your Droid X2 for you. Heck, they probably ripped the thing from the box, installed the battery, and maybe even walked you through the setup. That happens, and it might be a good thing. Even so, this section goes over some basic setup operations.

Looking in the box

Take a moment to locate and identify each of these goodies found inside the Droid X2 box:

- The Droid X2 phone
- Miscellaneous papers, the instructions, the warranty, and perhaps the *Master Your Device* manuelette (if it reads *Domina Tu Aparato,* turn the thing over)
- The phone's battery and back cover (if the battery isn't installed)
- A micro-USB cable
- A power adapter

The Droid X2 ships with a plastic cling sheet over its screen, which tells you where various features are located. You can remove the plastic if you haven't already.

Other things that you may want are not included in the Droid X2 box. Those things include:

- A smart-looking, leatherette belt-clip phone jacket
- A micro-USB car charger
- A docking stand
- An HDMI cable
- Headphones
- A large gemstone or gold nugget

These items, as well as other phone accessories, may have been included as bonus gifts by the people who sold you the phone. The large gemstone or gold nugget is simply something I'd enjoy finding in a Verizon tote bag, though I don't seem to be that fortunate.

I recommend keeping the instructions and other information as long as you own the phone: The phone's box makes an excellent storage place for that stuff — as well as for anything else you don't plan to use right away.

If anything is missing or appears to be damaged, contact the people who sold you the phone. The Droid X2 does come with a warranty, and most phone stores have a return policy if you're just completely grumpy about the phone.

Installing the phone's battery

When your phone comes disassembled inside its box, your first duty as a new Droid X2 owner is to install the battery. Your second duty is to charge the battery. Installing the battery is easy, and charging it doesn't require a lightning storm, Transylvanian castle, and 1930s lab equipment.

Install the battery by following these steps:

1. **Ensure that the phone is turned off.**

   Obviously if the battery isn't yet installed, you can pretty much be guaranteed that the phone is turned off. Otherwise, see Chapter 2 for information on turning off the phone.

2. **Flip the phone over so that the front (the glassy part) is facing away from you.**
3. **Disconnect any cables or the headset, if they're attached.**
4. **If necessary, remove the back cover: Place both thumbs on the center part of the back cover and gently slide the back cover downward using your thumbs. Lift the back cover and set it aside.**

   A gentle push is all that's required; feel free to squeeze the phone as you push downward. The back cover slides down a wee bit, about ⅛ of an inch.

5. **If you have a new phone and the battery hasn't yet been installed, unwrap the battery and the phone's back cover.**

   Toss out the plastic wrapping.

6. **Orient the battery so that its metallic contacts are in the lower-right corner as you're looking at the back of the phone.**

   The battery is shaped like a giant, square mint cookie, the fudgy kind that the doctor advised you not to eat.

7. **Insert the bottom edge of the battery first, and then lower the top edge like you're closing the lid on a tiny box.**

   See Figure 1-1 for help in positioning and inserting the battery. Its metal contacts should be on the lower-right edge as you insert the battery into the phone.

   When the battery is fully inserted, it snaps into place. The back of the battery is flush with the back of the phone; it doesn't stick up, not one itty bit.

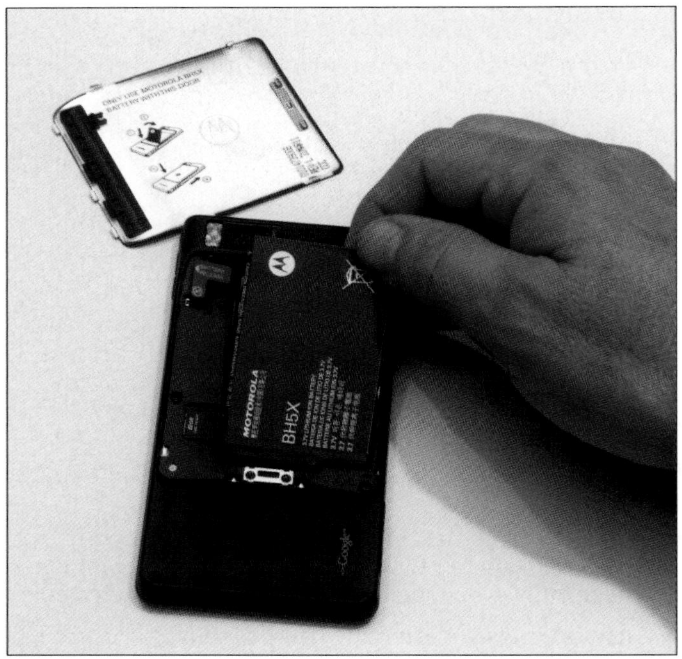

Figure 1-1: Inserting the phone's battery.

8. **Replace the phone's back cover.**

   The cover has four prongs that slide into four slots on the back of the phone. Position the cover over the slots and it falls into place. Then slide up the cover with your thumbs until it snaps into place.

After the battery is installed, the next step is to charge it. Continue reading in the next section.

Charging the battery

Forget the science and technical terms. To charge your phone's battery, follow these two steps:

1. **Plug the phone's power adapter into a wall socket.**

   Ensure that the power adapter is connected to the USB cable, which was included in the Droid X2 box.

2. **Plug the phone into the USB cable.**

   The cable connects to the phone's micro-USB hole, found on the phone's left side. The cable plugs in only one way.

As the phone charges, the notification light on the phone's front side glows. When the light is orange-yellow, the phone is charging. When the light is green, the phone is fully charged.

- When the phone is turned on while charging, you'll see the percentage that the battery is charged displayed on the touchscreen, such as *Charging (60%)*.
- The notification light uses three colors: amber for charging, green for fully charged, and red as the near-death battery-low warning light.
- You can use the phone while it's charging.
- The Droid X2 uses any standard cell phone charger that has a micro-USB connector.

- You can charge the Droid X2 in your car, assuming that you have a car cell phone charger that features a micro-USB connector. The folks at the Phone Store would be delighted to sell you such a contraption.
- The phone also charges itself when it's plugged into a computer using a USB cable. The computer must be on for charging to work.

- A micro-USB connector has a flat, trapezoid shape, which makes it different from the mini-USB connector, which is squat and slightly larger and used primarily on evil cell phones.

Droid X2 Orientation

No one dials a phone any more. I mean, phones don't really have dials, do they? It's like saying that you "roll down the windows" in your car. Unless you bought the bottom-line cheap car, you probably have power windows. (Although, in my Jeep, I have to unzip the windows.)

The Droid X2 has no dial. It has only a few buttons. And lots of other, mysterious crevasses and bumps are on the thing. To better know the purposes of all those greeblies, as well as their proper nomenclature, peruse this section.

Knowing what's what on your phone

To help you understand the intimidating onslaught of Droid X2 features and doodads, I present Figure 1-2, which illustrates interesting things found on the front of your phone. Figure 1-3 provides the same service, but for your phone's butt.

Figure 1-2: Your phone's face.

The terms referenced in both Figures 1-2 and 1-3 are the same as the ones used elsewhere in this book, as well as in whatever scant Droid X2 documentation exists.

- The phone's Power Lock button is found on top of the phone, as shown in Figures 1-2 and 1-3. See Chapter 2 for details on how it's used.
- The main part of the phone is the *touchscreen* display. You use the touchscreen with one or more of your fingers to control the phone, which is where it gets the name *touch*screen.
- *Soft buttons* appear below the touchscreen (refer to Figure 1-2). Some documentation may refer to these buttons as *keys*. They have no function unless the phone is turned on.
- Yes, the main microphone is on the bottom of the phone. Even so, it still picks up your voice, loud and clear. You don't need to hold the phone at an angle for the bottom microphone to work.

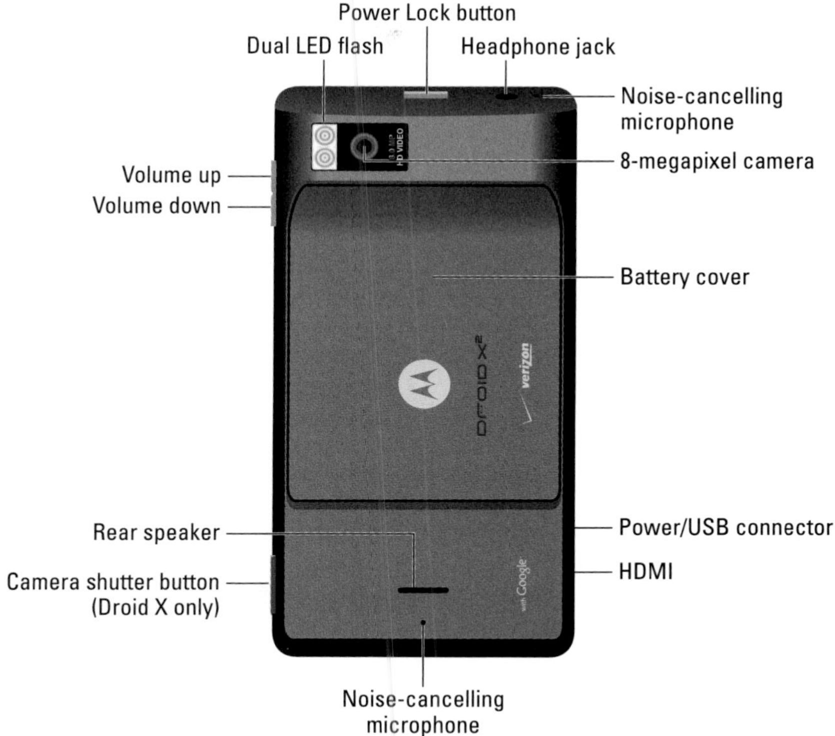

Figure 1-3: Your phone's rump.

- The two bonus microphones (refer to Figure 1-3) are for noise-cancelling purposes. They help reduce background noise, which means that you hear people on the phone more clearly and they hear you more clearly. You do not speak into the noise-cancelling microphones.
- The rear speaker is designed for video and other audio playback.
- You adjust the phone's volume by using the Volume button on the phone's right side (refer to Figure 1-2).
- The Volume button also serves as a Zoom function when using the Droid X2 as a camera. See Chapter 14 for additional details.
- The Droid X2, unlike the original Droid X, does not feature a camera shutter button.
- Yes, the Droid X2 lacks a physical keyboard. Instead, an onscreen keyboard is used, as covered in Chapter 4.

Listening with earphones

The nice people who sold you the Droid X2 might have tossed in a set of earbud-style earphones for you to use. If not, well then, they weren't that nice, were they? But that's not a reason to give up on the concept of using earphones or another form of headset.

You're probably familiar with earbud-type earphones: The buds are set into your ears. The sharp, pointy end of each earphone — what you don't want to stick into your ear — goes into the top of the phone.

Between the earbuds and the sharp, pointy thing is often found a control noodle on which a button sits. The button can be used to mute the phone or to start or stop playback of music when the Droid X2 is in its music-playing mode.

You can also use the control noodle to answer the phone when it rings.

Usually, a teensy hole on the back side of the noodle serves as the phone's microphone. The hole allows you to use the earphones as a hands-free headset with the Droid X2.

- You can purchase any cell phone headset for use with the Droid X2. Any standard earphones work, though some headsets may feature noodle buttons that may not work on the Droid X2.
- You want earphones that have a microphone. If you opt for the cheapest earphones, they probably don't have a microphone, which doesn't help.
- The earbuds are labeled R for right and L for left.
- You don't use the earphone's noodle to set the phone's volume, either in a call or while you're listening to music. Instead, the phone's volume is set by using the Volume button on the side of the phone, as illustrated in Figures 1-2 and 1-3.
- See Chapter 16 for more information on using your Droid X2 as a portable music player.

- Be sure to fully insert the earphone connector into the phone. The person you're talking with cannot hear you well when the earphones are plugged in only part of the way.
- You can also use a Bluetooth headset with your phone, to listen to a call or some music. See Chapter 19 for more information on Bluetooth attachments for the Droid X2.

- I find it best to fold the earphones when I don't need them, as opposed to wrapping them up in a loop: Put the earbuds and connector in one hand and then pull the wire out straight with the other hand. Fold the wire in half, and then in half again. You can then put the earphones in your pocket or on a tabletop. By folding the wires, you avoid creating the wire-ball-of-Christmas-tree-lights that would otherwise happen.

Exploring your phone's guts

It rarely happens, but occasionally you may need to access your phone's innards. Unlike some other cell phones, the Droid X2 is designed to have easily replaceable items that you can get to without having to sneak around behind the manufacturer's back, pry open the phone, and alert the warranty police.

Specifically, you might need to open your phone for two reasons:

- To install or replace the battery
- To access the microSD memory card

When you need to access one of these items, you can obey these steps:

1. **Turn off your phone.**

   See the section "Turning off the phone" in Chapter 2 for more information.

2. **Flip the phone over.**
3. **Use your thumbs to slide down the upper-back cover.**
4. **Set aside the back cover.**

   Use Figure 1-4 to identify the phone's battery and the microSD memory card.

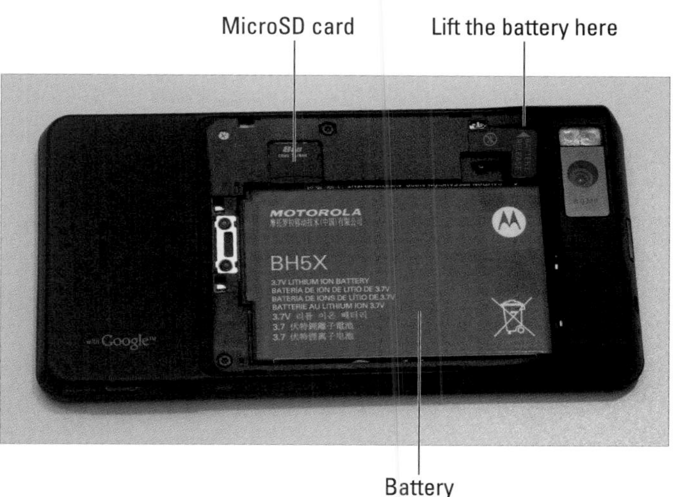

Figure 1-4: The guts of the Droid X2.

5. **To access the microSD card:**

   a. **First remove the battery by lifting the little tab illustrated in Figure 1-4.**

   b. **Remove the microSD card by sliding it to the right, toward the empty battery compartment. Pull the card all the way out until it's free.**

   When you're done rummaging around inside your phone, you close things up.

6. **Return the back cover to the phone; the little prongs on the cover fit into the four holes on either side of the phone.**

   The cover fits only one way.

7. **Slide up the cover until it snaps into position.**

You can turn on the phone again after the back cover is locked into place. See Chapter 2 for information on turning on your phone.

A SIM (subscriber identity module) card identifies the phone and does other things you need not care about. Other cell phones use one to access the cellular network, but the Droid X2 doesn't have or use a SIM card.

Using other phone accessories

The Droid X2 has available various optional accessories you can buy to enhance your mobile communications experience. In addition to a choice of cases, holsters, and charms, two accessories worth considering are the multimedia docking station and the car mount.

The multimedia docking station

In a nutshell, the *multimedia docking station* is a base into which you can set the phone. The station features both USB and HDMI connections so that the phone can recharge inside the docking station as well as communicate with a computer or share its touchscreen with an HD television set or monitor.

The multimedia docking station, which makes a helpful home for the phone (see the next section), can be used as a bedside alarm or, when connected to a stereo system, to delight you with its music.

- The multimedia docking station can be purchased at the same place where you obtained your Droid X2 or at any location where cell phone goodies are sold.
- The Droid X2 runs a special app when it's plugged into the docking station. That app typically displays a clock and the weather, plus it gives you quick access to the phone's music library.

- See Chapter 17 for more information about using your state-of-the-art cell phone as a digital clock.
- Chapter 16 covers playing music on the Droid X2.
- Viewing slideshows and managing pictures with the Droid X2 are covered in Chapter 15.

Car mount

The *car mount* has a cradle for the Droid X2 on one end and, when properly assembled, a suction cup on the other. You could probably stick it to any flat surface, but it's a *car* mount, so I assume that it will stick to the windshield or dashboard of your favorite auto.

When you stick the Droid X2 into the car mount, the phone automatically switches to the Car Dock screen, which provides you with quick access to handy phone features while you're operating a motor vehicle.

A car charger is also available for use with the car mount. It's one of those gizmos that plugs into what was once called a cigarette lighter. The other end of the car charger plugs into your Droid X2, which can be nestled in the car mount or just rattling loose inside your vehicle.

- Yes, you can use the car charger without having to use the car mount.
- For the suction cup on the car mount to work properly, use a hard, flat, smooth surface. An adhesive plastic disk comes with the car mount. Use it to ensure that the suction cup has a solid surface to suck on.

A Home for Your Phone

Where I grew up, the phone was always in the kitchen, on the wall. I remember that great day when my folks added a line in the living room — and then in the bedroom! You could even plug in an extension cord and take the phone outside to talk. Man, we were kings.

After charging the battery in your Droid X2, you can take it anywhere. Even so, I recommend keeping a home for your phone when you're not roaming about, even if that home is in your purse or pocket.

Carrying the Droid X2

The Droid X2 can still fit into a pocket or even the teensiest of party purses. It's well designed, so you can carry your phone in your pocket or purse without fear that something will accidentally turn it on, dial Mongolia, and run up a heck of a phone bill.

Because the Droid X2 features a proximity sensor, you can keep the phone in your pocket while you're on a call or listening to music on headphones. The proximity sensor disables the touchscreen, which ensures that nothing accidentally is activated when you don't want it to be.

- Although it's okay to place the phone somewhere when you're making a call, be careful not to touch the phone's Power Lock button (refer to Figure 1-3). Doing so may temporarily enable the touchscreen, which can hang up a call or mute the phone or do any of a number of other undesirable things.
- You can always store the Droid X2 in one of a variety of handsome carrying-case accessories, some of which come in fine Naugahyde or leatherette.

- Don't forget that the phone is in your pocket, especially when it's in your coat or jacket. You might accidentally sit on the phone, or it can fly out when you take off your coat. The worst fate for the Droid X2, or any cell phone, is to take a trip through the wash. I'm sure the phone has nightmares about it happening.

Storing the Droid X2

I recommend that you find a place for your phone when you're not taking it with you. Make the spot consistent: on top of your desk or workstation, in the kitchen, on the nightstand — you get the idea. Phones are as prone to loss as your car keys and glasses, so consistency is the key to keeping and finding your phone in one spot.

Then again, your phone does ring, so when you lose it, you can always have someone else call your number to help you locate the phone.

- I keep the Droid X2 on my desk, next to my computer. Conveniently, I have the charger plugged into the computer, so I keep it plugged in, connected, and charging when I'm not using it.
- Phones on coffee tables get buried under magazines and often squished when rude people put their feet on the furniture.
- Avoid putting the Droid X2 in direct sunlight; heat is a bad thing for any electronic gizmo.
- Do not wash your phone in the laundry (see the preceding section). See Chapter 23 for information on properly cleaning the phone.

2

Setup, Power, and Configuration

In This Chapter

- Turning on the phone
- Waking up the Droid X2
- Setting up your Google account
- Putting the phone to sleep
- Turning off your phone

The Droid X2 is possibly the most sophisticated phone you've ever owned, far more complex than the popular shoe phone from the 1960s TV series *Get Smart*. Saying the Droid X2 is just a phone is to do the gizmo a disservice. No, it's a *communications device*. It chats with the Internet, pays attention to satellites orbiting the earth, takes pictures and video, plays music, and does lots more things that I write about elsewhere in this book.

To make things work in your phone requires a modicum of setup. The setup is not that difficult but also not that obvious. This chapter helps you set up the options on your Droid X2 and describes the basic steps for turning it on and off.

©PhotoDisc/Getty Images

Hello, Phone

One of the most basic operations for any gizmo is turning it on. Don't bother looking for an on-off switch: The Droid X2 doesn't have one. Instead, it has a *Power Lock* button. It can be used in several ways, which is why I had to write this section to explain things.

Before you can turn on the phone, the battery must be installed. See Chapter 1.

Turning on the Droid X2 for the first time

To turn on the Droid X2 for the first time, press the Power Lock button. You may need to press and hold the button for a few moments. When the Motorola logo appears, you can stop pressing the button.

As the phone starts, you see some fancy graphics and animation. After a moment, you hear the phone say, in a robotic voice, "Droid!" Don't be alarmed. Well, at least that greeting is better than when you turn on one of those inexpensive phones and it greets you with, "You cheapskate."

When you turn on your phone the first time, you have to do some setup. This step was most likely completed at the Phone Store when you first got the phone. If not, work through the steps as presented on the screen.

It's perfectly acceptable to touch the Skip button during the first-time setup. You can do later anything you skip, such as setting up your Google account, configuring the Backup Assistant, and other annoying things.

After the initial setup, whether you plodded through it or chose to skip things, you're taken to the Home screen. Chapter 3 offers more information about the Home screen, which you should probably read right away, before the temptation to play with the Droid X2 becomes unbearable.

- The most important thing to configure on your Droid X2 is the Google account. See the later section "Google Account Setup."

- You may also be prompted for first-time setup information if you perform a factory data reset, which is a drastic step. See Chapter 23 for more information on resetting the phone's software.

Turning on the phone

Unlike turning on the phone for the first time, turning it on after that isn't complex. In fact, you probably won't turn off the phone much under normal circumstances.

To turn on the Droid X2, press and hold the Power Lock button. After a moment, you'll see the Motorola logo on the touchscreen. Release the Power Lock button, sit back, and watch the phone start.

Eventually, you're plopped into an unlocking screen.

The main unlocking screen is shown in Figure 2-1. To access your phone, use your finger to slide the white padlock icon to the right.

If you've added more security, you'll next see one of three additional unlocking screens: pattern lock, PIN lock, or password lock.

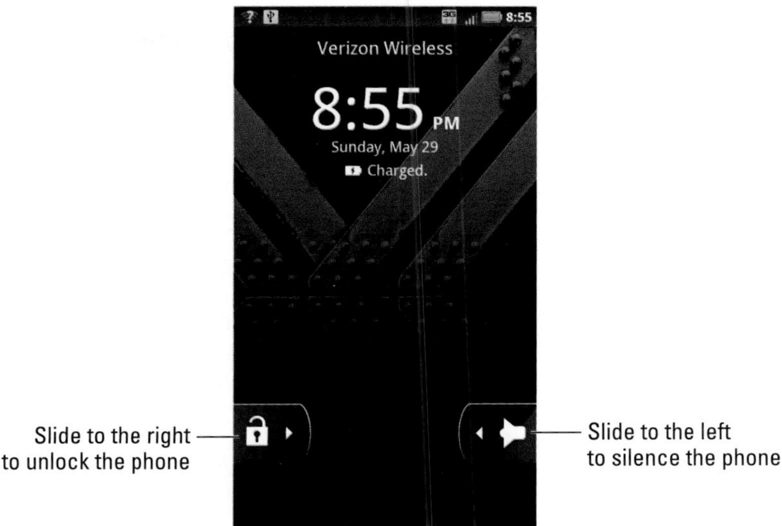

Figure 2-1: Unlocking the phone.

The pattern lock is shown in Figure 2-2. Drag your finger over the dots on the screen, duplicating the pattern you've preset. Only by dragging over the dots in the proper sequence does the phone unlock.

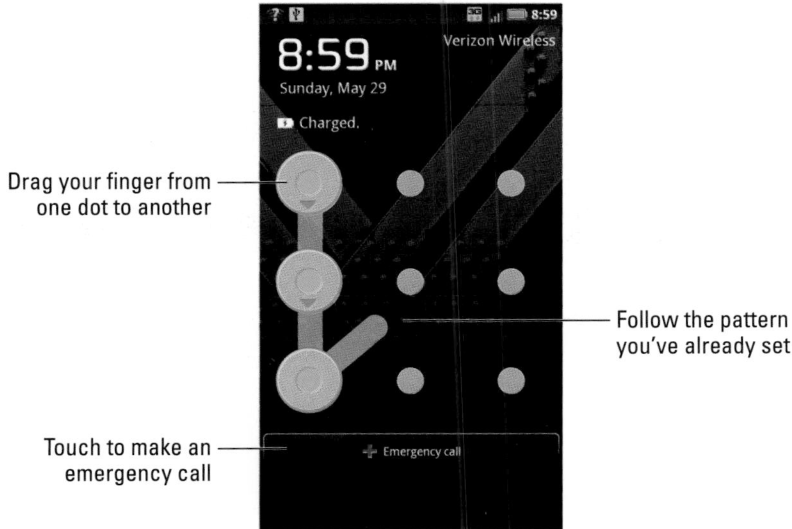

Figure 2-2: Inputting the phone's security pattern.

Another type of unlocking screen uses a *PIN,* or secret number, which must be input before you're allowed access to the phone. Type the number using the keypad. Touch the Return button to accept, as shown in Figure 2-3.

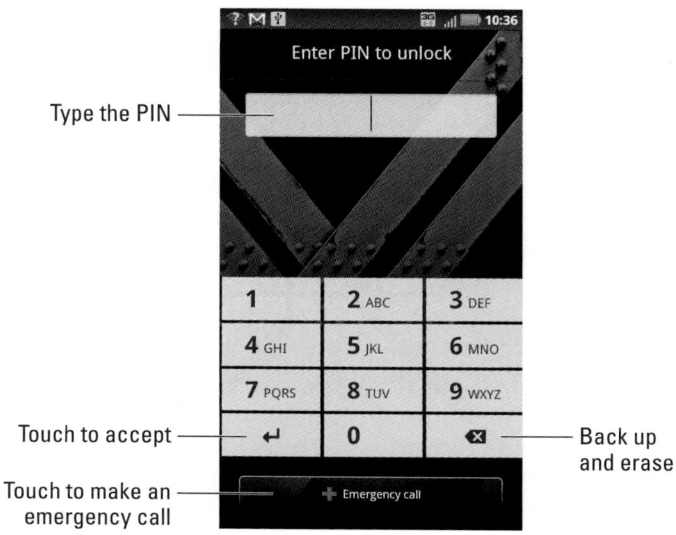

Figure 2-3: Typing the phone's PIN.

There may also be a password unlock screen, where you need to use the onscreen keyboard to type a password, just as you type a password to get into your computer or log in to a web site.

Eventually you see the Home screen, which is where you control the phone and run applications and do all sorts of other interesting things. The Home screen is covered in Chapter 3.

- After unlocking the phone, you may hear some alerts or see notifications. These messages inform you of various events going on in the phone, such as new email, scheduled appointments, and updates. See Chapter 3 for information on notifications.
- The locking screens (refer to Figures 2-2 and 2-3) add an extra level of protection in case the phone is ever lost or stolen. You can choose the pattern lock, a PIN, or password. See Chapter 22.
- Even if the phone has a locking screen, you can still make emergency calls by touching the Emergency Call button.
- For information on turning off the phone, see the section "Turning off the phone," later in this chapter.

There's an android in your phone

You might see or hear the term *android* used in association with your phone. That's because your phone, like your computer, has an *operating system,* the main program in charge of a computer's hardware. The operating system controls everything. On the Droid X2, the operating system is Android.

The Android operating system was developed by Google. Well, actually, it was developed by another company, which Google gobbled. Anyway: Android is based on the popular Linux operating system, used to power desktop computers and larger, more expensive computers all over the world. Android offers a version of Linux customized for mobile devices, such as the Droid X2, but also tablets as well as many other mobile devices I can't name off the top of my head.

Because the Droid X2 uses the Android operating system, your phone has access to thousands of software programs. The process of putting these programs on your phone is covered in Chapter 18.

Waking the phone

Most of the time, you don't turn off your phone. Instead, the phone does the electronic equivalent of falling asleep. Either it falls asleep on its own (after you've ignored it for a while) or you put it to sleep by singing it a lullaby or following the information in the section "Snoozing the phone," later in this chapter.

In sleep mode, the phone is still on and can still receive calls (as well as email and other notifications), but the touchscreen is turned off. See Chapter 5 for specifics on receiving a call on the Droid X2.

When the phone isn't ringing, you can wake it up at any time by pressing the Power Lock button. A simple, short press is all that's needed. The phone wakes up, yawns, and turns on the touchscreen display, and you can then unlock the phone, as described in the preceding section.

- Touching the touchscreen when it's off doesn't wake the phone.
- Pressing the Home soft button (shown in the margin) wakes the phone, though none of the other soft buttons wakes the phone.

- Loud noises don't wake the phone.

- The phone doesn't snore while it's sleeping.
- See the section "Snoozing the phone," later in this chapter, for information on manually putting the phone to sleep.
- When the Droid X2 is playing music, which it can do while it's sleeping, information about the song appears on the unlocking screen (not shown in Figure 2-1). You also find controls to play and pause or to skip to the next or previous song. See Chapter 16 for more information on using the Droid X2 to play music.

Google Account Setup

After initially turning on your phone and getting things configured, you're ready to go. Well, unless you opted to skip the Google account setup step. Having a Google account on your Droid X2 is very important. It's something that needs to be done to get the most from your phone. Follow along in this section and you'll be set up and running in no time.

Obtaining a Google account if you don't already have one

If you don't yet have a Google account, run — don't walk or mince — to a computer and follow these steps to create your own Google account.

1. **Open the computer's web browser program.**
2. **Visit the main Google page at `www.google.com`.**

   Type **www.google.com** on the web browser's address bar.
3. **Click the Sign In link.**

   Another page opens, where you can log in to your Google account. You don't have a Google account, so:
4. **Click the link to create a new account.**

   The link is typically found below the text boxes where you would log in to your Google account. As I write this chapter, the link is labeled Create an Account Now.
5. **Continue heeding the directions until you've created your own Google account.**

Eventually, your account is set up and configured. I recommend that you log off and then log back in to Google, just to ensure that you did everything properly. Also, create a bookmark for your account's Google page: Pressing Ctrl+D or Command+D does that job in just about any web browser.

Continue reading in the next section for information on synchronizing your new Google account with the Droid X2.

- A Google account is free. Google makes bazillions of dollars by selling advertising on the Web, so it doesn't charge you for your Google account or any of the fine services it offers.
- A Google account gives you access to a wide array of free services and online programs. They include Gmail for electronic messaging, Calendar for scheduling and appointments, the online picture-sharing program Picasa, an account on YouTube, Google Finance, blogs, Google Buzz, Google Latitude, and other features that are instantly shared with your phone.
- Information on using the various Google programs on your phone is covered throughout this book; specifically, in Part IV.

Setting up a Google account on your Droid X2

If you haven't yet configured a Google account, follow the steps in the preceding section and then continue with these steps:

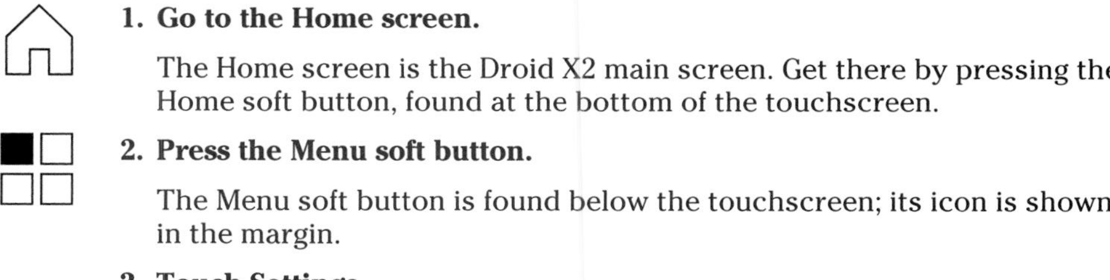

1. **Go to the Home screen.**

   The Home screen is the Droid X2 main screen. Get there by pressing the Home soft button, found at the bottom of the touchscreen.

2. **Press the Menu soft button.**

   The Menu soft button is found below the touchscreen; its icon is shown in the margin.

3. **Touch Settings.**

   The Settings window is where you configure many of the Droid X2 features and options.

4. **Choose Accounts.**
5. **Touch the Add Account button.**
6. **Choose Google.**
7. **Avoid reading the screen and quickly touch the Next button.**
8. **If you've already read the preceding section and have created your Google account on a computer, touch the Sign In button.**

   Yes, it's possible to create a Google account using your phone and not a computer. It's just easier to use a computer. Trust me.

9. **Touch the Username text box.**

   The onscreen keyboard appears.

10. **Type your Google account username.**

    Touch the Shift key on the keyboard to get capital letters. Touch the ?123 key to see numbers and symbols. Refer to Chapter 4 for detailed information on using the Droid X2's onscreen keyboard.

11. **Touch the Password text box.**

12. **Type your Google account password.**

    Each character you type appears briefly, but is then replaced by a black dot. The dot is for security purposes, so watch what you type!

13. **Touch the Sign In button.**

    If you need to, click the Done button on the onscreen keyboard so that you can see and touch the Sign In button.

14. **Ensure that there is a check mark by the option Back Up Data with My Google Account.**

    If not, touch the box to place a green check mark there.

15. **Touch the Next button.**

16. **Touch the Finish Setup button.**

    Wait while Google contacts your account and synchronizes any information. It takes longer when you have more information for Google to synchronize.

    And you're done.

After you're done, you're returned to the My Accounts window. You can press the Home soft button to return to the Home screen.

- If you change your Google password and forget to tell the phone about it, you'll see an alert notification on the Droid X2, as shown in the margin. Pull down the notifications and choose the Sign In Error for your Google account. Follow the directions on the screen to update your Google password.
- See Chapter 3 for more information about the Home screen.
- You can also add other accounts for synchronizing, such as Facebook, Twitter, and Skype Mobile. Other chapters in this book cover the specifics.

Goodbye, Phone

You can dismiss your Droid X2 from existence in three ways. The first way is to put the phone to sleep — to *snooze* it. The second is to turn off the phone. The third involves a blindfold and a foreign firing squad, but that method has yet to be approved by the FCC, so it isn't covered in this edition of the book.

Snoozing the phone

To snooze the phone, press and release the Power Lock button. No matter what you're doing, the phone's display turns off. The phone itself isn't off, but the touchscreen goes dark. The phone enters a low-power state to save battery life, and also to relax.

- You can snooze the phone while you're making a call. Simply press and release the Power Lock button. The phone stays connected, but the display is turned off.
- Snooze mode allows you to keep talking on the phone while you put it in your pocket. In snooze mode, there's no danger that your pocket will accidentally hang up or mute the phone in the middle of a call.

- Your Droid X2 will probably spend most of its time in snooze mode.
- Snoozing doesn't turn off the phone; you can still receive calls while it's asleep.
- Any timers or alarms you set still activate when the phone is snoozing. See Chapter 17 for information on setting timers and alarms.
- To wake up the phone, press and release the Power Lock button. See the section "Waking the phone," earlier in this chapter.
- Snoozing the phone doesn't stop any music from playing. See Chapter 16 for more information on using the Droid X2 as a portable music player.

Controlling snooze options

There's no need to manually snooze your Droid X2. That's because it has a built-in timeout: After a period of inactivity, or boredom, the phone snoozes itself automatically — just like Uncle Walt after Thanksgiving dinner.

You have control over the snooze timeout value, which can be set anywhere from 15 seconds to 30 minutes. Obey these steps:

1. **While viewing the Home screen, press the Menu soft button.**
2. **Choose Settings from the menu.**
3. **Choose Display.**

4. **Choose Screen Timeout.**
5. **Select a timeout value from the list provided.**

   The standard duration is 1 minute.

6. **Press the Home soft button to return to the Home screen.**

When you don't touch the screen or use the phone for a while, the sleep timer starts ticking. A few seconds before the timeout value you set (refer to Step 4), the touchscreen dims. Then it goes to sleep. If you touch the screen before then, the sleep timer is reset.

Turning off the phone

To turn off your phone, follow these steps:

1. **Press and hold the Power Lock button.**

   Eventually, you see the Phone Options menu, shown in Figure 2-4.

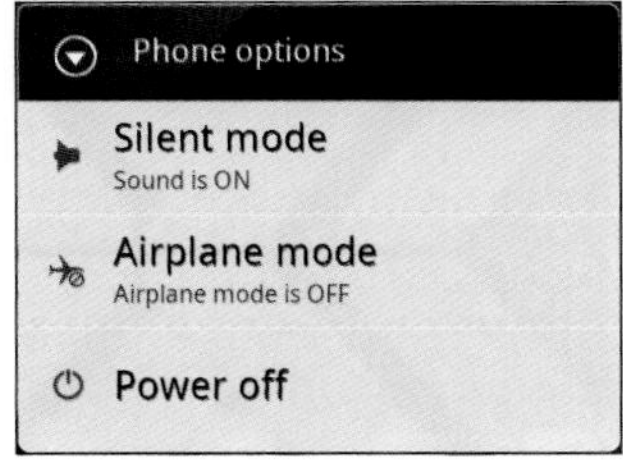

Figure 2-4: The Phone Options menu.

2. **Choose the Power Off item.**

   Off goes the phone, crying out "Droid" as it goes.

The phone doesn't receive calls when it's turned off. Those calls go instead to voice mail. See Chapter 7 for more information on voice mail.

If you change your mind and don't want to shut down the phone, press the Back soft button to cancel (after Step 1 in the preceding steps).

The original Droid X has an additional item on the Phone Options menu: Sleep. Choosing that option is as effective as turning the phone off, but with the advantage of it turning on faster the next time you press and hold the Power Lock button. See Chapter 21 for more information on how the Sleep command can be used.

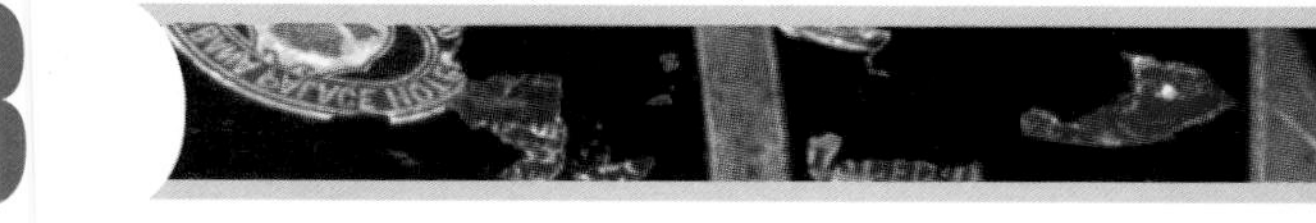

3

The Droid X2 Tour

In This Chapter

- Working the touchscreen
- Changing the phone's volume
- Entering vibration mode or silent mode
- Using the phone horizontally
- Checking notifications
- Running applications and working widgets
- Finding applications
- Accessing recently used apps

Do you remember when you first got your Droid X2? Do you remember how the person in the Phone Store showed you how the phone worked and how to use its basic features?

Me neither. That's why I wrote this chapter.

©ImageState

Some Basic Operations

The Droid X2 is most likely different from any other phone you've owned. As such, you should familiarize yourself with certain operations — basic things the phone does that you may not be aware of.

Using the soft buttons

Below the touchscreen are four buttons labeled with four icons. These *soft buttons* perform specific functions no matter what you're doing with the phone. Table 3-1 lists the soft-button functions.

Table 3-1 Droid X2 Soft-Button Functions

Button	*Name*	*Press Once*	*Press Twice*	*Press and Hold*
	Menu	Display menu	Dismiss menu	Nothing
	Home	Go to Home screen, display recent apps, view all Home screen panels, or wake the phone	Double-tap Home launch function	Recent applications
	Back	Go back, close, dismiss key-board	Nothing	Nothing
	Search	Open phone and web search	Nothing	Display Voice Actions menu/ Voice Search

Not every soft button always performs the actions listed in Table 3-1. For example, if there's no menu to open, pressing the Menu soft button does nothing.

Pressing the Home soft button always takes you to the main Home screen (the center one) — unless you're viewing the main Home screen, in which case pressing the Home soft button displays an overview of all seven Home screen panels. See the later section "Viewing all the Home screen panels" for more information.

Pressing the Home button twice activates the double-tap Home launch function. It's normally configured to do nothing, but you can direct the phone to run one of a smattering of apps by activating that function. Refer to Chapter 22 for more information.

Various sections throughout this book give examples of using the soft buttons.

Manipulating the touchscreen

The touchscreen works in combination with one or two of your fingers. You can choose which fingers to use, or whether to be adventurous and try using the tip of your nose, but touch the touchscreen you must. There are several techniques:

- **Touch:** In this simple operation, you touch the screen. Generally, you're touching an object, such as a program icon or a button, or a control, such as a gizmo you use to slide something around. You might also see the terms *press* or *tap* in addition to touch.
- **Double-tap:** Touch the screen in the same location twice. Double-tapping can be used to zoom in on an image or a map, but it can also zoom out. Because of the double-tap's dual nature, I recommend using the pinch or spread operation instead.
- **Long-press:** Touch and hold part of the screen. Some operations on the Droid X2, such as moving an icon on the Home screen, begin with a long press.
- **Swipe:** When you swipe, you start with your finger in one spot and then drag it to another spot. Swipes can be up, down, left, or right, which moves items displayed in the direction you swipe your finger. Swipes can be fast, flick-like actions, or they can be slow. This operation is also known as a *flick*.
- **Pinch:** A pinch involves two fingers, which start out separated and then are brought together. The effect is used to reduce an image or zoom out on a map or web page.
- **Spread:** The opposite of a pinch, you start out with your fingers together and then spread them. The spread is used to zoom in.
- **Rotate:** Use two fingers to twist around a central point on the touchscreen, which has the effect of rotating an object on the screen. If you have trouble with this operation, pretend that you're turning the dial on a safe.

You cannot use the touchscreen while wearing gloves, unless they're gloves specially designed for using an electronic touchscreen.

Setting the volume

The phone's volume control is found on the right side of the Droid X2 as it's facing you. Press the top part of the button to set the volume higher. Press the bottom part of the button to lower the volume.

The volume controls work for whatever noise the phone is making at the time: When you're on the phone, the volume controls set the level of the incoming phone call. When you're listening to music or watching a video, the volume controls set that media volume.

Volume can be preset for the phone, media, and notifications. See Chapter 22 for information.

"Silence your phone!"

You can't be a citizen of the 21st century and not have heard the admonition "Please silence your cell phones." Here's how to obey that command with your Droid X2 phone:

1. **Wake up the phone.**

   Obviously, if the phone is turned off, there's no need to turn it on just to make it silent. So, assuming that your phone is snoozing, press the Power Lock button to see the main screen (refer to Figure 2-1, in Chapter 2).

2. **Slide the Silencer button to the left.**

   You're good.

When you're using the phone and someone demands that you silence it, press and hold the Power Lock button until you see the Phone Options menu. From that menu, choose Silent Mode.

- Refer to Figure 2-1 in Chapter 2 for the location of the Silencer button.
- You can also silence the Droid X2 by setting the volume all the way down to zero: After you press the Volume down button one more time, the phone automatically enters vibration mode.

- When the phone is in vibration mode, the Vibration Mode status icon appears on the status bar, as shown in the margin.
- To make the phone noisy again, repeat the steps in this section.
- If you're concerned about missing a call, activate the phone's vibration mode. For details, see the section about setting incoming call signals in Chapter 5.

- When the phone is silenced but not in vibration mode, the Ringer Is Silenced icon appears on the status bar.
- Also see Chapter 22, which covers all the options for silencing the Droid X2, vibration mode, and all that noisy stuff.

Going horizontal

The Droid X2 features a gizmo called an *accelerometer*. It's used by various programs in the phone to determine in which direction the phone is pointed or whether you've reoriented the phone from an upright to a horizontal position or vice versa.

The easiest way to see how the vertical-horizontal orientation feature works is to view a web page on your Droid X2. Obey these steps:

1. **Touch the Browser application icon on the Home screen.**

   The Droid X2 launches its web browser program, venturing out to the Internet. Eventually, the browser's first page, its *home* page, appears on the touchscreen.

2. **Tilt the Droid X2 to the left.**

   As shown in Figure 3-1, the web page reorients itself to the new, horizontal way of looking at the web. For some applications, this method is truly the best way to see things.

3. **Tilt the phone upright again.**

   The web page redisplays itself in its original, upright mode.

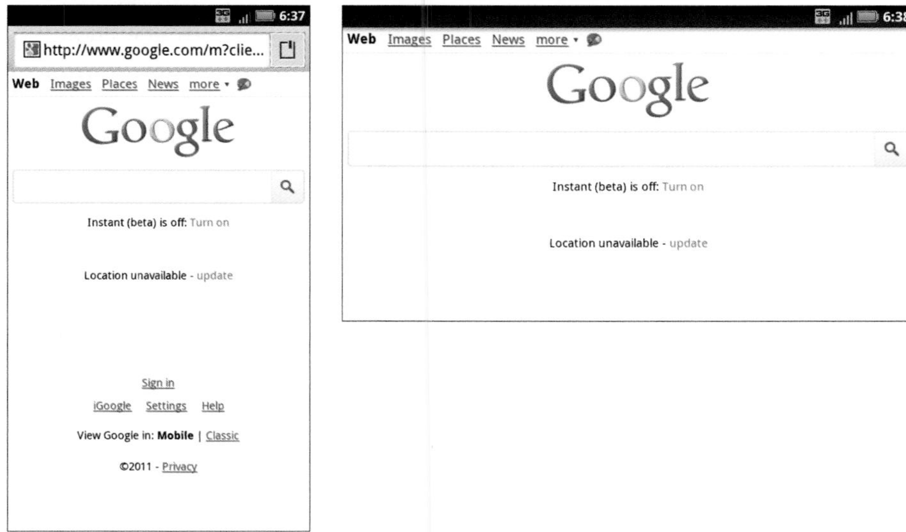

Figure 3-1: Vertical and horizontal orientations.

Landscape orientation works whether the phone is tilted to the left or the right. It does not work upside down — well, at least not in the Browser app.

- See Chapter 11 for more information on using your phone to browse the web.
- Some applications switch their view from portrait to landscape orientation whenever you tilt the phone. Other applications, however, appear only in portrait or landscape orientation, such as games.

- A great application for demonstrating the Droid X2 accelerometer is the game Labyrinth. You can purchase it at the Android Market or download the free version, Labyrinth Lite. See Chapter 18 for information on the Android Market.

There's No Screen Like Home

The first thing you see after you unlock your Droid X2 is the *Home* screen. It's also the place you'll return to when you quit an app, or anytime you press the Home soft button. Knowing how to work the Home screen is the key to getting the most from your Droid X2.

Looking at the Home screen

The main Home screen panel is illustrated in Figure 3-2. There are a few things to notice:

- **Status bar:** The top of the Home screen is a thin, informative strip I call the *status bar.* It contains notification icons and status icons, plus the current time.
- **Notification icons:** These icons come and go, depending on what happens in your digital life. For example, a new icon appears whenever you receive a new email message or have a pending appointment. The section "Reviewing notifications," later in this chapter, describes how to deal with notifications.
- **Status icons:** These icons represent the phone's current condition, such as the type of network it's connected to, its signal strength, and its battery status, as well as whether the speaker has been muted or a Wi-Fi network is connected.
- **Widgets:** A *widget* is a teensy program that can display information, let you control the phone, access features, or do something purely amusing. You can read more about widgets in Chapter 22.

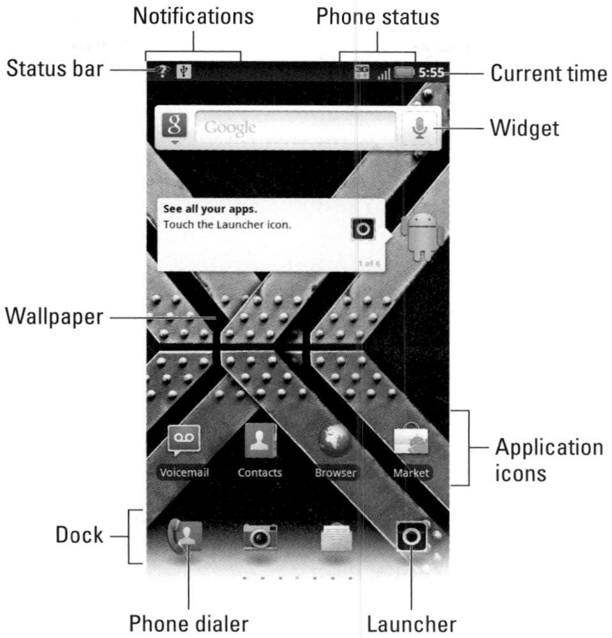

Figure 3-2: The Home screen.

- **Application icons:** The meat of the meal on the Home screen plate is the collection of application icons. Touching an icon runs the program.
- **Dock:** The bottom of each Home screen panel contains the same four icons in a place called the *dock.* You can change the first three icons; the fourth icon is the Launcher, which cannot be changed.
- **Phone Dialer:** It's really an application icon, but the phone dialer, dwelling on the dock, is what you use to make phone calls. It's kind of a big deal.
- **Launcher:** Touching the Launcher button icon displays the Apps Screen, where you can access all the applications installed on your phone. The section "The Apps Screen," later in this chapter, describes how it works.

The terms used in this section to describe items on the Home screen are used throughout this book, as well as in other Droid X2 documentation (if it exists). Specific directions for using the Home screen gizmos are found throughout this chapter.

- The Home screen doesn't do horizontal orientation.
- The Home screen is entirely customizable. You can add and remove icons from the Home screen, add widgets and shortcuts, even change the wallpaper images. Home screen *profiles* are available for changing everything on the Home screen at once. See Chapter 24 for more information.
- Touching part of the Home screen that doesn't feature an icon or a control doesn't do anything. That is, unless you're using the *live wallpaper* feature. In that case, touching the screen changes the wallpaper in some way, depending on the wallpaper selected. You can read more about live wallpaper in Chapter 24.
- Adding or removing app icons from the dock is covered in Chapter 22.

Viewing all the Home screen panels

And now, the secret: The Home screen is seven times wider than what you see on the front of your Droid X2. Three additional Home screen panels are to the left and to the right of the main Home screen panel, as illustrated in Figure 3-3.

To view the various Home screen panels, swipe your finger left or right across the touchscreen display. The Home screen slides over one page in each direction every time you swipe.

To see all seven Home screen panels at once, press the Home soft button twice. You'll see an overview similar to what's shown in Figure 3-4. Touch a Home screen panel thumbnail to visit that panel directly.

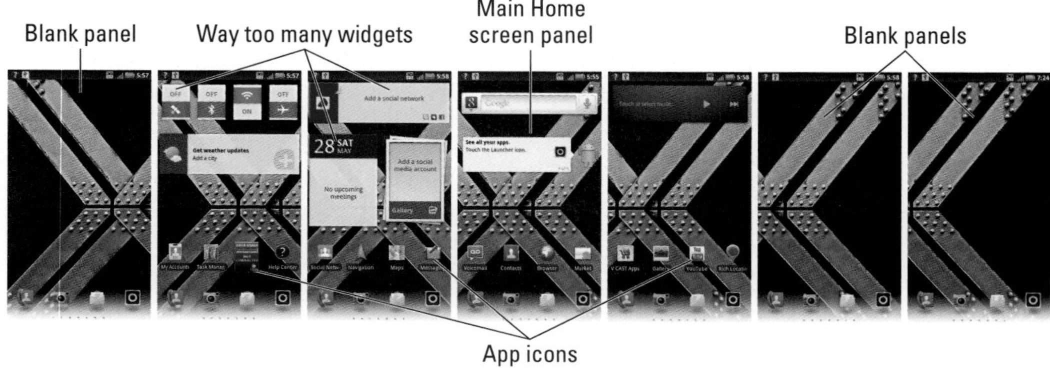

Figure 3-3: All the Home screen panels.

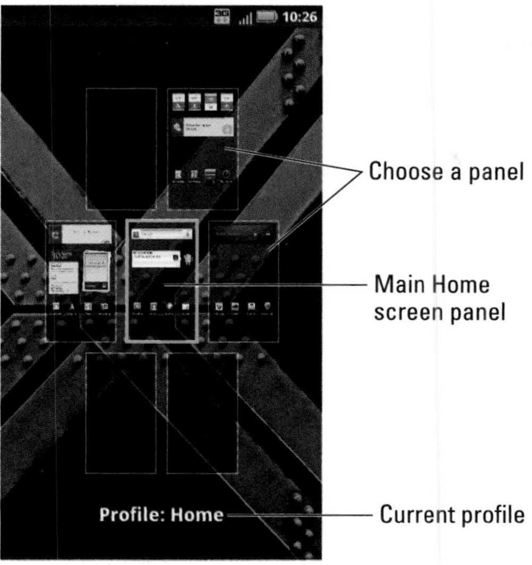

Figure 3-4: Home screen panel overview.

The various panels give you more opportunities to place applications and widgets on the Home screen.

- The Home screen panel overview (Figure 3-4) tells you which Home screen profile you're using. See Chapter 22 for more details on switching profiles.
- Tiny dots at the bottom of the Home screen tell you which panel you're currently viewing.
- No matter which part of the Home screen you're viewing, the status bar at the top of the touchscreen and the dock at the bottom of the screen stay the same.

I've Been Working on the Home Screen

I recommend getting to know three basic Home screen operations: reviewing notifications, starting applications, and using widgets.

Reviewing notifications

Notifications appear as icons at the top of the Home screen, as illustrated earlier, in Figure 3-2. To see the actual notifications, peel down the top part of the screen, as shown in Figure 3-5.

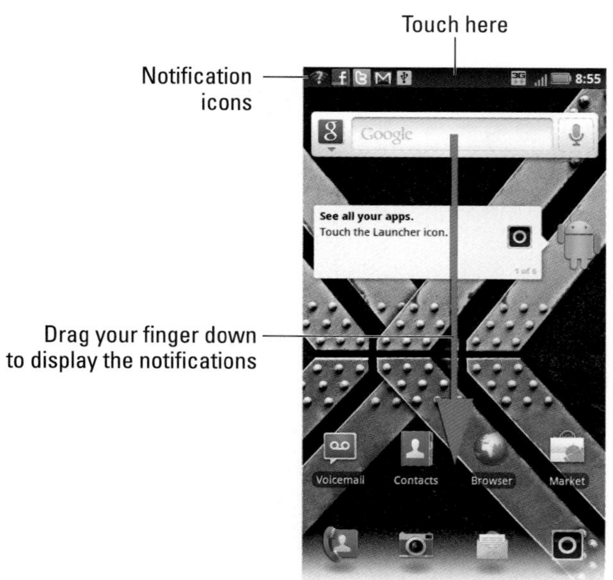

Figure 3-5: Accessing notifications.

The operation works like this:

1. **Swipe your finger from the top of the touchscreen all the way down to the bottom.**

   This step works like controlling a roll-down blind: You grab the top part of the touchscreen and drag it downward all the way. The notifications panel appears, as shown in Figure 3-6.

   You may need to drag the notification panel all the way to the bottom of the touchscreen to prevent it from rolling back up again. Use the Notification Panel control to pull it all the way down (refer to Figure 3-6).

2. **Touch a notification to see what's up.**

Touching a notification switches you to the program that generated the icon. For example, touching a New Email notification displays a new message or your inbox.

If you choose not to touch a notification, you can "roll up" the notification list by sliding the Notification Panel control back to the top of the touchscreen. Or you can press the Back soft button to dismiss the notifications.

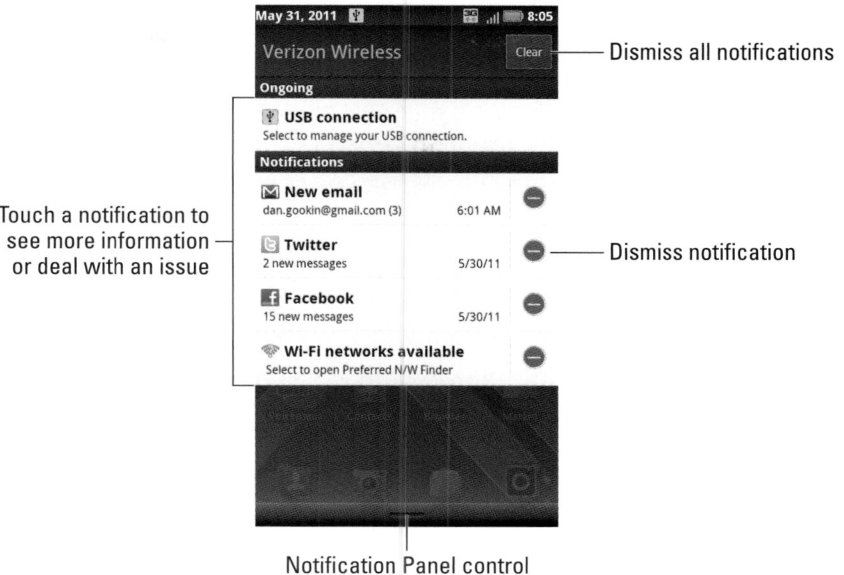

Figure 3-6: The notifications panel.

- The notification icons don't disappear until you've chosen each one — and sometimes those icons can stack up!
- Dismiss individual notifications by touching the red Delete button, as shown in Figure 3-6. There is no confirmation after you touch the Delete button.
- To dismiss all notification icons, touch the Clear button (refer to Figure 3-6).
- When more notifications are present than can be shown on the status bar, you see the More Notifications icon, as shown in the margin. The number on the icon indicates how many additional notifications are available.
- Dismissing notifications doesn't prevent them from appearing again in the future. For example, notifications to update your programs continue to appear, as do calendar reminders.
- Some programs, such as Facebook and the various Twitter apps, don't display notifications unless they're running. See Chapter 12.

- When new notifications are available, the Droid X2 notification light flashes. Refer to Chapter 1 for information on locating the notification light.
- See Chapter 17 for information on dismissing calendar reminders.

- Notification icons appear on the screen when the phone is locked. Remember that you must unlock the phone before you can drag down the status bar to display notifications.

Starting an application

Running an application on the Home screen is cinchy: Touch its icon. The application starts.

- Not all applications appear on the Home screen, but all of them can appear when you display the Apps screen. See the section "The Apps Screen," later in this chapter.
- When an application closes or you quit that application, you return to the Home screen.
- *Application* is often abbreviated as *app*.

Accessing a widget

A *widget* is a teensy program that floats over the Home screen (refer to Figure 3-3). To use a widget, simply touch it. What happens after that depends on the widget.

For example, touching the Calendar widget displays a list of today's appointments in the Calendar app. Touching the Google widget displays the onscreen keyboard and lets you type, or dictate, something to search for on the Internet. The Power Control widgets turn various phone features off or on.

Information on these and other widgets appears elsewhere in this book. See Chapter 22 for information on working with widgets.

The Apps Screen

Although some app icons can be found on the Home screen, the place where you can find all applications installed on your Droid X2 is the *Apps screen*. It's accessed by touching the Launcher button, found at the bottom-right corner of the Home screen.

Starting an app from the Apps screen

To start a program — an *app* — on the Droid X2, heed these steps:

1. **Touch the Launcher button on the Home screen.**

   The Launcher is the far-right button on the bottom of the Home screen, as shown in the margin; the original Droid X Launcher looks similar to what's shown in the margin, though its icon has a tiny triangle in the middle.

   After touching the Launcher button, you see the Apps screen, shown in Figure 3-7.

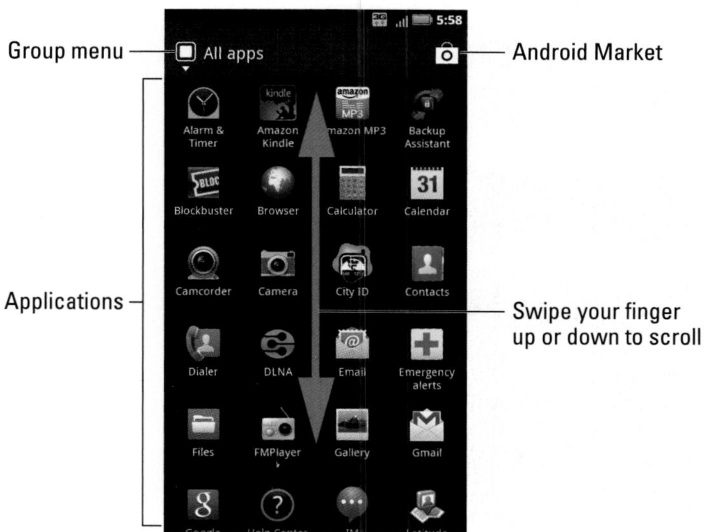

Figure 3-7: The Applications screen shows your phone's apps.

2. **If you don't see All Apps displayed, choose All Apps from the Group menu.**

   Refer to Figure 3-7 for the Group menu's location.

3. **Scroll the list of app icons by swiping your finger up or down.**
4. **Touch an icon to start that app.**

The app that starts takes over the screen and then does whatever good thing it's supposed to do.

- Use the Group menu to view recently opened apps, apps you've downloaded, as well as apps you've categorized into groups.
- See the next section for information on viewing recently opened apps.
- Refer to Chapter 18 for information on apps you can download from the Android Market, as well as information on creating app groups on the Apps screen.

- The terms *program*, *application,* and *app* all mean the same thing.

Reviewing your most recently used apps

If you're like me, you probably use the same apps repeatedly, on both your computer and your phone. You can easily access the list of recent programs on the Droid X2 by pressing and holding the Home soft button. When you do, you see the most recently accessed programs, similar to the ones shown in Figure 3-8.

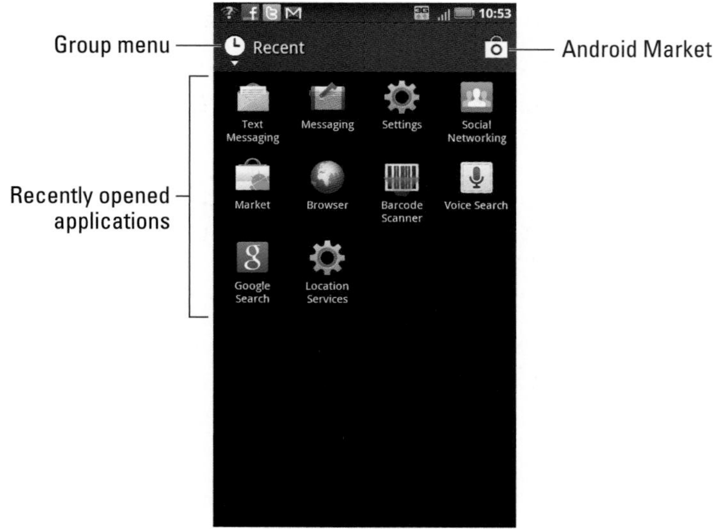

Figure 3-8: Recently used apps.

You can see your recent apps also by choosing Recent from the Group menu, as illustrated in Figure 3-8.

For programs you use all the time, consider creating shortcuts on the Home screen. Chapter 22 describes how to create shortcuts for apps, shortcuts to people, shortcuts for instant messaging, and all sorts of fun stuff.

Finding a lost app

The problem isn't that you'll lose apps on your Droid X2. No, the problem is that you'll forget the app's name. It happens. For example, I have a translator app I use occasionally, but I forget its exact name. By searching for **translator** I can always find it. Here's what to do:

1. **Press the Search soft button.**
2. **Use your finger to type all or part of the app's name.**

   As you type, items matching the text you've typed appear in the list. The items include applications, music, contacts, and even locations on the Internet. When you're looking for a program, you see the text *Application* appear beneath the program name.
3. **Scroll the list to explore the apps that have been found.**

   Use your finger to swipe the list up and down.
4. **Touch the name of the app you're looking for.**

   The app starts.

Searching for apps is a small part of searching for all kinds of information on the Droid X2, such as contact information, appointments, and email. Various chapters throughout this book describe other ways you can use the Droid X2 search function.

See Chapter 18 for information on how to shop the Android Market to find more apps for your phone.

4

Text to Type and Edit

In This Chapter

- Using the multitouch keyboard
- Getting at special characters
- Typing with the Swype keyboard
- Editing text on the screen
- Selecting, cutting, copying, and pasting text
- Dictating text with voice input

You just can't escape it. Despite all the touchscreen goodness and portability of your Droid X2, you need to use a keyboard to get the most from the phone. That means typing, that means working with text, that means editing and all that keyboardy-texty nonsense. To help you cope, this chapter covers the whole typing-text-editing ordeal, plus it introduces you to a non-keyboard way of typing text: Dictation.

Keyboard Mania

Don't fret if you can't find a keyboard on your Droid X2. The keyboard is not a physical one but an *onscreen keyboard*. It looks and works similar to the keyboard on your computer, and it's pretty easy to figure out — until you get all frustrated and want to hurl the phone into a brick oven. This section was written to help you fight that urge.

©PhotoDisc/Getty Images

- The Droid X2's primary onscreen keyboard is called the *multitouch keyboard* and is covered in this section.
- An alternative onscreen keyboard is also available for typing in a new way. See the later section "Take a Swype at the Old Hunt-and-Peck."
- The Droid X2 also lets you dictate text into your phone. See the section "Voice Input," later in this chapter.

Displaying the multitouch keyboard

The multitouch keyboard shows up any time the phone demands text as input, such as when you're composing email, typing a text message, or using any application where text is required.

Normally, the keyboard just pops up — for example, when you touch a text field or an input box on a web page. Then you start typing with your finger or — if you're good — your thumbs.

The QWERTY version of the multitouch keyboard is shown in Figure 4-1. The keys A through Z (lowercase) are there, plus a Shift/Caps Lock key, a Delete key, and other common keys and characters.

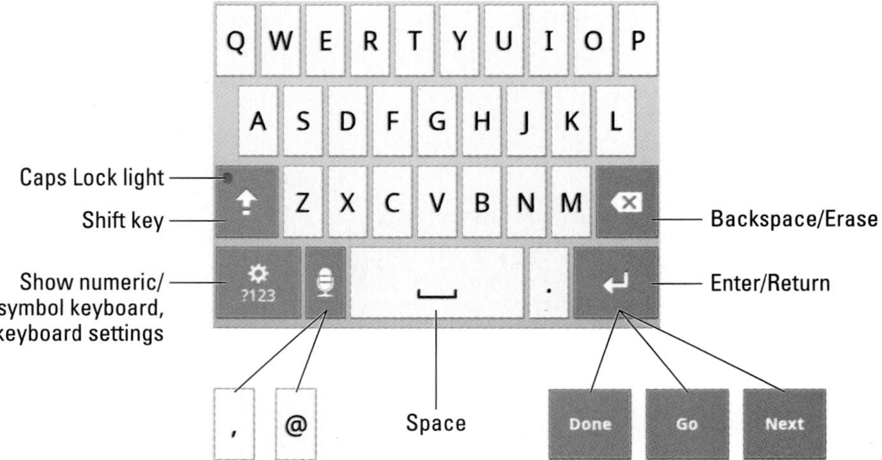

Figure 4-1: The onscreen keyboard.

The Microphone and Enter/Return keys change, depending on what you're typing. For example, when typing an email address, the Microphone key changes to an @ key. Likewise, the Enter/Return key has its variations, as shown in Figure 4-1. Here's what those special keys do:

- **Done:** The Done key is used to tell the Droid X2 that you're finished typing and want the keyboard to go away.
- **Go:** The Go key directs the phone to perform some action, such as searching for something, opening a web page, or some other process that can immediately proceed when you're finished typing.

- **Next:** The Next key is used when filling in multiple fields in a form. You touch it to move to the next field, which comes in handy when you can't see the next field on the touchscreen.

Touch the ?123 key to see the number keys as well as a smattering of punctuation symbols, as shown in Figure 4-2. You can then touch the ALT key to see even more symbols (also shown in Figure 4-2). Press the ABC key to return to the standard *alpha* keyboard (refer to Figure 4-1).

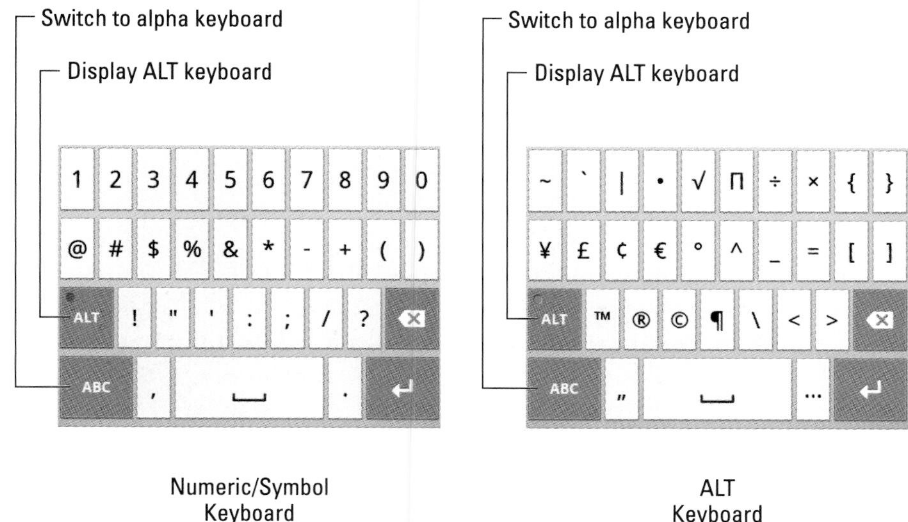

Figure 4-2: Onscreen keyboard variations.

Some applications show the onscreen keyboard when the phone is in landscape orientation. If so, the keyboard displays the same keys but offers more room for your stump-like fingers to type. Not every application features a horizontal keyboard, however, so you might be stuck using the narrower version of the keyboard.

On the original Droid X, the top row of keys on the alpha keyboard (refer to Figure 4-1) have little numbers on them. To produce those numbers, press and hold the key. For example, pressing and holding the R key generates the number 4.

Typing on the Droid X2

Using the Droid X2 multitouch keyboard works just as you'd expect: Touch the key you want and that character appears in the program you're using. It's magic! A blinking cursor on the touchscreen shows where new text appears, which is similar to how text input works on your computer.

As you type on the onscreen keyboard, the key you touch appears enlarged on the screen, as shown in Figure 4-3. That's how you can confirm that your finger is touching the character you intend to type.

Figure 4-3: Typing the g key.

The characters you type appear in whichever application accepts text input. You see what you type as you type it, just like on a computer. Also, similar to when you use a computer, when you type a password on your phone, the character you type appears briefly on the screen and is then replaced by a black dot.

- Above all, it helps to *type slowly* until you get used to the keyboard.
- When you make a mistake, press the Delete key to back up and erase.
- To set the Caps Lock, press the Shift key twice. A little light comes on (refer to Figure 4-1), indicating that Caps Lock is on.

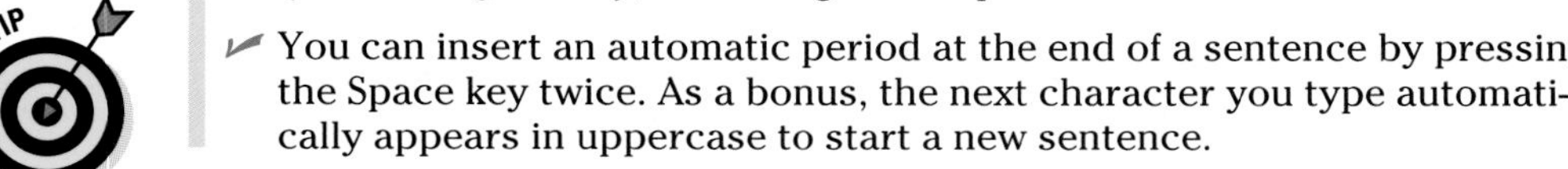

- You can insert an automatic period at the end of a sentence by pressing the Space key twice. As a bonus, the next character you type automatically appears in uppercase to start a new sentence.

- People generally accept that typing on a phone isn't perfect. Don't sweat it if you make a few mistakes as you type instant messages or email, though you should expect some curious replies about unintended typos.
- See the later section "Choosing a word as you type" to find out how to deal with automatic typo and spell correction.
- See the later section "Text Editing" for more details on editing your text.

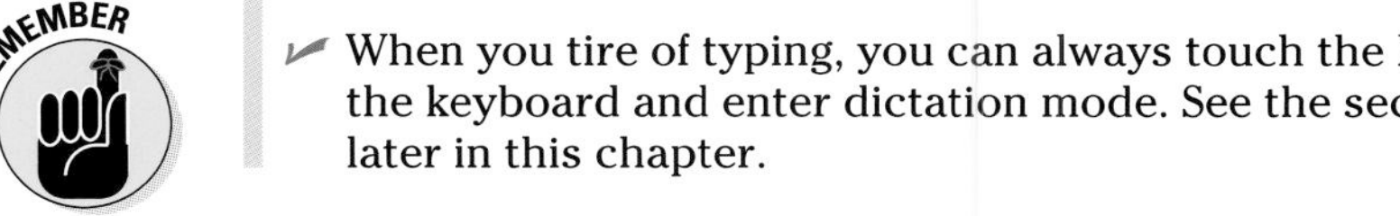

- When you tire of typing, you can always touch the Microphone key on the keyboard and enter dictation mode. See the section "Voice Input," later in this chapter.

Accessing extra special characters

You can type more characters on your phone than are shown on all three variations of the onscreen keyboard (refer to Figures 4-1 and 4-2). To access those characters, you press and hold a specific key to see a pop-up palette of options from which you choose a special character.

Figure 4-4 illustrates the pop-up palette for the O key. Pressing and holding down the O key displays that palette, from which you can choose a special character variation or touch the X button to cancel.

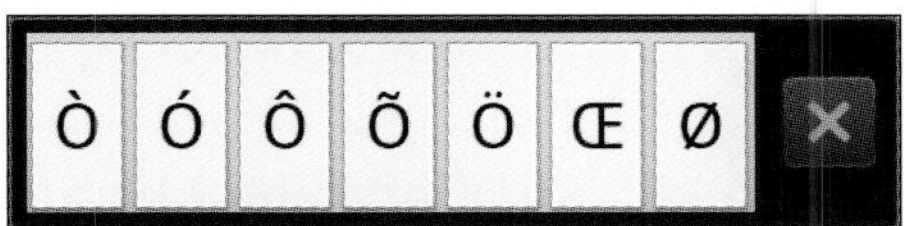

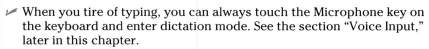

Figure 4-4: Optional characters on the O key.

Extra characters are available in uppercase as well. To get uppercase, press the Shift key before you long-press a key on the multitouch keyboard.

Certain symbol keys on the onscreen keyboard also sport extra characters. For example, various currency symbols are available when you long-press the $ key.

Choosing a word as you type

As a *smart*phone, the Droid X2 makes a guess at the words you're typing as you type them. A list of suggestions appears, as shown in Figure 4-5. You can choose a suggestion by touching it with your finger; the word instantly appears on the screen, saving you time (and potentially fixing your terrible spelling or typing, or both).

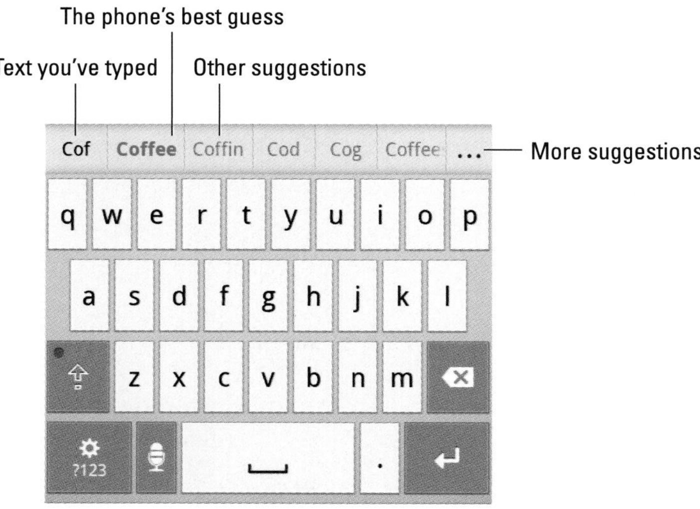

Figure 4-5: Suggestions for typing *Cof.*

You can press the Space key to automatically choose the word suggestion highlighted in orange (refer to Figure 4-5). That's a good way to save on typing but also a source of miscommunication when the phone guesses wrong.

To fix an incorrectly chosen word, use the Del key to back up and erase. Type slower next time.

Take a Swype at the Old Hunt-and-Peck

The Swype utility is designed to let you type like greased lightning on a touchscreen. The secret is that Swype allows you to type without lifting your finger from the keyboard; you literally swipe your finger over the touchscreen to rapidly type words.

Although Swype is an amazing tool, it's not for everyone. It appeals most to the younger crowd, who send text messages like crazy. Still, Swype is a worthy alternative to using the normal onscreen keyboard: Even when you're new and slow with Swype, you'll probably create text faster than doing the old touchscreen hunt-and-peck.

- Swype may be fast, but it's not as fast as using dictation. See the later section "Voice Input."
- Don't confuse Swype with Skype, which is a utility you can use to place free phone calls and send instant text messages over the Internet. See Chapter 21 for details on Skype Mobile.

Activating Swype

You can turn on Swype any time you see the onscreen keyboard. Follow these steps:

1. **Press and hold the ?123 key to summon the Multi-Touch Keyboard menu.**

   Refer to Figure 4-1 for the key's location on the keyboard.

   On the original Droid X, you cannot use the ?123 key to see the Multi-Touch Keyboard menu. Instead, press the Menu soft button at the Home screen, choose Settings, and then choose Language & Keyboard.

2. **Choose Input Method.**
3. **Choose Swype.**

   If you are given the option to view a Swype tutorial, do so.

After switching to the Swype input method, you see a new keyboard, as shown in Figure 4-6. You're now ready to start using Swype for typing text. Or, rather, for *swyping* text.

Figure 4-6: The Swype keyboard.

Even though Swype is active, you can continue to use your finger (or thumbs) to touch-type on the keyboard. And, as shown in Figure 4-6, you can still use dictation when the Swype keyboard is active.

- To view the Swype tutorial, press the Swype key on the keyboard (refer to Figure 4-6) and then touch the Tutorial button.
- See the section "Deactivating Swype" for when you want to return to the multitouch keyboard.

Using Swype to create text

The key to using Swype is to not lift your finger from the keyboard. The secret to learning to use Swype is to start slowly; don't worry that the teenager sitting next to you is swiping so fast it looks like he's writing Chinese characters on his phone.

Your first task in Swype is to learn how to type simple, short words: Keep your finger on the touchscreen and drag it over the letters in the word, such as the word *howdy,* shown in Figure 4-7. Lift your finger when you've completed the word, and the word appears in whichever app you're using.

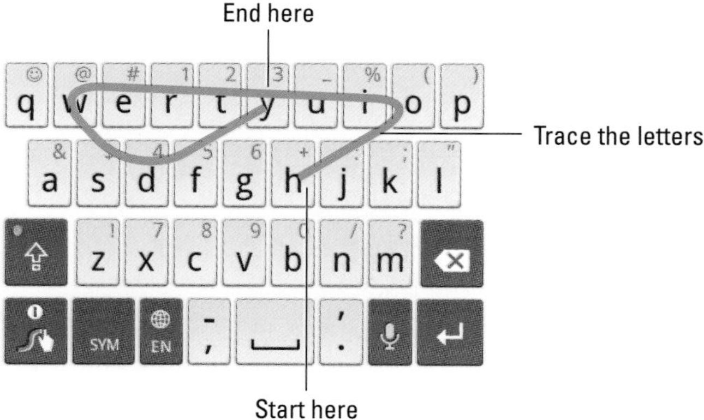

Figure 4-7: Swipe the word *howdy.*

Capital letters are typed by dragging your finger above the keyboard after touching the letter, as shown in Figure 4-8, where *Idaho* is typed.

Figure 4-8: Swiping a capital letter.

To create a double letter, such as the *oo* in *book*, you do a little loop on that key. In Figure 4-9, the word *Hello* is typed, using both the capital letter trick and the double-letter trick.

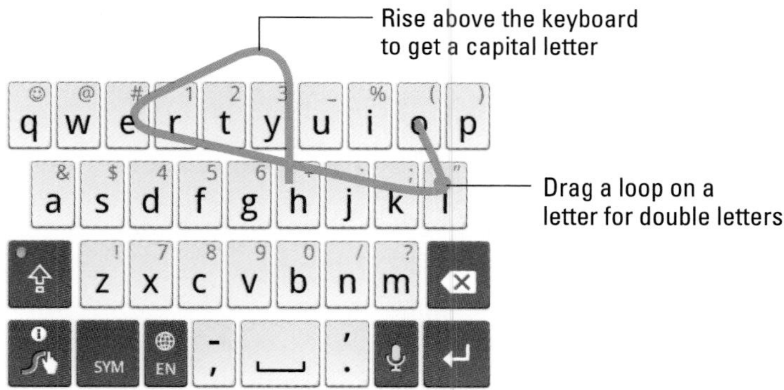
Rise above the keyboard
to get a capital letter
Drag a loop on a
letter for double letters

Figure 4-9: Swiping double letters.

When Swype is confused about the characters you type, a pop-up window appears containing word suggestions, as shown in Figure 4-10.

Choose a suggestion from the list or switch to the alternative suggestions, as illustrated in Figure 4-10.

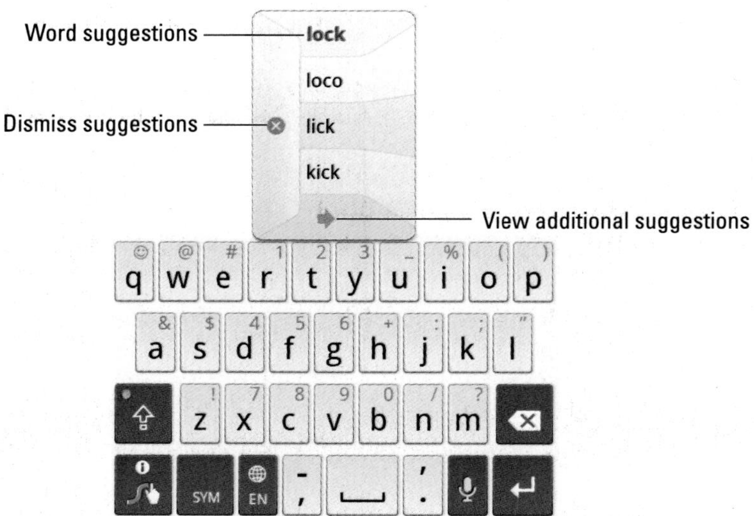

Figure 4-10: Choose the right word.

For more information on Swype typing tips, refer to the tutorial found by touching the Swype key on the keyboard (refer to Figure 4-6).

- The Swype software interprets your intent as much as it interprets your accuracy. Even being *close to* the target letter is good enough; as long as you create the correct pattern over the keyboard, Swype usually displays the right word.
- Slow down and you'll get the hang of it.

Deactivating Swype

To return to the multitouch keyboard and disable Swype, follow these steps:

1. **At the Home screen, press the Menu soft button.**
2. **Choose Settings.**
3. **Choose Language & Keyboard.**
4. **Choose Input Method.**
5. **Choose Multi-Touch Keyboard.**

You can press the Home soft button to return to the Home screen when you're done with the Language & Keyboard Settings window.

Text Editing

Editing is the part of writing where you admit that nothing <ahem> reads good the first time. Though you may not be editing on your cell phone for content reasons, you'll probably want to fix the typos and ensure that the automatic word selection thing did its job properly.

Moving the cursor

The first task in editing text is to move the *cursor,* that blinking vertical line where text appears, to the correct spot. To move the cursor, simply touch that part of the text where you want the cursor to blink. This method works but, because your finger is probably fatter than the spot where you want the cursor, is not quite effective.

To better position the cursor on the Droid X2, touch the screen quickly. A Target icon appears where the cursor is located, as shown in the margin. While that icon is visible, touch the screen again right on the icon and keep your finger down. A pop-up magnification bubble appears, which lets you better position the cursor.

The Target icon for the original Droid X is different, as shown in the margin. It doesn't display a magnifier as you move the target around.

If a pop-up menu appears instead of the Target icon, press the Back soft button to dismiss the pop-up menu and try again.

Selecting text

If you're familiar with selecting text in a word processor, you'll find that selecting text on the Droid X2 works the same. Well, *theoretically,* it works the same: Selected text appears highlighted on the touchscreen. You can then delete, cut, or copy that block of selected text. It's the method of selecting text on a phone that's different.

Start selecting text on the Droid X2 by double-tapping a word on the touchscreen. When you do so, the word becomes highlighted, as shown in Figure 4-11. You can then use the markers at the start and end of the word to extend the selection, as illustrated in the figure.

Another way to select text is to long-press the text on the touchscreen. When this method works, you'll see the Edit Text menu, as shown in Figure 4-12.

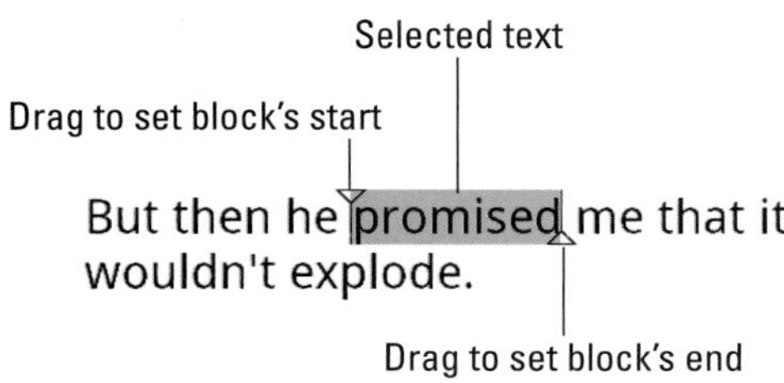

Figure 4-11: Selecting a block of text.

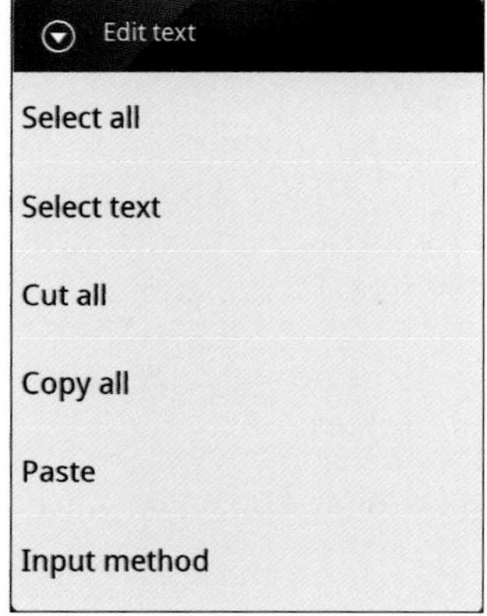

Figure 4-12: The Edit Text menu.

The first two options on the Edit Text menu (refer to Figure 4-12) deal with selecting text:

- **Select All:** Choose this option to select all text, either in an input box or whatever text you've been entering or editing in the current application.
- **Select Text:** Choose this option to select a block of text starting at the cursor's location, similar to what's shown in Figure 4-11.

On the original Droid X, select text by long-pressing the screen near the text you want to select. Choose the Select Word command from the Edit Text menu, then use the start and ending markers to extend the selection, if necessary.

After the text is selected, you can do four things with it: Delete it, replace it, copy it, or cut it. Delete text by touching the Delete key on the keyboard. You replace text by typing something new while the text is selected. The later section "Cutting, copying, and pasting text" describes how to cut or copy the text.

- To dismiss the Edit Text menu, press the Back soft button.
- You can cancel a text selection by tapping elsewhere on the text

Selecting text on a web page

When you're browsing the web on your Droid X2, text is selected by summoning a special menu item. Obey these steps:

1. **Press the Menu soft button to summon the web browser's menu.**

2. **Choose More, then Select Text.**
3. **Drag your finger over the web page text you want to copy, and then lift your finger to complete selecting the text.**

   On the original Droid X, you can use the start and ending block markers to refine or extend the text selection. You then need to touch the block of text to see the Select Text menu.
4. **Choose the Copy command from the Select Text menu.**

You can paste the copied text into any application on your phone that accepts text input. See the next section.

Refer to Chapter 11 for more information on surfing the web with your phone.

Cutting, copying, and pasting text

After selecting a chunk of text — or all the text — on the screen, you can then cut or copy that text and paste it elsewhere. Copying or cutting and then pasting text works just like it does on your computer.

Follow these steps to cut or copy text on your phone:

1. **Select the text you want to cut or copy.**

   Selecting text is covered earlier in this chapter.
2. **Long-press the selected text.**

   Touch the text on the touchscreen and keep your finger down. You see the Edit Text menu, similar to the one shown in Figure 4-12.
3. **Choose Cut or Copy on the menu to cut or copy the text.**

   The commands Cut All and Copy All, shown in Figure 4-12, change to Cut and Copy when text is selected. When you choose Cut, the text is removed. Choose the Paste command afterward to move that cut chunk of text.
4. **If necessary, start the application you want to paste text into.**

5. **Choose the input box or text area where you want to paste the copied or cut text.**
6. **Move the cursor to the exact spot where the text is to be pasted.**
7. **Long-press the text box or area.**
8. **Choose the Paste command from the Edit Text menu (refer to Figure 4-12).**

   The text you cut or copied appears where the cursor was blinking.

The text you paste can be pasted again and again. Until you cut or copy additional text, you can use the Paste command to your heart's content.

You can paste text only into locations where text is allowed. Odds are good that if you can type, or whenever you see the onscreen keyboard, you can paste text.

Voice Input

One of the most amazing things about the Droid X2 is its uncanny capability to interpret your dictation as text. Yes, it's almost as good as Mr. Spock talking to the computer on *Star Trek*. In fact, it should amaze you — which I admit is impressive for a cell phone.

Dictating to your phone

Voice input is available anytime you see the Microphone icon, similar to the one shown in the margin. To begin voice input, touch the icon. A voice input screen appears, as shown in Figure 4-13.

When you see the text *Speak now,* speak directly at the phone.

Figure 4-13: The Voice Input prompt.

After you stop talking, the phone digests what you said. Eventually, the text you spoke — or a close approximation — appears on the screen. It's magical, and sometimes comical.

- The first time you try voice input, you might see a description displayed. Touch the OK button to continue.
- A Microphone icon shows up on the onscreen keyboard variations. Touch that Microphone key to dictate, rather than type, to your phone.
- The Microphone icon appears only when voice input is allowed. Not every application features voice input as an option. You cannot, for example, use dictation to enter a password.

- The better your diction, the better the result. Also, try to speak in short sentences.
- You can edit your voice input just as you edit any text. See the section "Text Editing," earlier in this chapter.

- You have to speak any punctuation in your text. For example, you would need to say, "I'm sorry comma Belinda period" to have the phone produce the text *I'm sorry, Belinda.*.
- Common punctuation marks you can dictate include the comma, period, exclamation point, question mark, and colon.

- Pause your speech before and after speaking punctuation.
- Dictation requires a data connection on your phone. If that connection is unavailable, or the dictation servers are down, dictation won't work.

Controlling the Droid X2 with voice commands

The Voice Command app, found in the Apps screen, can be used to blast out vocal orders to your Droid X2. Start the app and wait a second to see a list of potential commands.

Try a few of the commands, such as the Call command. The phone may ask for more detailed information, requiring you to say "yes" or "no" as various options are presented.

I admit that this feature is a bit rough around the edges, especially compared with the Droid X2 text-input dictation capabilities. Still, it's a unique and interesting way to use the phone without suffering the burdens of typing text.

Uttering b*** words

The Droid X2 features a voice censor. It replaces any naughty words you might utter, placing the word's first letter on the screen, followed by the appropriate number of asterisks.

For example, if *spatula* were a blue word, and you uttered *spatula* when using the Droid X2's dictation feature, you would see *s****** on the screen instead of the word *spatula*.

The phone knows a lot of blue terms, including the famous "Seven Words You Can Never Say On Television," but apparently the terms *crap* and *damn* are fine. Don't ask me how much time I spent researching this topic.

Part II
It's the Phone!

In this part . . .

Any gizmo can be distilled down to its most basic function. A microwave oven may sport dozens of buttons and features, but it just heats things up. A Swiss Army Knife is basically a knife. And a computer, despite all its features and software, is simply a gizmo designed to help you more efficiently waste time. The same philosophy can be applied to a smartphone.

At its most basic, the Droid X2 is a phone. It's used to make and receive phone calls. All the other features — the fancy stuff covered in Parts III and IV, stuff that you're probably aware of but intimidated by — are really extras and bonus goodies. Take them away and you're left with using the Droid X2 as a phone, which is the subject of this part of the book.

5

The Telephone Thing

In This Chapter

- Calling someone
- Connecting with a contact
- Getting a call
- Replying to missed calls with a text message
- Checking into a missed call
- Perusing the call log

Oh, I remember the days when all a cell phone could do was make a phone call. You could store names and addresses, but the process was a pain so no one did it. The phone had no Internet access, no music, no camera. Sure, the thing may have weighed 8 pounds and had a full four-hour battery life, but all you needed it for was mobile calls, so who cared?

The Droid X2 is far lighter than 8 pounds and its battery can last all day for typical usage. It can do a lot more than make phone calls, but at its core, that's what it does, as this chapter gladly describes.

Reach Out and Touch Someone

Email may have killed off the personal letter, but nothing replaces a phone call. It's special. It's good to hear someone's voice. Making phone calls on the Droid X2 is cinchy, if you've mulled through the information in this section.

Making a phone call

To place a call on your phone, heed these steps:

1. **Touch the Dialer app, on the bottom left of the Home screen.**

The Dialer app can be found also on the Apps screen.

After starting the Dialer app, you see the Phone dialpad, similar to the one shown in Figure 5-1. If you don't see the dialpad, touch the Dialer tab (labeled in the figure).

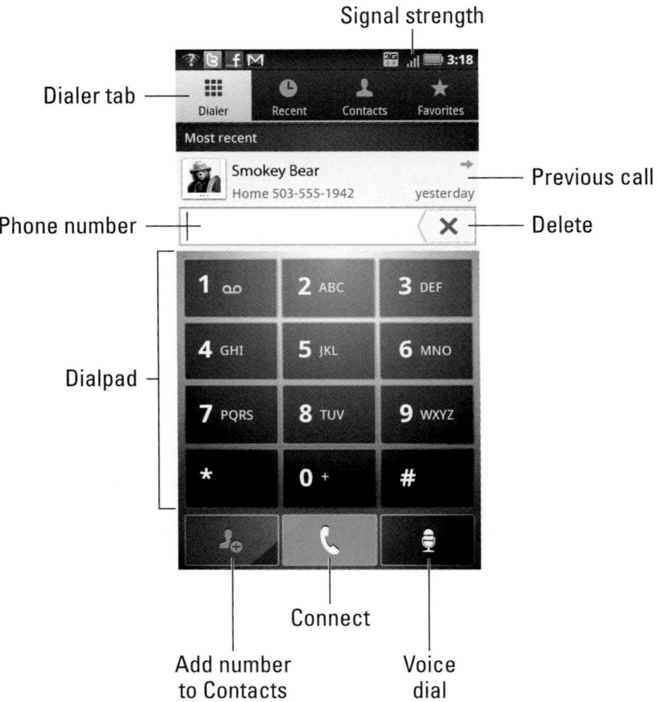

Figure 5-1: Dialing a phone number.

2. **Input the number to call.**

   Touch the keys on the dialpad to input the number. If you make a mistake, use the Delete key (refer to Figure 5-1) to back up and erase.

   As you dial, any matching phone numbers found in your Contacts list appear. You can touch a found contact to have that phone number copied to the input area.

3. **Touch the green Phone button to make the call.**

   The phone doesn't make the call until you touch the green button.

   As the phone attempts to make the connection, two things happen:

- First, the Call in Progress notification icon appears on the status bar. The icon is a big clue that the phone is making a call or is actively connected.
- Second, the screen changes to show the number that was dialed, similar to the one shown in Figure 5-2. When the recipient is in your Contacts list, the name appears as shown in the figure. Further, if a picture is part of the person's contact information, the picture appears, as shown in the figure.

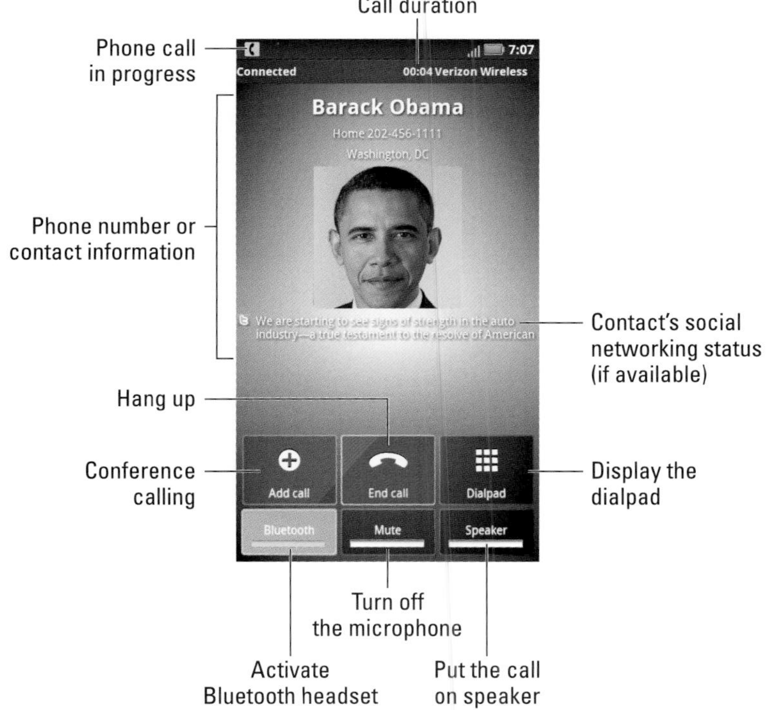

Figure 5-2: Your call has gone through!

Even though the touchscreen is pretty, at this point you need to listen to the phone: Put it to your ear or listen on earphones or a Bluetooth headset.

4. **When the person answers the phone, talk.**

   What you say is up to you, though I can recommend from experience that it's a bad idea to coldly open your conversation with your spouse by saying, "My dream of having my own elephant has come one step closer."

   Use the phone's Volume button (on the side of the Droid X2) to adjust the speaker volume during the call.

5. **To end the call, touch the red End button.**

   The phone disconnects. The phone Call in Progress notification goes away.

You can do other things while you're making a call on the Droid X2. Just press the Home button to run an application, check an appointment time, play a game, or do whatever. These activities don't disconnect you, though your cellular carrier may not allow you to do everything with the phone (such as browse the web) while you're on a call.

You can also listen to music while you're making a call, though I don't recommend it because the music volume and call volume cannot be set separately.

To return to the call after doing something else, swipe down the notifications at the top of the screen and touch the notification for the current call. You return to the call screen, similar to the one shown earlier, in Figure 5-2. Continue yapping. (See Chapter 3 for information on reviewing notifications.)

- You can connect or remove the earphones at any time during the call. The call is neither disconnected nor interrupted by doing so.
- If you're using the earphones, you can press the phone's Power Lock button during the call to turn off the display and lock the phone. I recommend turning off the display so that you don't accidentally touch the Mute or End button during the call.
- You can't accidentally mute or end a call when the phone is pressed against your face; a proximity sensor in the phone detects when it's close to something and the touchscreen is automatically disabled.
- Don't worry about holding the phone too far away from your mouth; it picks up your voice just fine.

- To mute the call, touch the Mute button (refer to Figure 5-2). A Mute icon, shown in the margin, appears as the phone's status (atop the touchscreen).

- Touching the Speaker button lets you hold the phone at a distance to listen and talk, which allows you to let others listen and share in the conversation. The Speaker icon appears on the status bar when the speaker is active.
- Don't hold the phone to your ear when the speaker is active.
- If you're wading through one of those nasty voice mail systems, touch the Dialpad button (refer to Figure 5-2) so that you can "Press 1 for English" when necessary.
- See Chapter 6 for information on using the Add Call button.
- The contact picture (refer to Figure 5-2) appears if you've assigned a picture to the contact. Or the picture may be pulled from one of your social networking sites — if you've set up those sites on the Droid X2. See Chapter 12.

- If you've logged into your social networking sites and the person you're calling is one of your friends or followers, that person's recent social networking status appears below the contact icon. For example, in Figure 5-2, President Obama's Twitter status appears. His Facebook status would appear as well, were President Obama one of your Facebook friends.
- When using a Bluetooth headset, connect the headset *before* you make the call. See Chapter 19.
- If you need to dial an international number, press and hold the 0 (zero) key until the plus sign (+) character appears. Then input the rest of the international number. Refer to Chapter 21 for more information on making international calls.
- You hear a beep when the call is dropped or if the other party hangs up on you. You can confirm the disconnection by looking at the phone, which shows that the call has ended.
- You cannot place a phone call when your phone has no service; check its signal strength (refer to Figure 5-1). Also see the nearby sidebar, "Signal strength and network information you don't have to read."
- You cannot place a phone call when the phone is in airplane mode. See Chapter 21 for information.
- The Call in Progress notification icon (refer to Figure 5-2) is a useful indicator. When you see the notification, it means the phone is connected to another party. To return to the phone screen, swipe down the status bar and touch the phone call's notification. You can then press the End button to disconnect or just put the phone to your face to see who's on the line.

Signal strength and network information you don't have to read

Two technical status icons appear to the left of the current time and battery status at the top of the Droid X2 screen. These icons represent the network the phone is connected to as well as the signal strength.

The Signal Strength icon displays the familiar bars, rising from left to right. The more bars you see, the stronger the signal. A lack of a signal is shown by zero bars, often with an X over the bars.

When the phone is out of its service area but still receiving a signal, you see a Roaming icon, where an *R* appears near the bars. See Chapter 21 for more information on roaming.

To the left of the signal bar icon is the digital network icon. No icon means that no network is available, which happens when the network is down or you're out of range. Otherwise, you see an icon representing one of the different types of cellular data networks to which the Droid X2 can connect. The 3G icon represents the fastest network with which the Droid X2 communicates.

See Chapter 19 for more information on the network connection and how it plays a role in your phone's Internet access.

Dialing a contact

Because your Droid X2 is also your digital Little Black Book, an easy method for placing a phone call is to simply dial one of the folks on your Contacts list. Follow these steps:

1. **On the Home screen, touch the Dialer app icon.**
2. **Choose the Contacts tab at the top of the screen.**

   See Figure 5-3 for the location of the Contacts tab.
3. **Scroll the list of contacts to find the person you want to call.**

   To rapidly scroll, you can swipe the list with your finger or use the index on the right side of the list (refer to Figure 5-3).
4. **Touch the contact to display their detailed information.**
5. **Touch the green Phone icon by the contact's phone number you want to call.**

   The contact is dialed immediately.

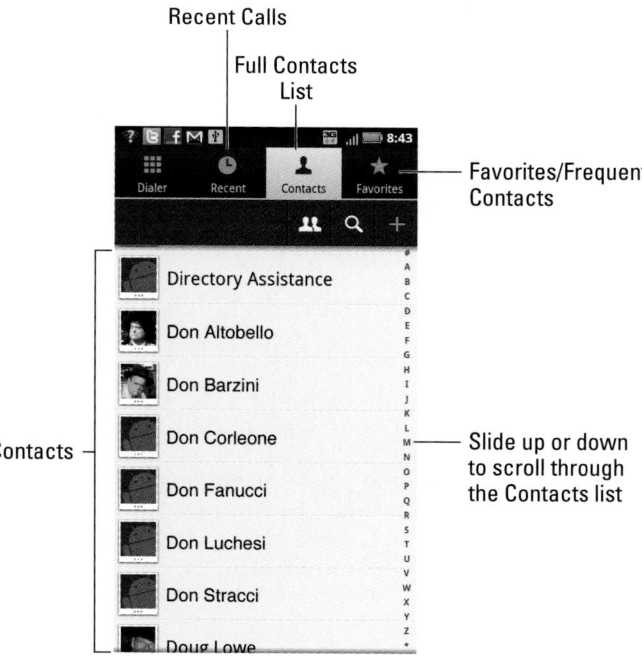

Figure 5-3: Choosing a contact to dial!

At this point, dialing proceeds as described earlier in this chapter.

- See Chapter 8 for more information about the Contacts list.
- To quickly dial contacts, refer to Chapter 22 for information on placing contact shortcut icons on the Home screen.

Phoning someone you call often

As sort of a computer, the Droid X2 keeps track of your phone calls. Also, you can flag certain people whose numbers you want to keep handy as your favorites. You can take advantage of these two features to quickly call the numbers you phone most often or to redial a number.

To use the call log to return a call, or to call someone right back, follow these steps:

1. **Open the Dialer app on the Home screen.**
2. **Touch the Recent tab, found at the top of the window.**

   (Refer to Figure 5-3.) You see a list of recent calls you've made or calls that came in. You can choose an item to see more information; to call someone back, though, it's just quicker to move to Step 3.
3. **Touch the Phone button by the entry.**

   The Droid X2 dials the contact.

People you call frequently, or contacts you've added to your Favorites list, can be accessed by touching the Favorites tab (refer to Figure 5-3). Scroll the list to find a favorite contact, and then touch the green phone button to dial.

Refer to Chapter 8 for information on how to make one of your contacts a favorite.

It's the Phone!

Once upon a time, getting a phone call was quite an exciting event. Heck, you didn't even know who was calling you until you picked the thing up and eagerly said "Hello!" You may not be as excited to receive a phone call these days, what with the popularity of cell phones, but it's still exciting to know that someone out there cares enough to call — even when it's a bill collector.

Well, maybe not when it's a bill collector, but you get the idea.

Receiving a call

Several things can happen when you receive a phone call on your Droid X2:

- The phone rings or plays a ringtone signaling you to an incoming call.
- The phone may vibrate.
- The touchscreen display turns on, as shown in Figure 5-4.
- The car in front of you explodes and your crazy passenger starts screaming in an incoherent yet comical manner.

Only the last item happens in a Bruce Willis movie. The other three possibilities, or a combination thereof, are your signals that you have an incoming call. A simple look at the touchscreen tells you more information, as illustrated in Figure 5-4.

To answer the call, slide the green Answer button to the right. Then place the phone to your ear or use the headset, if one is attached.

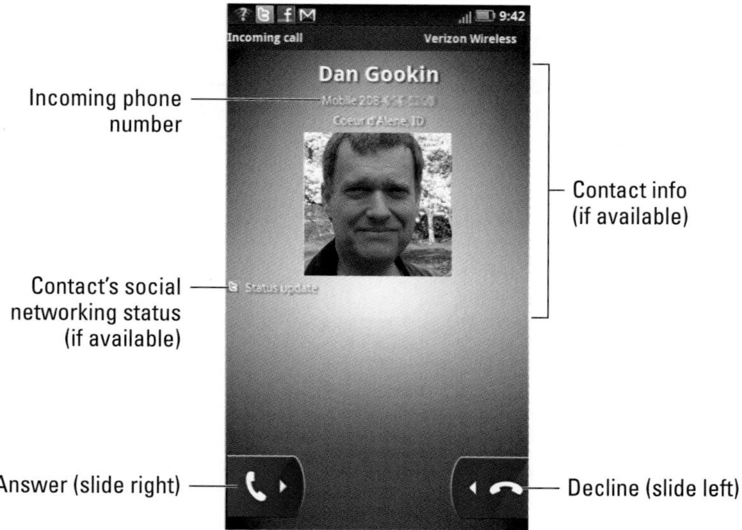

Figure 5-4: You have an incoming call.

To ignore the call, slide the red Decline button to the left. The phone stops ringing and the call is immediately sent to voice mail.

You can also press the Volume button (up or down) to silence the ringer.

If you're already on the phone when you receive an incoming call, you hear a tone. At that point, the touchscreen displays information about the incoming call, similar to the one shown in Figure 5-4. You can choose to answer or ignore the call. When you choose to answer, the current call is placed on hold. See Chapter 6 for more information on handling multiple calls.

- The contact's picture (refer to Figure 5-4) appears only when you've assigned a picture to that contact or the picture has been imported from your social networking sites. Otherwise, a generic silhouette icon shows up.
- Touch the control on your Bluetooth headset to answer an incoming call. See Chapter 19 for more information on using Bluetooth gizmos.
- The sound you hear when the phone rings is known as the *ringtone*. You can configure the Droid X2 to play a number of ringtones, depending on who is calling, or you can set a universal ringtone. Ringtones are covered in Chapter 6.

Using text message reply

When you dismiss an incoming call, you may see a pop-up menu such as the one shown in Figure 5-5. That's the feature Text Message Reply in action: Choose an option to send the caller a quick text message, explaining why you didn't answer.

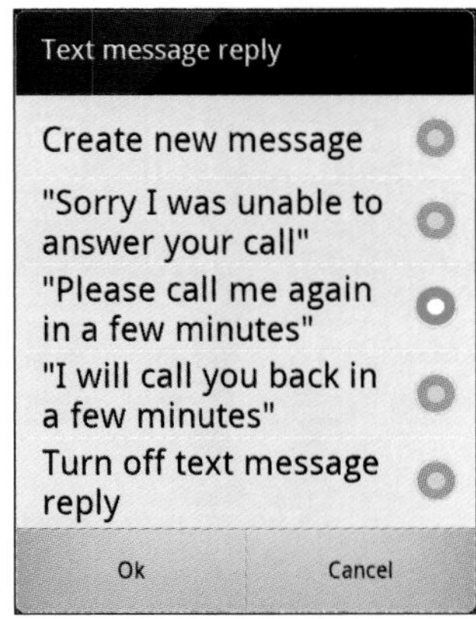

Figure 5-5: Choose a text message reply.

Where is that call coming from?

The Droid X2 can display the location for both incoming and outgoing calls, similar to the ones shown in Figures 5-2 and 5-4. That feature works courtesy of the City ID app.

City ID is a subscription service, though you get a free 15-day trial with your Droid X2. After that, you have to sign up to pay for the service. Although it may not help you identify callers you know, it is a handy tool for gleaning information about unknown incoming calls.

Open the City ID app on the Apps screen to learn more information about City ID.

Text Message Reply must be activated before it shows up. Follow these steps:

1. **At the Home screen, press the Menu soft button.**
2. **Choose Settings.**
3. **Choose Call Settings, and then Text Message Reply.**
4. **Ensure that there is a green check mark by the option Text Message Reply.**
5. **You can choose the option Edit Messages to remove existing text message replies or create your own.**

After the feature is activated, you'll see the Text Message Reply menu when you dismiss or ignore a call while you're on the line.

Setting the incoming call-signal volume

Whether the phone rings, vibrates, or explodes depends on how you configure the Droid X2 to signal you for an incoming call. Abide by these steps to set the various options (but not explosion) for your phone:

1. **On the Home screen, touch the Launcher to view all apps on the phone.**
2. **Choose the Settings icon to open the phone's settings screen.**
3. **Choose Sound.**
4. **Set the phone's ringer volume by touching Volume.**
5. **Manipulate the Ringtone slider left or right to specify how loud the phone rings for an incoming call.**

   After you release the slider, you hear an example of how loudly the phone rings.
6. **Touch OK to set the ringer volume.**

   If you'd rather just mute the phone, touch the Silent Mode option on the Sound Settings screen.

7. **To activate vibration when the phone rings, touch the Vibrate option and choose Always from the Vibrate menu.**
8. **Touch the Home button when you're done.**

When the next call comes in, the phone alerts you by using the volume setting or vibration options you've just set.

- When the phone is silenced, the Ringer Is Silenced icon appears on the status bar.
- Turning on vibration puts an extra drain on the battery. See Chapter 23 for more information on power management for your phone.
- See Chapter 6 for information on changing the Droid X2 ringtone.

Who's Calling Who When?

Before answering machines, there were teenagers. They would pick up the phone, promise that they'd pass along a message, then promptly forget the message, who called, or that anyone called. Answering machines fixed that problem, but still left open the question of who called when no one left a number. Thankfully, the Droid X2 is smart enough to remember not only who called but when they called. It even makes it easy to phone someone back.

Dealing with a missed call

The notification icon for a missed call looming at the top of the screen means that someone called and you didn't pick up. Oops.

To deal with a missed call, follow these steps:

1. **Display the notifications.**

   See Chapter 3 for details on how to deal with notifications.
2. **Touch the Missed Call notification.**

   A list of missed calls is displayed.
3. **To return a call, touch the green Phone icon by the person you want to call back.**

Reviewing recent calls

The key to knowing who called and when is to use the Droid X2 Recent call log. Here's how it works:

1. **Open the Dialer app.**

2. **Choose the Recent tab.**

   The Recent call log is displayed in Figure 5-6. You see the list of people who have phoned you, starting with the most recent call in chronological order. Icons next to each entry describe whether the call was incoming, outgoing, or missed, as illustrated in the figure.

Each entry in the Recent call log displays information about the call, and if the call was from one of your contacts, you see contact information, as shown in Figure 5-6.

The call log can be quite long. Use your finger to scroll the list.

You can filter the list of recent calls, directing the phone to show only missed calls, received calls, or outgoing calls. To do so, touch the Menu button (labeled in Figure 5-6). Choose which type of calls you want to see from the View menu, or choose All Calls to display all recent calls.

Using the Recent call log is a quick way to add a recent call as a contact. Simply touch the recent call and choose the command Add to Contacts from the menu. See Chapter 8 for more information about contacts.

To clear the call log, press the Menu soft button and then choose the Clear List command.

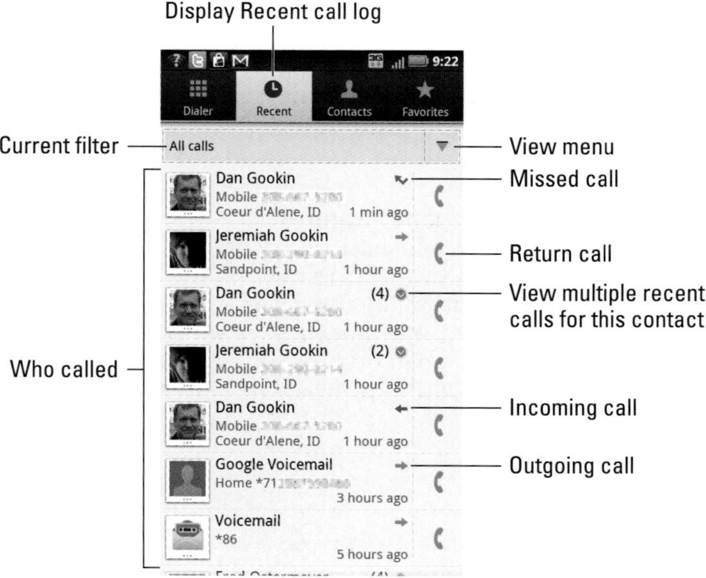

Figure 5-6: The Recent call log.

6

More Telephone Things

In This Chapter

- Setting up speed dial
- Handling multiple incoming calls
- Making a conference call
- Configuring call forwarding options
- Banishing a contact forever to voice mail
- Finding a better ringtone
- Assigning ringtones to your contacts
- Using your favorite song or sound as a ringtone

Some of the features considered standard on a cell phone weren't always so standard — or included at no additional charge. I remember paying an extra $7.95 a month for caller ID. The call waiting feature was more. Three-way calling? Even more. Sure, the old landline could pull off those useful functions, but only when you were willing to pay outrageous fees.

Your Droid X2 comes with fancy features such as speed dial, call waiting, and call forwarding. They're part of the phone's repertoire of basic features. Plus you have the ability to play with ringtones, or change the sound the phone makes when it rings. You can even have different ringtones for different contacts. It's easy to set up, providing you read through this informative and humor-laden chapter.

Speed Dial

How fast can you dial a phone? Pretty fast — specifically, for eight of your friends or the folks you phone most often. The feature is *speed dial,* and you can set it up by obeying these steps:

1. **Open the Dialer app.**

   The Dialer app's icon is found to on the bottom left of the Home screen.
2. **Ensure that either the Dialer or Recent tab is chosen.**
3. **Press the Menu soft button.**
4. **Choose Speed Dial Setup.**

   The first speed dial number is already configured to your carrier's voice mail. The remaining numbers, 2 through 9, are blank (unless you've already configured them).
5. **Touch a blank item in the list.**

   The blank lines contain the text *Add Speed Dial.*
6. **Choose a contact to speed-dial.**

   Contacts with multiple phone numbers have multiple entries; ensure that you choose the right one.
7. **Repeat Steps 4 and 5 to add more speed dial numbers.**

When you're done adding numbers, press the Back or Home button to exit the Speed Dial Setup screen.

Using speed dial is simple: Summon the Dialer (refer to Figure 5-1, in Chapter 5), and then *long-press* (press and hold) a number on the dialpad. When you release your finger, the speed dial number is dialed.

To remove a speed dial number, follow Steps 1 through 4 in this section. Touch the minus button to the right of the speed dial number to remove it. You can then add another speed dial number in that slot or just leave it empty.

To add a recently called number to the speed dial list, long-press the recent caller from the Recent call log. Choose the option Add to Speed Dial from the menu that appears. This trick works only when speed dial numbers are available. See Chapter 5 for more information on the Recent call log.

Multiple Call Mania

I remember hearing in a psychology class lecture the theory that human beings can hold only one conversation at a time, but then the guy next to me started talking and I couldn't focus on what the professor was saying. So, I'll never know for certain. I do know, however, that the Droid X2 is capable of handling more than one call at a time. This section explains how it works.

Receiving a new call when you're on the phone

You're on the phone, chatting it up. Suddenly, someone else calls you. What happens next?

The Droid X2 alerts you to a new call. The phone may vibrate or make a sound. Look at the front of the phone to see what's up with the incoming call, as shown in Figure 6-1.

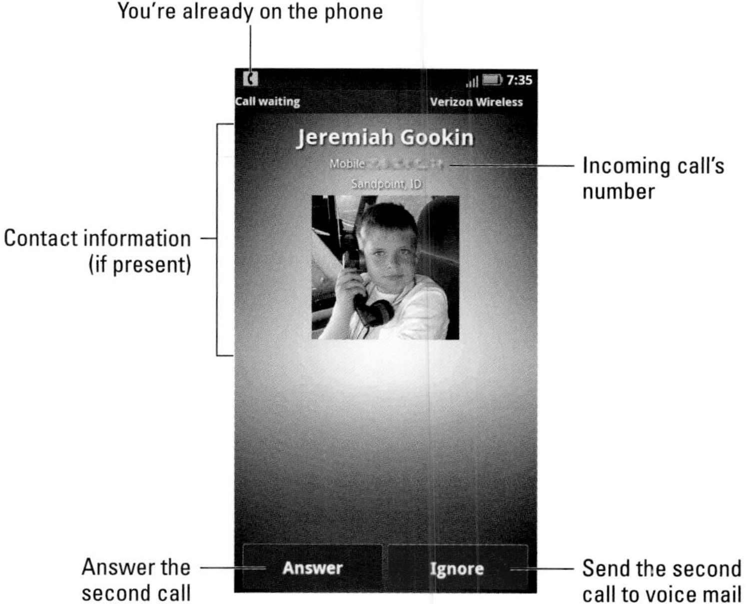

Figure 6-1: Suddenly, you have an incoming call!

You have three options:

- **Answer the call.** Touch the big, green Answer button to answer the incoming call just as you answer any call on your phone. The call you're on is placed on hold.
- **Send the call directly to voice mail.** Touch the big, red Ignore button to send the incoming call directly to voice mail.
- **Do nothing.** The call eventually goes into voice mail.

When you choose to answer the call and the call you're on is placed on hold, you return to the first call when you end the second call. Or you can manage multiple calls as described in the next section.

Contact information about the incoming call (refer to Figure 6-1) appears only when that caller is on your phone's Contacts list.

Juggling two calls

After answering a second call, as described in the preceding section, your Droid X2 is now working with two calls at a time. You can speak with only one person at a time; juggling two calls isn't the same thing as a conference call.

To switch callers, touch the Switch Calls button. Every time you touch the Switch Calls button, you connect to the other caller.

To end a call, touch the End button, just as you normally would. It might appear as though both calls have been disconnected, but that's not the case: In a few moments, the call you didn't disconnect "rings" as though the person called you back. Actually, the person didn't call you back; the Droid X2 is simply returning you to that ongoing conversation.

- Lamentably, the screen doesn't show you which call you're on; you have to figure out on your own whom you're switching to when you touch the Switch Calls button.
- The number of different calls your phone can handle depends on your carrier. For the Verizon network, that's only two calls at a time. In that case, a third person calling you either hears a busy signal or is sent directly to voice mail.
- If the person on hold hangs up, you may hear a sound or feel the phone vibrate when the call is dropped.

Making a conference call

Unlike an incoming call that interrupts a conversation, a *conference call* is one that you set out to make intentionally. Here's how it works:

1. **Phone up the first person.**

   Refer to Chapter 5 if you need to hone your Droid X2 phone-calling skills.

2. **After your phone connects and you complete a few pleasantries, touch the Add Call button.**

   The first person is put on hold, and you see the dialpad.

3. **Dial the second person.**

   Or you can summon the number from the Contacts list.

   Say your pleasantries and inform the party that the call is about to be merged.

4. **Touch the Merge button.**

   The two calls are now joined. Everyone you've dialed can talk to and hear each other.

5. **To end the conference call, disconnect the last person you called by touching the End Last Call button.**

   The second person you dialed is disconnected; the call ends. You're still taking to the first person.

6. **To end the first conversation, touch the End Call button.**

   The conference call is over.

When several people are in a room and want to participate in a call, you can always put the phone in speaker mode by simply touching the Speaker button.

Send a Call Elsewhere

Banishing unwanted calls on the Droid X2 is relatively easy. You can dismiss the phone's ring by touching the Volume button. Or you can send the call scurrying into voice mail by sliding the red Ignore button to the left when you receive a call. Other options exist for the special handling of incoming calls. They're the forwarding options, described in this section.

Forwarding phone calls

Call forwarding is the process by which you send elsewhere a phone call coming into your Droid X2. For example, when you're on vacation, you can send your calls to your office. You then have the luxury of having your cell phone while still making calls but freely ignoring anyone who calls you.

The options for call forwarding on the Droid X2 are set by the cell carrier and not by the phone itself. In the United States, when Verizon is your cellular provider, the call forwarding options work as described in Table 6-1.

Table 6-1 Verizon Call Forwarding Commands

Number to Input First	*Number to Input Second*	*Result*
*71	Forwarding number	Forward unanswered incoming calls
*72	Forwarding number	Forward all incoming calls
*73	(Nothing)	Cancel call forwarding

For example, to forward all calls to (714) 555-4565, you input ***727145554565** and touch the green Dial button on the Droid X2. You hear just a brief tone after dialing, and then the call ends. After that, any call coming into your phone rings at the other number.

- You must disable call forwarding for your Droid X2 to return to normal cell phone operations. Dial *73.
- The Droid X2 doesn't even ring when you forward a call using *72. Only the phone number you've chosen to forward to rings.
- You don't need to input the area code for the forwarding number when it's a local call. In other words, if you need to dial only 555-4565 to call the forwarding number, you need to input only ***725554565** to forward your calls.

- Call forwarding affects Google Voice. If you're using Google Voice as your voice mail service, you'll need to re-enable it after you deactivate the call forwarding feature on your Droid X2.

Sending a contact directly to voice mail

You can configure the Droid X2 to forward any of your cell phone contacts directly to voice mail. It's a great way to deal with a pest! Follow these steps:

1. **Open the Dialer app.**

   The Dialer app is found on the bottom left of the Home screen.

2. **If necessary, touch the Contacts tab at the top of the screen.**

   The Contacts list opens.

3. **Choose a contact.**

   Use your finger to scroll the list of contacts until you find the annoying person you want to eternally banish to voice mail.

4. **Press the Menu soft button.**

5. **Choose Options, and then touch the gray square next to Incoming Calls.**

   Touching the square places a green check mark in the square, which activates the Banish to Voicemail feature.

6. **Press the Back soft button.**

   Now all incoming calls from that contact are instantly sent to voice mail.

To unbanish your contact, repeat these steps to remove the green check mark.

- This feature is one reason you might want to keep contact information for someone with whom you really don't ever want to have contact.
- See Chapter 8 for more information on contacts.
- Also see Chapter 7, on voice mail.

Fun with Ringtones

I confess: Ringtones can be fun. They uniquely identify your phone's ring, especially when you forget to mute your phone and you're hustling to turn the thing off because everyone in the room is annoyed by your ringtone choice of *Soul Bossa Nova*.

On the Droid X2, you can choose which ringtone you want for your phone. You can create your own ringtones or use snippets from your favorite tunes. You can also assign ringtones for individual contacts. This section explains how it's done.

Choosing the phone's ringtone

To select a new ringtone for your phone, or to simply confirm which ringtone you're using already, follow these steps:

1. **From the Home screen, touch the Launcher button.**
2. **Choose Settings.**
3. **Choose Sound, and then Phone Ringtone.**

   If you have a ringtone application, you may see a menu asking you which source to use for the phone's ringtone. Choose Android System.

4. **Choose a ringtone from the list that's displayed.**

   Scroll the list. Tap a ringtone to hear a preview.

5. **Touch OK to accept the new ringtone or touch Cancel to keep the phone's ringtone as is.**

You can also specify the ringtone used for notifications: in Step 3 of the preceding list, choose Notification Ringtone instead of Phone Ringtone. The notification ringtone plays when the Droid X2 generates a new notification.

Setting a contact's ringtone

Ringtones can be assigned by contact so that when your annoying friend Larry calls, you can have your phone yelp like a whiny puppy. Here's how to set a ringtone for a contact:

1. **Open the Contacts app.**
2. **From the list, choose the contact to which you want to assign a ringtone.**
3. **Press the Menu soft button.**
4. **Choose Options, and then choose Ringtone.**

   If you see a Complete Action Using menu, choose the option Android System to select one of the phone's ringtones. Otherwise, you can use another listed application to choose a ringtone.
5. **Choose a ringtone from the list.**

   The same list is displayed for the phone's ringtones.
6. **Touch OK to assign the ringtone to that contact.**

Whenever that contact calls, the Droid X2 rings using the ringtone you've specified.

Using music as a ringtone

You can use any tune from the Droid X2 music library as the phone's ringtone. The first part of the process is finding a good tune to use. Follow along with these steps:

1. **Touch the Launcher button on the Home screen to display all apps on the phone.**
2. **Touch Music to open the music player.**
3. **Choose a tune to play.**

   See Chapter 16 for specific information on how to use the Music application and use your Droid X2 as a portable music player.

   The song you want must appear on the screen, or it can be playing, for you to select it as a ringtone.
4. **Press the Menu soft button, and then choose Use As Ringtone.**

   The song — the entire thing — is set as the phone's ringtone.

Whenever you receive a call, the song you've chosen plays from the beginning. It plays until you answer the phone, banish the call to voice mail, silence the phone, or just sit and wait.

The song you've added appears in the phone's list of ringtones. That way, the song can also be assigned as the notification ringtone, or set as an individual contact's ringtone, as discussed earlier in this chapter.

You can add ringtones for as many songs as you like by repeating the steps in this section. Follow the steps in the earlier section "Choosing the phone's ringtone" for information on switching between different song ringtones. Refer to the steps in the earlier section "Setting a contact's ringtone" to assign a specific song to one of your contacts.

A free app at the Android Market, Zedge, has oodles of free ringtones available for preview and download, all shared by Android users around the world. See Chapter 19 for information about the Android Market and how to download and install Zedge.

Creating your own ringtones

You can use any MP3 or WAV audio file as a ringtone for the Droid X2, such as a personalized message, a sound you record on your computer, or an audio file you stole from the Internet. As long as the sound is in either MP3 or WAV format, it can work as a ringtone on your phone.

The secret to creating your own ringtone is to transfer the audio file from your computer to the Droid X2. You can do that by synchronizing the audio file to the phone's Music app, as covered in Chapter 16, or by copying the audio file over directly, which is covered in Chapter 20. After the audio file is on the phone, you can choose it as a ringtone as described in the preceding section.

7

Message for You!

In This Chapter

- Configuring basic voice mail
- Retrieving messages
- Setting up Visual Voice Mail
- Using Google Voice for voice mail
- Reviewing your Google Voice messages

Long ago, Caveman Og showed up at his friend Gronk's cave. It was empty. How would Gronk know that Og stopped by? Well, rather than invent writing, Og decided to place a large rock at the opening of Gronk's cave. Believe it or not, that was the dawn of the voice mail era. Never mind that Gronk was utterly confused by the rock. When Og explained the rock to Gronk, Gronk was pleasantly surprised and decided not to kill Og for missing the appointment.

Voice mail has come a long way from the days of leaving rocks at cave openings. Your Droid X2 comes with a smattering of methods by which people can leave a message when you miss a call, or even when you don't want to talk with them and banish them into the voice mail holding pen.

Carrier Voice Mail

Your cell phone provider most likely offers a basic, and therefore stupid, voice mail feature. No fancy features, nothing special that requires a touchscreen or a smartphone. As long as you don't read the later parts of this chapter, which discuss much superior and better forms of voice mail, you won't be disappointed.

Basically, carrier voice mail is what you pay for with your cellular service. It provides a simple voice interface for retrieving and storing messages. You use the phone's dialpad to control things. Try not to yawn as you read this section.

- Voice mail is where calls go that you miss or dismiss. See Chapter 5 for information on dismissing calls.
- You cannot use Visual Voice Mail, covered later in this chapter, until you've first setup carrier voice mail.
- Even if you plan on using something sophisticated like Google Voice as your voice mail service, I still recommend setting up basic carrier voice mail as described in this section.

Setting up carrier voice mail

If you haven't yet done it, you need to set up voice mail on your phone. Even if you believe it to be already set up and configured, consider mincing through these steps, just to be sure:

1. **At the Home screen, press the Menu soft button.**
2. **Choose Settings.**
3. **Choose Call Settings.**
4. **Choose Voicemail Service.**
5. **Choose My Carrier, if it isn't chosen already.**

You can use the Voicemail Settings command to confirm or change the voice mail phone number. For Verizon in the United States, the number is *86.

After performing the steps in this section, the next step is to call into the carrier's voice mail service to complete the setup: You can dial *86, or touch the Launcher button on the Home screen and open the Voicemail app on the Apps screen.

In the Voicemail app, touch the Call Voicemail button. Set up voice mail for your Droid X2 by configuring your language, setting a voice mail password, and then recording a greeting. The Cheerful Verizon Robot will guide you. Complete those steps even if you plan to use an alternative voice mail service, as covered elsewhere in this chapter.

Don't forget to complete your voice mailbox setup by creating a customized greeting. When you don't, you may not receive voice mail messages because people may believe that they've dialed the wrong number.

Getting your messages

When you have voice mail, you see a New Voicemail icon on the status bar. It's your clue to voice mail looming in your carrier's voice mail system.

To access your messages, pull down the notifications. Touch the New Voicemail notification. The Droid X2 dials the carrier voice mail.

Table 7-1 lists the commands that are current for Verizon voice mail service at the time this book goes to press. These commands may change later.

Table 7-1 Verizon Voice Mail System Commands

Dial	*What You Can Do*
*	Go to the Main menu or, if you're at the Main menu, disconnect from voice mail
0	Help
1	Listen to messages/rewind
2	Send a message to another phone number on the Verizon system
3	Fast-forward
4	Review or change your personal options, such as the message greeting
5	Restart the session/Get date time information on a message
6	Send the message to someone else
7	Delete the message you just heard

Some numbers, such as 1 and 5, have different commands depending on where you are in the Verizon voice mail system. For example, when you're listening to a message, pressing the 1 button rewinds the message.

- You don't have to venture into carrier voice mail just to see who's called you. Instead, check your call log to review recent calls. Refer to Chapter 5 for information on reviewing the call log.
- Calls you exile into voice mail are not flagged as Missed in the Recent call log.
- See Chapter 3 for more information on reviewing notifications.
- Thank you for not yawning.

Visual Voice Mail

A less-boring option than carrier voice mail is something Verizon calls Visual Voice Mail. It's an app that lets you organize and listen to your messages in an interactive way. The only drawback to using the app is that you must subscribe to the service, which runs $2.99 per month as this book goes to press.

Setting up Visual Voice Mail

To configure Visual Voice Mail to work on your Droid X2, first set up carrier voice mail as covered earlier in this chapter. Visual Voice Mail is simply an interface into your existing carrier voice mail.

After you have carrier voice mail up and running, and especially after you set your password or PIN, touch the Launcher button to pop up the list of all apps installed on your phone and then choose Voicemail. Touch the button labeled Subscribe to Visual Voice Mail. Follow the directions on the screen to sign up and subscribe to the service.

You'll have to input your existing voice mail PIN to proceed, which is why I suggested that you first set up carrier voice mail earlier in this chapter.

You may also be required to download an update to the Visual Voice Mail app. Refer to Chapter 18 for information on downloading and updating apps on your Droid X2.

It may take a few moments for Visual Voice Mail to be configured. When it's ready, you see the Visual Voice Mail notification on the status bar. See the next section to find out how to deal with the notification.

The steps listed in this section may vary, depending on updates and enhancements to the Visual Voice Mail system.

Accessing your Visual Voice Mail

Visual Voice Mail serves as your access to all voice mail left on your phone. After it's configured (see the preceding section), you never need to dial carrier voice mail again. Simply pull down a voice mail notification or start the Voicemail app, and all your messages are instantly available on the screen.

When new voice mail arrives, you see the notification icon. The number in the icon indicates how many new messages are available. To access your message, pull down the notifications and choose Voicemail.

Use the controls in the Visual Voice Mail app to listen to your messages, call the person back, or delete the messages.

Visual Voice Mail uses the same greeting set as when you first configured carrier voice mail. To change the greeting, you have to dial carrier voice mail and follow the menu prompts.

The Wonders of Google Voice

Perhaps the best option I've found for working your voice mail is something called Google Voice. It's more than just a voice mail system: You can use Google Voice to make phone calls in the United States, place cheap international calls, and perform other amazing feats. But for the purposes of this section, the topic is using Google Voice as the Droid X2's voice mail system.

- Even when you choose to use Google Voice, I still recommend setting up and configuring the stupid carrier voice mail as covered earlier in this chapter.

- You may need to reset Google Voice after using call forwarding. See Chapter 6 for more information on call forwarding, and see the section "Adding your phone to Google Voice," in this chapter, for information on reestablishing Google Voice as your phone's voice mail service.

Setting up a Google Voice account

I recommend getting a Google Voice account on the Internet before you configure the Droid X2 for Google Voice. Start your adventure by visiting the Google Voice home page on the Internet: `http://voice.google.com/`.

If necessary, sign into your Google account. You use the same account name and password you use to access your Gmail.

Your next task is to configure a Google Voice number to be used for your Droid X2, as covered in the next section.

- If all you want is to use Google Voice as your voice mail service, choose the option that says Just Want Voicemail for Your Cell.
- Google Voice offers a host of features: international dialing, call forwarding, and other stuff I'm not aware of.

Adding your phone to Google Voice

After you have a Google Voice account, you need to add your Droid X2's phone number to the list of phone numbers registered for Google Voice. As in the preceding section, I recommend that you complete these steps on a computer connected to the Internet, but keep your phone handy:

1. **Click the Gear icon in the upper-right corner of the Google Voice home page.**

   You need to access the Voice Settings command, which may change its location in a future update to the Google Voice web page.

2. **Choose the Voice Settings command.**

   You need to access the Settings screen, where you register phone numbers for use with Google Voice.

3. **Click the link Add Another Phone.**

4. **Work the steps to verify your phone for use with Google Voice.**

   Eventually, Google Voice needs to phone your Droid X2. When it does, use the dialpad to type the code number you see on your computer screen. After confirming the Droid X2, you see it listed as a registered phone, though you're not done yet:

5. **Click the Activate Voicemail link.**

   This is the most important step! You must activate your phone for it to work with Google Voice.

6. **On your Droid X2, dial the number you see on your computer screen.**

   The number starts with *71, which is the command to forward unanswered calls on your phone. Note that the number you're dialing is not the same as your Google Voice phone number.

   The number dials and then the Droid X2 hangs up right away. That's normal.

7. **On your computer screen, click the Done button.**

Your Droid X2 is now registered for use with Google Voice.

Getting your Google Voice messages

Google Voice transcribes your voice mail messages. They all show up eventually in your Gmail account, just as if someone sent you an email instead of left you a voice mail. That's a good way to deal with your messages, but it's not the best way.

The best way to handle Google Voice is to use the Voice app, available from the Android Market. Use the QR code in the margin, or visit the Android Market to search for and install the Google Voice app. (See Chapter 18 for details.)

Once installed, the Google Voice app provides the best interface for getting your messages. You'll have to work through some setup, which isn't difficult. Eventually you'll see the app's main interface, which looks and works similar to an email program. You can review your messages or touch a message to read or play the message, as illustrated in Figure 7-1.

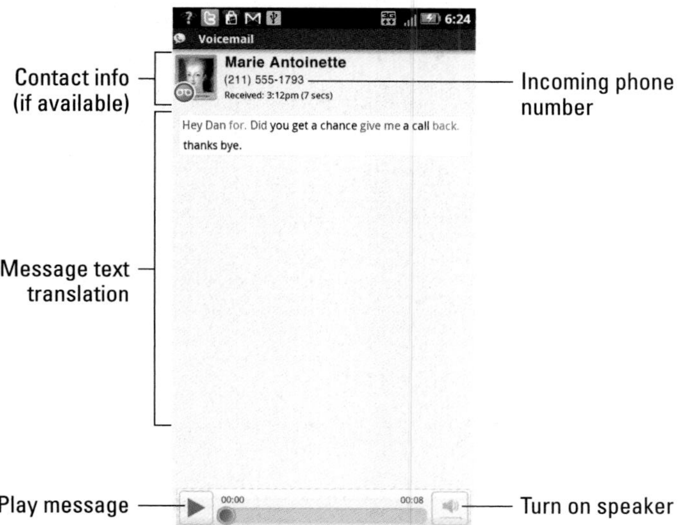

Figure 7-1: Voice mail with the Google Voice app.

When new Google Voice messages come in, you'll see the Google Voice notification icon appear, as shown in the margin. Pull down the notifications and choose the Voicemail from *whomever* item to read or listen to the message.

- With Google Voice installed, you'll get two notices for each voice mail message left: One from Google Voice and another for the Gmail message that comes in.
- The Google Voice app works only when you've activated Google Voice for your Droid X2, as described in the preceding section.
- You can best listen to the message when using the Google Voice app. In Gmail, you'll see a transcript of the message, but you must touch the Play Message link to visit the Internet and then listen to the message.
- The text translation feature in Google Voice is at times astonishingly accurate and at other times not so good.
- The text *Transcript Not Available* appears when Google Voice is unable to create a text message from your voice mail, or when the Google Voice service is temporarily unavailable.

8

The Address Book

In This Chapter

- Using the Contacts list
- Finding contacts
- Creating contacts
- Finding a contact from a map search
- Editing a contact
- Putting a picture on a contact
- Working with favorites
- Deleting contacts

At some point, you recognize that you can't keep contact information inside your head. Maybe when you were younger you could remember a few key phone numbers or an address or two. But eventually, you end up writing things down. Then you get organized and maybe keep things in an address book or — dare I say it — a computer.

The problem with any address book, real-world or digital, is that you need to have it with you all the time. So the geniuses at Motorola smooshed the address book into your Droid X2, combining it with your Gmail contact list, Facebook friends, and other sources. The result is the Contacts app, where all the people you know and all the information about them is stored on your phone.

The People You Know

Given that the Droid X2 can phone, email, text, or socially network with your friends, it just makes sense to keep all your friends inside the phone.

No. Wait. It makes sense to keep *information* about your friends in the phone. Not only your friends, but work associates, professionals, restaurants, businesses, and even those people whose name you don't know that you smile at when you go to church — all that information can be accessed on your Droid X2, thanks to the Contacts app.

Presenting the Contacts list

View the Droid X2 address book by opening the Contacts app, which can be found on the main Home screen or on the Apps screen.

The full contact list can also be accessed from the Dialer app. In fact, the Dialer app and the Contacts app both go to the same screen. The difference is that when you open the Contacts app, you see the Contacts tab, as shown in Figure 8-1.

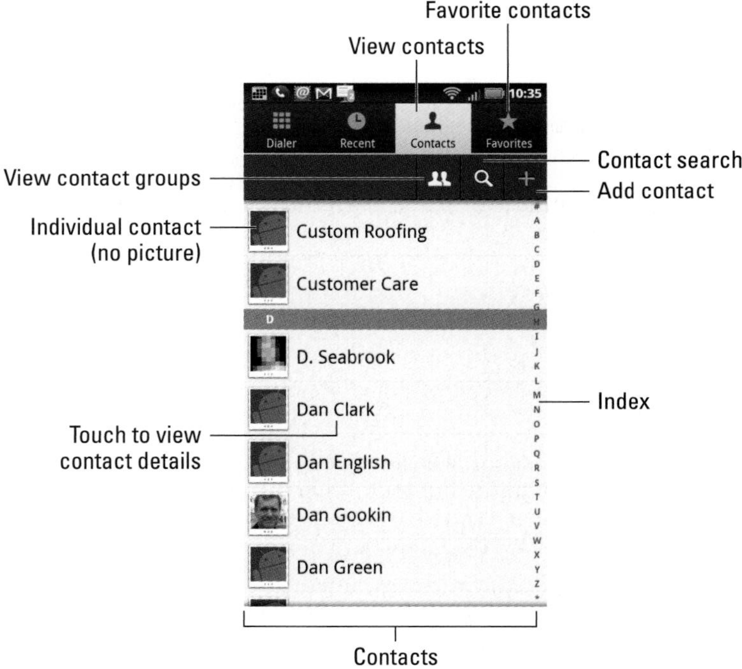

Figure 8-1: The Contacts list.

Scroll the list by swiping with your finger. You can use the index on the right side of the screen (refer to Figure 8-1) to quickly navigate up and down the list.

To do anything with a contact, you first have to choose it: Touch a contact name and you see more information, as shown in Figure 8-2.

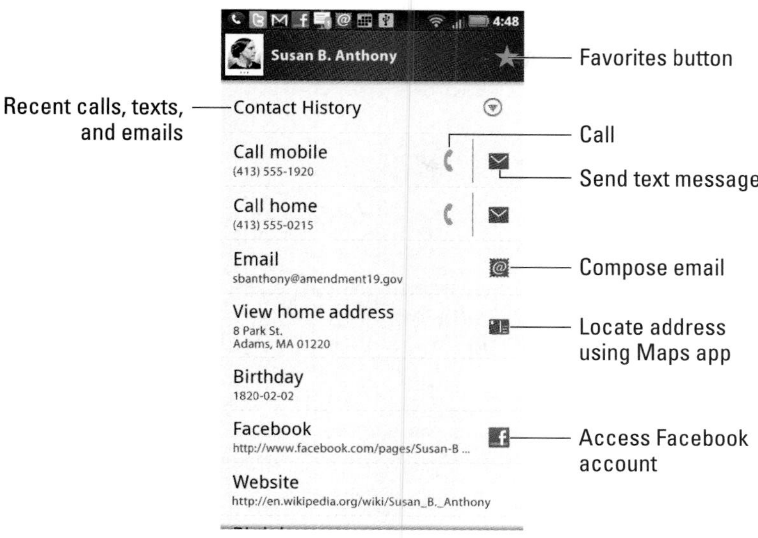

Figure 8-2: More details for a contact.

You can do a multitude of things with the contact after it's displayed, as shown in the figure:

Make a phone call. To call a contact, touch one of the contact's Call entries, such as Home or Mobile. See Chapter 5.

Send a text message. Touch the Text Message icon (refer to Figure 8-2) to open the Messaging app and send that contact a message. See Chapter 9 for information about text messaging on your Droid X2.

Compose an email message. Touch the Email link to compose an email message to the contact. When a contact has more than one email address, you can choose to which one you want to send the message. Chapter 10 covers using email on your phone.

View social networking info. Visit the contact's Facebook, Twitter, or other social networking accounts by touching the appropriate item. See Chapter 12 for more information on accessing social networking sites using your Droid X2.

Locate your contact on a map. When a contact has a home or business address, you can touch the little doohickey next to the address (refer to Figure 8-2) to summon the Maps application. Refer to Chapter 13 for all the fun stuff you can do with Maps.

Oh, and if you have added birthday information, you can view it as well. Singing "Happy Birthday" is something you have to do on your own.

Those weird people

Some people in the Contacts list aren't people at all. They're preset contacts, which represent various phone company services. Here's the list:

- **#BAL:** Receive a free text message indicating your current cell phone charges as well as any previous payments you've made.
- **#DATA:** Receive a free text message indicating your text message or data usage.
- **#MIN:** Receive a free text message indicating the minutes you've used on the Droid X2.
- **#PMT:** Make a payment using your phone, but only when you've configured your account to make payments that way.
- **Customer Care:** Contact Verizon support for your phone. (The contact is actually a shortcut for the number 611, which is the support number for your cell phone.)

See Chapter 9 for more information on text messaging.

When you're done viewing the contact, press the Back soft button.

Information for your contacts is pulled from multiple sources: from your Google account, in the phone's storage, and from your social networking sites. When you see duplicated information for a contact, it's often because the information comes from two or more locations. You can view sources for a contact when you edit the contact's information, as covered later in this chapter.

Sorting the contact list

Your contacts are displayed in the Contact list in a certain order: alphabetically by first name and listed first name first. You can change that order, if you like:

1. **Start the Contacts app.**
2. **Press the Menu soft button and choose Display Options.**
3. **Choose Sort List By.**
4. **Select Last Name or First Name to sort the list accordingly.**

   I prefer last name, which is how most rolodexes are organized.
5. **Choose View Contact Names As.**
6. **Choose First Name First or Last Name First, which sets how the contacts are displayed in the list.**

   The way the name is displayed does not affect the sort order. So if you choose First Name First (as I have) as well as Last Name for the sort order (as I have), you still see the list sorted by last name.
7. **Press the Back soft button when you're done.**

The contact list is updated, displayed per your preferences.

Searching contacts

Rather than scroll the Contacts list with angst-riddled desperation, press the Search soft button or choose the Search button in the Contacts app (refer to Figure 8-1). A Search Contacts text box appears. Type a few letters from the contact's name and you see the list of contacts narrowed to those few whose names match the letters you type. Touch a name from the search list to view the contact's information.

No correlation exists between the number of contacts you have and the number of bestest friends you have — none at all.

Make New Friends

You have many ways to put contact information into your phone. You can build a list of contacts from scratch, but that method is tedious. More likely, you collect contacts as you use your phone. Or you can borrow contacts from your Gmail, Facebook, Twitter, or other contacts. In no time, you have a phone full of contact information.

Adding a new contact from the Recent call log

One of the quickest ways to build your Contacts list is to add people as they phone you — assuming that you've told them about your new phone number. After someone calls, you can use the call log to add the person to your Contacts list. Obey these steps:

1. **Open the Dialer or Contacts app.**

   They both take you to the same basic place.

2. **Touch the Recent tab at the top of the screen.**
3. **Choose the phone number you want to create a contact for.**
4. **Choose Add to Contacts.**
5. **Choose Create a New Contact.**
6. **Choose Google.**

   I recommend creating the new contact using your Google account, which means whatever information you supply about the contact is duplicated on the Internet.

   You can place a check mark by Remember this Choice to ensure that you won't be prompted again

7. **Touch OK.**

8. **Fill in the contact's information.**

   Fill in the blanks — as many as you know about the caller: first name and family name and other information. If you know no additional information, that's fine; just filling in the name helps clue you in to who is calling the next time that person calls (using that number).

9. **Touch the Save button to create the contact.**

You can use these steps to add a new phone number to an existing contact. In Step 5, choose a person from your contacts list. The phone number is added to that existing contact's information.

Creating a new contact from scratch

Sometimes, you must create a contact when you meet another human being in the real world. In that case, you have more information to input, and the process starts like this:

1. **Open the Contacts app.**

2. **Touch the Add Contact button found near the top of the screen.**

3. **If prompted, choose Google as the account to store the contact.**

   I recommend using Google because its contacts are automatically synchronized and backed up on the Internet.

4. **Touch the OK button.**

5. **Fill in the information about the contact.**

   - Fill in the text fields with the information you know: first name, family name, and phone number plus perhaps an email address. That's all good, basic information for a contact.
   - Use the green plus sign button to add another item, such as a second phone number or an email address.
   - Touch the gray button to the left of the phone number or email address to choose the location for that item, such as Home, Work, or Mobile.
   - Touch the More button at the bottom of the list to add *even more* information!

6. **Touch the Save button to finish editing and add the new contact.**

If you'd rather not go through the toil of creating a contact on the phone using the onscreen keyboard, just use a computer instead: Visit your Gmail account on the Internet and use the computer's full-size keyboard and screen to create the contact.

Importing contacts from your computer

Your computer's email program is doubtless a useful repository of contacts that you've built up over the years. You can export those contacts from your email program and then import them into the Droid X2. It's not the simplest process, but it's possible.

The key is to save or export the records in the *vCard* (`.vcf`) file format, which can then be read by the phone. The technique for exporting your contacts varies depending on the email program:

- In the Windows Live Mail program, choose Go⇨Contacts and then choose File⇨Export⇨Business Card (.VCF) to export the contacts.
- In Windows Mail, choose File⇨Export⇨Windows Contacts and then choose vCards (Folder of .VCF Files) from the Export Windows Contacts dialog box. Click the Export button.
- On the Mac, open the Address Book program and choose File⇨Export⇨Export vCard.

After the vCard files are created, connect the Droid X2 to your computer and transfer the vCard files from your computer to the phone. Directions for making such a transfer can be found in Chapter 20.

Once the vCard files are on the Droid X2, follow these steps in the Contacts app to complete the process:

1. **Press the Menu soft button.**
2. **Choose the Import/Export command.**
3. **Choose the SD Card command below the heading Import Contacts From.**

   Yeah, it's a dumb design decision to have two SD Card commands on the same menu. Bad, Motorola. Bad!
4. **Choose Google, then touch the OK button.**
5. **If prompted, choose Import All vCard Files.**
6. **Touch the OK button.**

   The contacts are saved on your phone, and also to your Gmail account, which instantly creates a backup copy.

Build up contacts from your social networking sites

After you tell your Droid X2 which social networking sites you use, the phone scours those sites, looking for your friends and followers for information. New contacts are built automatically from that information and automatically placed into your phone's Contacts list. Even the avatar images associated with the accounts are imported.

The key to pulling in contacts from your social networking sites is to use the Social Networking app on the Droid X2. Using that app is covered in Chapter 12.

Finding a new contact by using its location

When you use the Maps application to locate a restaurant, haberdashery, or public defender, you can quickly create a contact for that location. Here's how:

1. **After searching for your location, touch the cartoon bubble that appears on the map.**

   See Chapter 13 for more information on the cartoon bubble thing.

2. **Touch the More button.**
3. **Choose Add as a Contact.**
4. **If prompted, choose Google to create the contact as a Gmail contact; touch the OK button to confirm.**

   The information from the Maps application is copied into the proper fields for the contact, including the address and phone number, plus other information (if available).

5. **Touch the Save button.**

   The new contact is created.

Contact Management

When information about a contact changes, or perhaps if your thumbs were a bit too big when you created the contact while riding a bus during an earthquake, you can edit the contact's information. Aside from just editing existing information or adding new items, you can do a smattering of interesting things, as covered in this section.

- See Chapter 6 for information on configuring contacts so that all their incoming calls go to voice mail.
- Also refer to Chapter 6 on how to set a contact's ringtone.

Making basic changes

To make minor touch-ups on any contact, start by locating and displaying the contact's information. Press the Menu soft button and choose Edit Contact.

The contact's information is displayed, organized by source. You may see Google contact information, information stored on the phone, or information culled from web email services or online social networking sites.

Change or add information by touching a field and using the onscreen keyboard.

Some information cannot be edited. For example, fields pulled in from social networking sites can be edited only by that account holder on the social networking site.

When you're done editing, touch the Save button.

Adding a picture to a contact

Displaying a contact with a pretty picture is so much nicer than using just the generic android icon. Well, unless your contact is, in fact, an android.

To add a picture to your contact, it helps to already have the picture stored on the phone. You can transfer the picture from a computer (covered in Chapter 20) or snap a shot with the phone anytime you see the contact or a person or an object that resembles the contact.

After the contact's photo, or any other suitable image, is stored on the phone, follow these steps to update the contact's information:

1. **Locate and display the contact's information.**
2. **Press the Menu soft button and choose the Edit Contact command.**
3. **Touch the contact's picture icon.**

4a. **To pull a picture from the phone's photo gallery, choose Select Photo from Gallery.**

You may be prompted to choose the Gallery app; do so. After browsing your photos, touch one to instantly assign it to the contact. You're done.

4b. **If the contact is in front of you and willing to have a picture taken, choose the Take Photo command.**

5. **Use the Droid X2 camera to take the contact's photo.**

   Chapter 14 discusses using the Droid X2's camera.

6. **Choose Retake to try again, Done to keep the photo, or Cancel to give up.**
7. **After choosing Done, select the size and portion of the image you want to use for the contact.**

   Use Figure 8-3 as your guide. You can choose which portion of the image to use by moving the cropping box; resize the cropping box to select more or less of the image; and rotate the image.

8. **Touch Save to assign the image to the contact.**
9. **Touch the Save button to complete the editing of the contact.**

   The image is now assigned, and it appears whenever you phone the contact or they phone you.

Figure 8-3: Cropping a contact's image.

To change an existing photograph, follow Steps 1 through 3 in this section, then choose Change Icon. Or to remove a contact's photo, choose the command Remove Icon.

- Refer to Chapter 14 for more information on how the Droid X2 camera works.
- Chapter 15 has information on using the Gallery.

Making a favorite

A *favorite* contact is someone you stay in touch with more often than others. It doesn't have to be someone you like — just someone you (perhaps unfortunately) phone often, like your dentist.

When you touch the Favorites button in the Contacts list, you see a list of favorites, similar to what's shown in Figure 8-4. The top part of the list shows favorite favorites, or those favorite contacts you contact frequently.

To add a contact to the Favorites list, display the contact's information and touch the Favorites button (the star) in the upper-right corner of the Contacts screen (refer to Figure 8-2). When the star is green, as shown in Figure 8-2, the contact is one of your favorites.

To remove a favorite, touch the contact's star until it loses its color. Removing a favorite doesn't delete the contact but does remove it from the Favorites list.

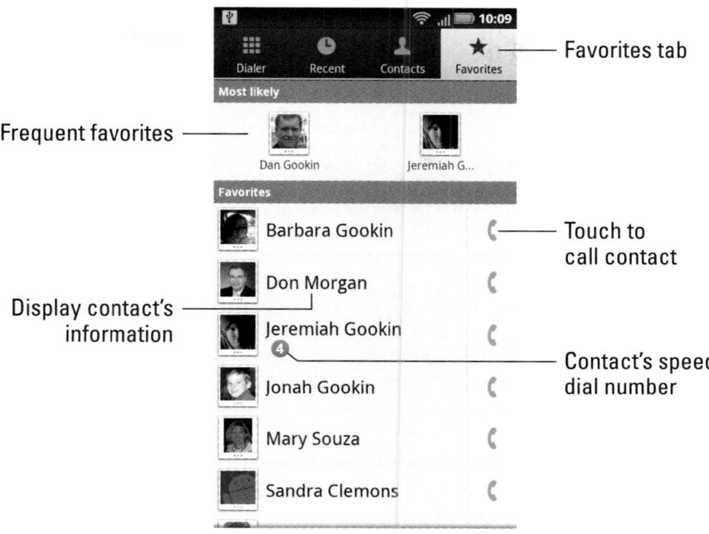

Figure 8-4: Favorite contacts.

Sharing a contact

You know Bill? I know Bill, too! But you don't have his contact information? Allow me to share that with you. Here's what I do:

1. **Summon the contact you want to share from your Contacts list.**
2. **Press the Menu soft button.**
3. **Choose Share.**
4. **Choose which items to share.**

   All the contact's information is selected; touch a green check mark to remove an item if you don't want to share it.
5. **Touch the OK button.**
6. **Choose a method to share the contact, such as Gmail or Text Messaging.**
7. **Proceed with composing an email message, typing a text message, or completing whatever action is necessary to send the contact information.**

In a few Internet moments, the message is received. It contains an attachment, which is the contact's *vCard* information. The recipient can then import that card or do whatever else with it to add it to his or her own Contacts list.

Removing a contact

Every so often, consider reviewing your phone's contacts. Purge those folks whom you no longer recognize or you've forgotten. It's simple:

1. **Locate the contact in your Contacts list and display the contact's information.**
2. **Press the Menu soft button.**
3. **Choose Delete Contact.**
4. **Touch the OK button.**

   The contact is removed from your phone's address books, and potentially from your Gmail contact list as well.

For some linked accounts, such as Facebook, deleting the contact from your phone doesn't remove the human from your Facebook account. You have to unfriend the person on Facebook to remove them.

Part III
Other Ways to Stay in Touch

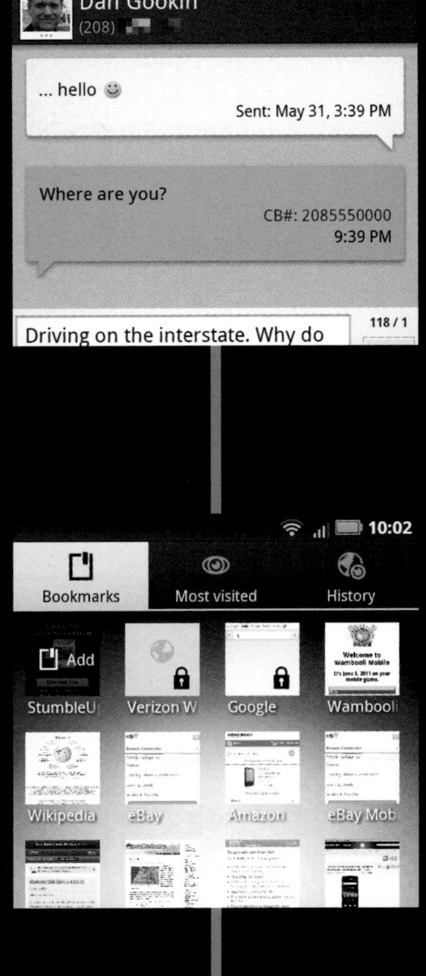

In this part . . .

In 1844, the official message sent to open the first telegraph line was What hath God wrought. In 1876, Alexander Graham Bell said, “Mr. Watson, come here, I want to see you” over his telephone invention. And in 1973, the first email message was sent between two computer scientists, the first asking the second whether he was interested in purchasing some low-cost Viagra. Communications has come a long way.

You can employ your Droid X2 smartphone in a variety of ways to send messages using multiple methods. The most obvious way is making a phone call. And while the Droid X lacks a telegraph feature, you can use it to send email as well as other forms of communications far and wide, obvious or not, as covered in this part of the book.

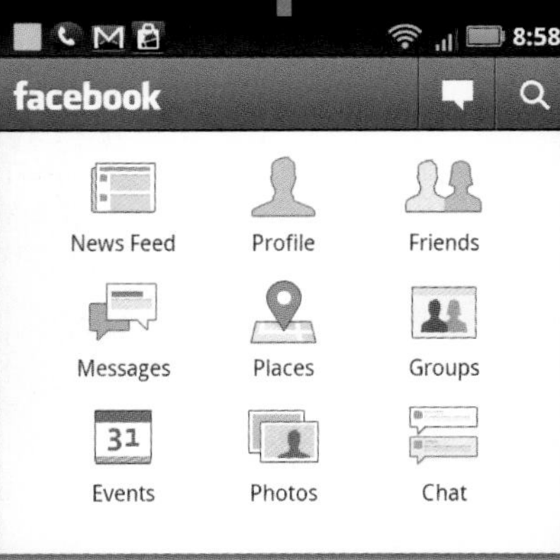

9

When Your Thumbs Do the Talking

In This Chapter

- Creating a text message
- Getting a text message
- Forwarding text messages
- Texting pictures, videos, and media
- Managing your text messages

The whole text-message enchilada should be instantly familiar with you if you're under 25. My guess is that you're not under 25. In fact, you probably purchased this book because it's lighter and cheaper than hauling a 25-year-old around with you wherever you go. Minus that 25-year-old, you'll need the information in this chapter to understand, appreciate, and use the texting feature on your Droid X2. It's handy, even if your 25th birthday was around the time NBC was announcing that its evening TV programs were broadcast "in living color."

Message for You!

The common term for using a cell phone to send a text message to another cell phone is *texting*. I prefer to say "sending a text message." The app that handles this job on your Droid X2 is called Text Messaging.

- Some Android applications can affect messaging. You're alerted to whether the app affects messaging before the app is installed. See Chapter 18.
- Your cellular service plan may charge you per message for every text message you send. Some plans feature a given number of free messages per month. Other plans, favored by teenagers (and their parents), feature unlimited texting.

- The nerdy term for texting is *SMS*, which stands for Short Message Service.

Composing a new text message to a contact

Because most cell phones sport a text-messaging feature, you can send a text message to just about any mobile number. It works like this:

1. **Open the Contacts app.**
2. **Choose a contact, someone to whom you want to send a text message.**
3. **Touch the Message icon next to the contact's mobile number.**

The Message icon looks like an envelope, as shown in the margin. A message composition window appears, which also tracks your text conversation, similar to the one shown in Figure 9-1.

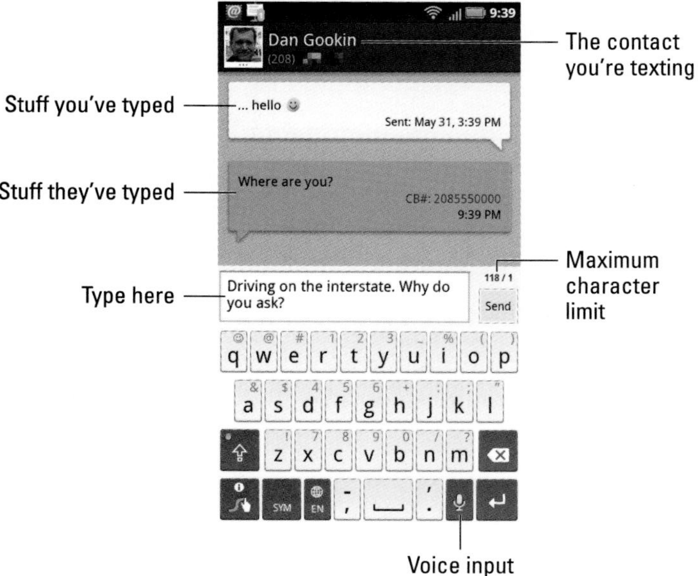

Figure 9-1: Typing a text message.

4. **Type the message text.**

Be brief. A text message has a 160-character limit. See the later sidebar "Common text-message abbreviations," for some useful text-message shortcuts and acronyms.

5. **Touch the Send button.**

   The message is sent instantly. Whether the contact replies instantly depends. When the person replies, you see the message (refer to Figure 9-1).

6. **Read the reply.**

7. **Repeat Steps 4 through 6 as needed — or eternally, whichever comes first.**

There's no need to continually look at the phone, waiting for a text message. Whenever your contact chooses to reply, you see the message recorded as part of an ongoing conversation. See the later section "Receiving a text message."

- You can send text messages only to cell phones. Grandma cannot receive text messages on her landline that she's had since the 1960s.
- Yes, using Swype to type is much faster than using the standard onscreen keyboard. See Chapter 4.
- You can also dictate text messages by clicking the Microphone button on the onscreen keyboard. See Chapter 4 for more information on voice input.
- Add a subject to your message by touching the Menu soft button, then Add Subject. On the original Droid X, choose the More command, then Add Subject.
- Phone numbers and email addresses sent in text messages become links. You can touch a link to call that number or visit the web page.

- Press the Back soft button to dismiss the onscreen keyboard, which can be useful when the keyboard obscures all or part of a message.
- Continue a conversation at any time: Open the Text Messaging application, peruse the list of existing conversations, and touch one to review what has been said or to pick up the conversation.

- Do not text and drive. Do not text and drive. Do not text and drive.

Common text-message abbreviations

Texting isn't about proper English. Indeed, many of the abbreviations and shortcuts used in texting are slowly becoming part of the English language, such as LOL and BRB.

The weird news is that these acronyms weren't invented by teenagers. Sure, the kids use them, but the acronyms find their roots in the Internet chat rooms of yesteryear. Regardless of their source, you might find them handy for typing messages quickly. Or maybe you can use this reference for deciphering an acronym's meaning. You can type acronyms in either uppercase or lowercase.

2	To, also
411	Information
BRB	Be right back
BTW	By the way
CYA	See you
FWIW	For what it's worth
FYI	For your information
GB	Goodbye
GJ	Good job
GR8	Great
GTG	Got to go
HOAS	Hold on a second
IC	I see
IDK	I don't know
IMO	In my opinion
JK	Just kidding
K	Okay
L8R	Later
LMAO	Laughing my [rear] off
LMK	Let me know
LOL	Laugh out loud
NC	No comment
NP	No problem
OMG	Oh my goodness!
PIR	People in room (watching)
POS	Person over shoulder (watching)
QT	Cutie
ROFL	Rolling on the floor, laughing
SOS	Someone over shoulder (watching)
TC	Take care
THX	Thanks
TIA	Thanks in advance
TMI	Too much information
TTFN	Ta-ta for now (goodbye)
TTYL	Talk to you later
TY	Thank you
U2	You, too
UR	Your, you are
VM	Voice mail
W8	Wait
XOXO	Hugs and kisses
Y	Why?
YW	You're welcome
ZZZ	Sleeping

Sending a text message when you know only the phone number

I recommend that you create a contact for anyone you plan to message. It just saves time to have the contact there, with — at minimum — a name and phone number. When you don't want to create a contact first, send any cell phone a text message by following these steps:

1. **Open the Text Messaging app.**

   The Text Messaging app, like all apps installed on the Droid X2, can be found on the Apps screen: Touch the Launcher button on the Home screen.

   You see a list of current conversations (if any), organized by contact name or phone number.

2. **Touch the green plus button, found at the top of the touchscreen.**
3. **Input a cell phone number in the To field.**

   When the number you type matches one or more existing contacts, those contacts are displayed. Choose one to send a message to that person; otherwise, continue typing the phone number.

4. **Touch the Enter Message Here text box.**
5. **Type your text message.**
6. **Touch the Send button to send the message.**

The message is sent instantly. You can wait for a reply or do something else with the phone, such as snooze it or choose to talk with a real person, face to face. Or you can always get back to work.

Whether to send a text message or an email?

Sending a text message is similar to sending an email message. Both involve sending a message instantly to someone else. Yet both methods of communication have their advantages and disadvantages.

Text messages are short and to the point. They're informal, more like quick chats. Indeed, the speed of reply is often what makes text messaging useful. But like sending email, sending a text message doesn't guarantee a reply.

An email message can be longer than a text message. You can receive email on any computer or device that can access the Internet, such as your Droid X2. Email message attachments (pictures, documents) are handled better, and more consistently, than text message (MMS) media. You can also reply to everyone in an email message (Reply All), but you can only send an initial text message to multiple recipients.

Finally, though email isn't considered formal communication, not like a paper letter or a phone call, it ranks higher in formality than a text message.

Receiving a text message

Whenever a new text message comes in, you see a message appear at the top of the Droid X2 touchscreen. The message goes away quickly, and then you see the New Text Message notification, shown in the margin.

To view the message, pull down the notifications, as described in Chapter 3. Touch the messaging notification and that conversation window immediately opens.

Forwarding a text message

It's possible to forward a text message, but it's not the same as forwarding email. In fact, when it comes to forwarding information, email has text messaging beat by well over 160 characters.

The bottom line is, you can forward only the information in a text-messaging cartoon bubble, not the entire conversation. Here's how it works:

1. **If necessary, open a conversation in the Messages app.**
2. **Long-press the text entry (the cartoon bubble) you want to forward.**
3. **From the menu that appears, choose Forward Message.**

   From this point on, forwarding the message works like sending a new message from scratch:
4. **Type the recipient's name (if he or she is a contact) or type a phone number.**

   The text you're forwarding appears already written in the text field.
5. **Touch the Send button to forward the message.**

Opting out of text messaging

You don't have to be a part of the text-messaging craze. Indeed, it's entirely possible to opt out of text messaging altogether. Simply contact your cellular provider and tell them that you'd like to disable text messaging on your phone. They will happily comply, and you'll never be able to send or receive a text message again.

People opt out of text messaging for a number of reasons. A big one is cost: If the kids keep running up the text messaging bill, it's often easier to simply disable the feature than to keep paying all the usage surcharges. Another reason is security: viruses and spam can be sent via text message. If you opt out, you don't have to worry about receiving unwanted text messages.

Multimedia Messages

When a text message contains a bit of audio or video or a picture, it ceases becoming a mere text message and transforms into — *ta-da!* — a multimedia message. This type of message even has its own acronym, MMS, which supposedly stands for Multimedia Messaging Service.

- You can send pictures, video, and audio using multimedia messaging.
- There's no need to run a separate program or do anything fancy to send media in a text message; the same Messaging app is used on the Droid X2 for sending both text and media messages. Just follow the advice in this section.
- Not every mobile phone has the capability to receive MMS messages. Rather than get the media, the recipient is directed to a web page where the media can be viewed on the Internet.

Attaching media to a message

You don't need to go hunting for already created multimedia to send in a message; you can attach media directly to any message or ongoing conversation. It works like this:

1. **Compose a text message as you normally do.**

   Refer to the directions earlier in this chapter.

2. **Press the Menu soft button.**
3. **Choose Insert.**

   A pop-up menu appears, listing various media items you can attach to a text message.

   Here's a summary:

   Existing Picture: Choose an image stored in the phone's Gallery.

   New Picture: Take a picture right now and send it in a text message.

   Existing Audio: Attach a song from the music library.

   New Audio: Record an audio clip, such as your voice, and then send it.

   Existing Video: Choose a video you've taken with the phone and stored in the Gallery.

   New Video: Record a video and then send it as media in a text message.

   Slideshow: Create a collection of photos to send together.

Location: Send your latitude and longitude, address, or a Google Maps web link.

Name card: Attach contact information in the form of a vCard.

More options may appear on the menu, depending on which apps you have installed on your Droid X2.

4. **If prompted, choose which app to use for obtaining or creating the media.**
5. **Choose a media attachment from the pop-up menu.**

   What happens next depends on the attachment you've selected.

   For existing media, you choose from among media stored on your phone.

   For creating new media, you use various apps on the phone to record or capture the image, video, or audio.

   The Slideshow option presents a second screen, where you collect media stored on the Droid X2. Use the icons on top of that screen to add items to the slideshow.

   The Name Card option displays the phone's address book. Choose a contact and that contact's information is then translated into a vCard file and attached to your text message.
6. **(Optional) Compose a message to go with the media attachment.**
7. **Touch the Send button to send your media text message.**

In just a few, short, cellular moments, the receiving party will enjoy your multimedia text message.

- Not every phone is capable of receiving multimedia messages.

- It's also possible to create a multimedia message by choosing one of the many Share commands found in media apps. Touch the Share button, or choose the Share command, then select Text Messaging as the method by which you'll share the media.
- Pictures and videos may need to be resized (compressed) to send as a text-message attachment. If so, you'll be prompted and the Droid X2 resizes the media automatically.

- A *vCard* is a contact-information file format, commonly used by email programs and contact management software. Whether the recipient can do anything with a vCard in a multimedia text message is up to the recipient's phone software.

It's an emergency alert!

Another type of message you can receive on your Droid X2 is the emergency alert. To peruse your options, open the Apps screen and then the Emergency Alerts app. On the main Emergency Alerts screen, you see any pending alerts, such as evacuation alerts for your area or even AMBER Alerts.

To configure emergency alerts, press the Menu soft button when viewing the main Emergency Alerts screen. Choose the Settings command. You can review the types of available alerts by choosing the Receive Alerts menu command.

Press the Home soft button to exit the Emergency Alerts app.

Receiving a multimedia message

Multimedia attachments come into your Droid X2 just like any other text message does, but you see a thumbnail preview of whatever media was sent, such as an image, a still from a video, or a Play button to listen to audio. To preview the attachment, touch it. To do more with the multimedia attachment, long-press it. Choose how to deal with the attachment by selecting an option from the menu that's displayed.

For example, to save an image attachment in a text message, long-press the image thumbnail and choose the Save Picture command.

Some types of attachments, such as audio, cannot be saved.

Clean Up Your Conversations

Even though I'm a stickler for deleting email after I read it, I don't bother deleting my text message threads. That might be because I get far more email than text messages. Anyway, were I to delete a text message conversation, I would follow these exact steps:

1. **Open the conversation you want to remove.**

   Choose the conversation from the main Messaging screen. You get to that screen from any conversation by pressing the Back soft button.

2. **Touch the Menu soft button.**
3. **Choose Delete.**
4. **Touch the Delete button to confirm.**

   The conversation is gone.

If I wanted to delete every dangdoodle conversation shown on the main Messaging screen, I'd follow these steps:

1. **Touch the Menu soft button.**
2. **Choose Select Multiple.**
3. **Touch the box next to each conversation you want to zap.**

   Obviously, if you want to keep one, don't touch its box; touch all boxes to delete all conversations.

   A green check mark appears by conversations slated for execution.
4. **Touch the Delete button.**
5. **Touch the Delete button again to confirm.**

The selected messages are gone.

10

Email This and That

In This Chapter

- Understanding email on the Droid X2
- Configuring a new email account
- Receiving a new message
- Finding messages and email text
- Creating and sending email
- Working with email attachments
- Making an email signature
- Changing various email options and settings

It's number two! It's number two!

Once upon a time, email was the number-one reason for people to use the Internet. That's no longer true, with Facebook and social networking now the number one reason. Still, email has its place: It's faster than a telegraph and cheaper than a first class stamp. Your email is also available wherever you go, because the Droid X2 can both send and receive your electronic missives.

Mail Call!

Electronic mail is handled on the Droid X2 by two apps: Gmail and Email.

The Gmail app hooks directly into the Gmail account associated with your Google account, which you already have on your Droid X2. In fact, the accounts are exact echoes of each other: The Gmail you receive on your computer is also received on your phone.

You can also use the Email app on your phone to connect to non-Gmail electronic mail, such as the standard mail service provided by your ISP or a web-based email system such as Yahoo! Mail or Microsoft Live Mail.

Regardless of the app, electronic mail on your phone works just like it does on your computer: You can receive mail, create new messages, forward email, send messages to a group of contacts, work with attachments, and so on. As long as your phone has a data connection, email works just peachy.

- You can run the Gmail and Email apps by touching the Launcher on the Home screen and then locating the apps on the Apps screen.
- Adding the Gmail or Email app icon to the Home screen is easy: See Chapter 22.
- The Email program can be configured to handle multiple email accounts, as discussed in the next section.
- Although you can use your phone's web browser to visit the Gmail web site, you should use the Gmail app to pick up your Gmail.
- If you forget your Gmail password, visit this web address: `www.google.com/accounts/ForgotPasswd`.

Setting up a web-based email account

You need to configure the Droid X2 to access any non-Gmail email account. The process is easy for web-based email accounts such as Yahoo Mail. The process is not as easy for ISP mail accounts. Either way, follow through with these steps to get things set up:

1. **Start the My Accounts app.**

   The My Accounts app is found in the Apps screen, which you access by touching the Launcher button at the bottom of the Home screen.

2. **Touch the Add Account button.**
3. **If your account type, such as Yahoo Mail, is shown in the list, choose it. Otherwise, choose the Email icon.**
4. **Type the account's email address and password.**
5. **Press the Back soft button to dismiss the onscreen keyboard.**
6. **Touch the Next button.**

   In a few magical moments, the email account is configured and added to the account list.

   If you goofed up the account name or password, you'll be warned: Try again.

7. **Touch the Done button.**

If your attempt is not met with success, you'll have to configure the account manually. That's the bad news. The good news is that the phone may help you by providing suggestions. Follow them.

It might also be necessary to work through the steps in the next section to configure your email account.

Setting up an ISP email account

Setting up a traditional email account, such as the one you have with your ISP, requires a bit of work. You'll need to know basic information provided by your ISP, such as the POP3 and SMTP server names, passwords, and stuff like that. Then you follow these steps:

1. **Start the My Accounts app.**

   Look for the app on the Apps screen.

2. **Touch the Add Account button.**
3. **Choose the Email icon to add your Internet email account.**
4. **Type the email address you use for the account and its password.**
5. **Remove the check mark by the option Automatically Configure Account.**

   You need to supply more information for the Droid X2 to configure a standard Internet email account, such as the one given to you by your ISP.

6. **Touch the Next button.**

   If necessary, press the Back soft button to dismiss the onscreen keyboard so that you can see the Next button.

7. **Choose General Settings.**
8. **Fill in the information for account name, real name, and email address:**

   - For the Account Name field, type a name to help you recognize the account, such as Comcast Email. For my main email account, I used the name *Main*.
   - In the Real Name field, type your name, screen name, or whatever name you want to appear in the From field of your outgoing email messages.
   - The Email Address field is the address your recipients use when replying to your messages.

9. **Touch the OK button.**

   Press the Back soft button, if necessary, to dismiss the onscreen keyboard so that you can see the OK button.

10. Choose Incoming Server.

11. Fill in the fields per the information provided by your Internet service provider (ISP):

- For most ISP email, the server type is a POP mail server, shown at the top of the screen.
- The Server field contains the name of the ISP's POP server. The Droid X2 may guess at the name; confirm that it's correct. If not, type the correct server name.
- The username is the name you use to log in to your ISP to retrieve email. The password is your ISP email password. Both fields should be preset for you.

12. Touch the OK button.

13. Choose Outgoing Server.

14. Fill in the fields.

- Fill in the SMTP Server name as provided by your ISP.
- Type your username and password, if they aren't already filled in for you.

15. Touch the OK button, and then touch OK to create the email account.

The account is now listed in the My Accounts screen, along with Google and Facebook and whatever other accounts you're accessing from your Droid X2.

You can set up a ton of email accounts on the Droid X2, one for each email account you have.

You've Got Mail

The Droid X2 works flawlessly with Gmail. In fact, if Gmail is already set up to be your main email address, you'll enjoy having access to your messages all the time by using your phone.

Regular email, handled by the Email program, must be set up before it can be used, as discussed earlier in this chapter. After completing that quick and relatively painful setup process, you can receive email on your phone just as you can on a computer.

Getting a new message

You're alerted to the arrival of a new email message in your phone by a notification icon. The icon differs between a new Gmail message and an Email message.

For a new Gmail message, you see the New Gmail notification, shown in the margin, at the top of the touchscreen.

For a new email message, you see the New Email notification.

Yahoo Mail also features its own new mail notification icon.

To deal with the new-message notification, drag down the notifications and choose the appropriate one. You're taken right to your inbox to read the new message.

- See the later section "Setting email options" to set up how the phone reacts when you get a new email message.
- Refer to Chapter 3 for information on notifications and how to peruse them.

Checking the inbox

To check the mail you have, start your email program — Gmail for your Google mail or Email for other mail you have configured to work with the Droid X2 — and open your electronic inbox.

To check your Gmail inbox, start the Gmail app, which can be found on the Apps screen. The Gmail inbox is shown in Figure 10-1.

To get to the inbox screen when you're reading a message, touch the Menu soft button and choose the command Go to Inbox.

To check your Email inbox, open the Email app. You're taken to the inbox for your primary email account. However, when you have multiple email accounts on your Droid X2, you should use the Messaging app, covered in the next section.

Search through your Gmail messages by pressing the Search soft key when you're viewing the Gmail inbox.

Gmail is organized using *labels*, not folders. To see your Gmail labels from the inbox, touch the Menu soft button and choose Go To Labels.

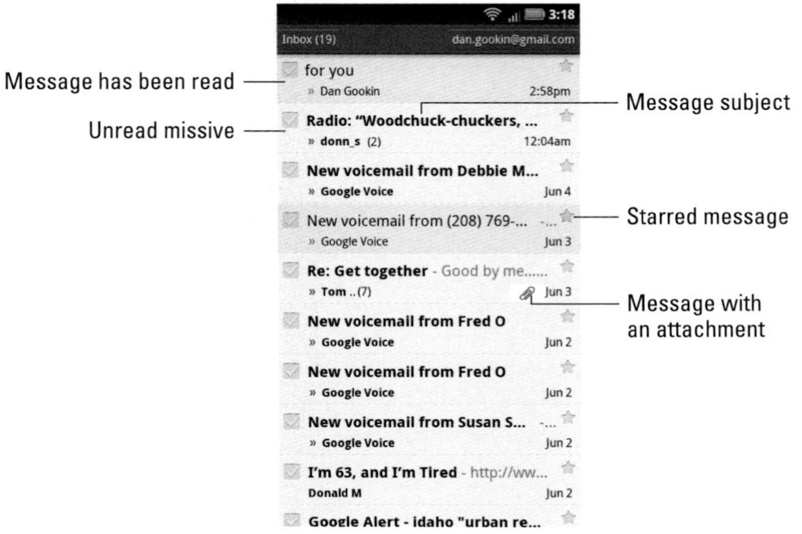

Figure 10-1: The Gmail inbox.

Visiting the universal inbox

An app in the Apps screen called Messaging is the home plate for every account on your Droid X2 that receives messages. It includes your email accounts, both Gmail and Email, as well as social networking sites and even text messaging.

To view all your messages, open the Messaging app. You see the main screen, shown in Figure 10-2.

New messages for an account are noted by a number shown in a blue circle (refer to Figure 10-2).

To view all messages — from email to Facebook updates — touch the Universal Inbox icon.

To compose a new message, touch the green plus-sign button (refer to Figure 10-2). Choose an account or a method for creating the new message from the menu that appears. You're then taken to the appropriate program (Email, Facebook, Text Messaging) to craft the new message.

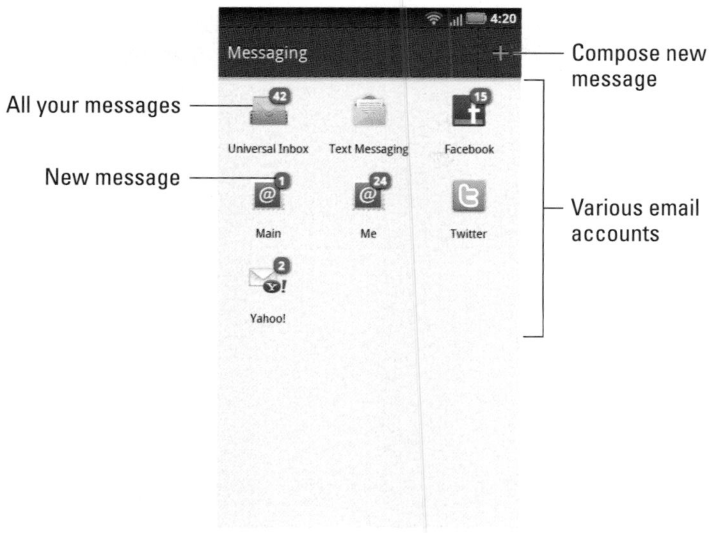

Figure 10-2: All your messages in one place.

Note that your Gmail inbox is missing from the Messaging window. Gmail is its own program on the Droid X2; your Gmail messages don't show up in the universal inbox.

Reading an email message

As mail comes in, you can read it by choosing one of the new email notifications, described earlier in this chapter. You can also choose new email by viewing the inbox in the Gmail or Email program. The message appears on the screen, as shown in Figure 10-3. Reading and working with the message operate much the same as in any email program you've used.

In the Email or Messaging program, you browse the messages in your inbox by touching the arrow button, found at the bottom of the message window.

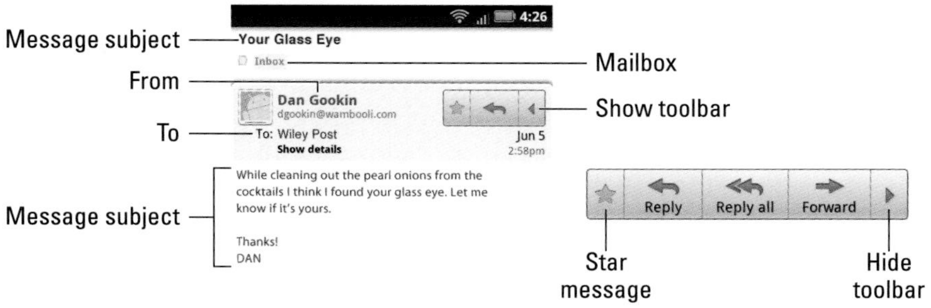

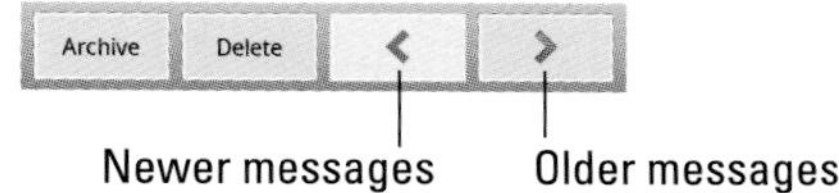

Figure 10-3: Reading a Gmail message on your phone.

Here are some things you can do with an email message you read on your Droid X2:

- To reply to the message, touch the Reply button, as shown in Figure 10-4. See the upcoming section "Composing a new electronic message" for information on working the reply screen, which behaves similarly to writing a new message.
- Touch the Reply All button to send a response to everyone in the original message's To and CC fields.

- Because most people find endless Reply All email threads annoying, use the Reply All option judiciously.
- Type or dictate your message reply; refer to Chapter 4 for information on typing and talking, if you're unfamiliar with either.
- To forward a Gmail message, touch the Forward button.
- When you touch the star icon in a Gmail message, you're flagging the message. Those starred messages can be viewed or searched separately, making them easier to locate later.

- To delete a message, touch the Delete button. I see no reason to delete messages in the Email program because they're deleted when your computer's email program picks them up later.
- I find it easier to delete (and manage) Gmail using a computer.

Figure 10-4: The Email app's Reply button.

Make Your Own Mail

Every so often, someone comes up to me and says, "Dan, you're a computer freak. You probably get a lot of email." I generally nod and smile. Then they say, "How can I get more email?" The answer is simple: To get mail, you have to send mail. Or you can just be a jerk on a blog and leave your email address there. That works, too, though I don't recommend it.

Composing a new electronic message

Crafting an email epistle on your Droid X2 works exactly like creating one on your computer. Figure 10-5 shows the basic setup.

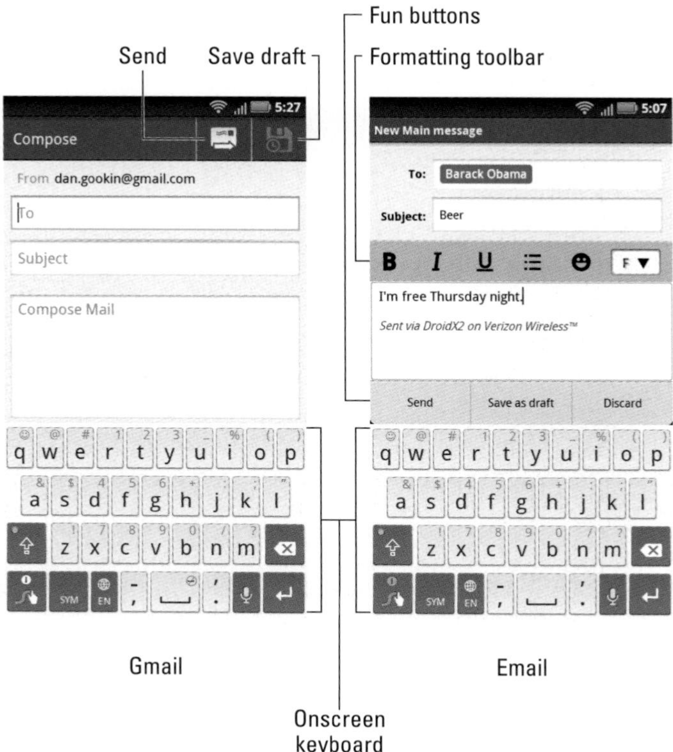

Figure 10-5: Writing a new email message.

Here's how to get there:

1. **Start an email program, either Gmail or Email, or use the Messaging app.**

2. **Press the Menu soft button.**
3. **Choose Compose.**

   You need to be viewing the inbox, not a specific message, for the Compose command to be available.

4. **If you are using the Messaging app, choose an account to send the message.**

   A new message screen appears, looking similar to Figure 10-4 but with none of the fields filled in. Text-formatting options are available only with the Email program, as shown in the figure.

5. **If necessary, touch the To field to select it.**
6. **Type the first few letters of a contact name, and then choose a matching contact from the list that's displayed.**

   You can also send to any valid email address not found in your Contacts list by typing that address.
7. **Type a subject.**

   Touch the Subject field and use the onscreen keyboard to type a subject. Or you can dictate the subject using voice input, as described in Chapter 4.
8. **Type the message.**
9. **Touch the Send button to whisk your missive to the Internet for immediate delivery.**

   In Gmail, you can touch the Save Draft button, which can be accessed by the Menu soft key; the message is stored in the Drafts folder. Open this folder to reedit the message. Touch Send to send it.

Copies of the messages you send in the Email program are stored in the Sent mailbox. If you're using Gmail, copies are saved in your Gmail account, which is accessed both from your phone and from any computer connected to the Internet.

- To cancel a message, press the Menu soft button and choose the Discard command. Touch the OK or Discard button to confirm.
- To summon the CC field in Gmail, press the Menu soft button and choose the command Add Cc/Bcc. In the Email program, press the Menu soft button and choose the Add CC button .
- Refer to Chapter 8 for more information on the Contacts list.
- Chapter 4 covers typing, voice input, and message editing.

Starting a new message from a contact

A quick and easy way to compose a new message is to find a contact and then create a message using that contact's information. Heed these steps:

1. **Open the Contacts list.**
2. **View the information for the contact to whom you want to send an electronic message.**

   Review Chapter 8 for ways to hunt down contacts in a long list.

3. **Touch the contact's email address.**
4. **Choose Email or Gmail to send the message.**

   At this point, creating the message works as described in the preceding section; refer to it for additional information.

Message Attachments

The Droid X2 lets you view most email attachments, depending on what's attached. You can also send attachments, though it's more of a computer thing, not something that's wholly useful on a cell phone. That's because cell phones, unlike computers, aren't really designed for creating or manipulating information.

Email messages with attachments are flagged in the inbox with paper clip icons, which seems to be the standard I-have-an-attachment icon for most email programs. When you open one of these files, you may see the attachment name, as shown in Figure 10-6. Touch the icon or the Preview button to witness the attachment on your phone; touch the Save button to save the attachment to the phone's storage.

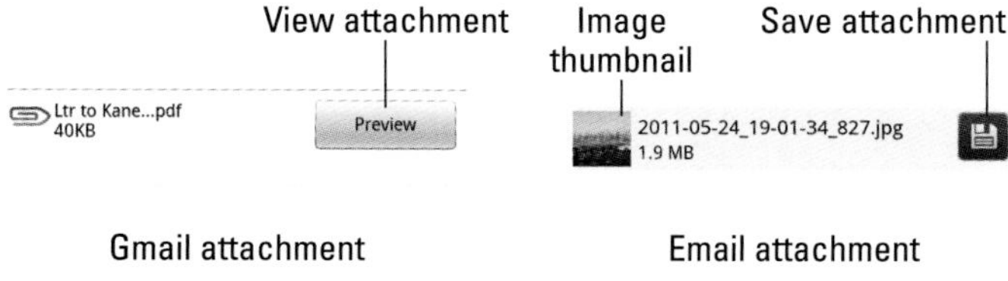

Figure 10-6: An email attachment.

Some attachments cannot be opened. In those cases, use a computer to fetch the message and attempt to open the attachment. Or you can reply to the message and inform the sender that you cannot open the attachment on your phone.

- Sometimes, pictures included in an email message aren't displayed. You find a Show Pictures button in the message, which you can touch to display the pictures.
- You cannot save certain email attachments on your phone. Wait until you retrieve these messages on your computer to save the attachments.

- You can add an attachment to an email message you create, though attachments are limited to photos and videos. Touch the Menu soft button, choose either the Attach or Attach Files command, and then choose what to attach.

- You can browse the Gallery and choose a photo or video to email. Long-press the photo and choose the Share command from the bottom of the screen. Choose Email or Gmail from the pop-up menu to begin a new message with that photo or video attached.
- See Chapter 15 for more information on the Gallery.

Email Configuration

You can do plenty of things to customize the email experience on your Droid X2. The most interesting are modifying or creating an email signature, as well as setting a smattering of options, as noted in this section.

Creating a signature

I highly recommend that you create a custom email signature for sending messages from your phone. Here's my signature:

```
DAN

This was sent from my Droid X2.
Typos, no matter how hilarious, are unintentional.
```

To create a signature for Gmail, obey these directions:

1. **Visit the Gmail inbox**
2. **Press the Menu soft button.**
3. **Choose More, then Settings.**
4. **Choose Signature.**
5. **Type or dictate your signature.**
6. **Touch OK.**

To set a signature for the Email app, heed these steps:

1. **Press the Menu soft button.**
2. **Choose Email Settings.**

3. **Choose Compose Options.**
4. **If you've set up more than one email account, choose the account to which you want to apply or edit a signature.**
5. **Edit the Email Signature area to reflect your new signature.**

   The preset signature is *Sent via DROIDX2 on Verizon Wireless™.* Feel free to edit it at your whim.
6. **Touch the Done button.**

Repeat Steps 1–6 for the Email app to set your signature for each email account you've set up.

Setting email options

A clutch of interesting email settings are worth looking into. To reach the Settings screen in Gmail, follow Steps 1–3 in the first set of steps in the preceding section; for Email, follow Steps 1 and 2 in the second set of steps.

Here are some items worthy of note:

- To specify how frequently the Email program checks for new messages, choose Email Delivery on the Email settings screen. Put a check mark by Data Push and then set the check frequency by choosing the Fetch Schedule item.
- Choose Email Notifications in Gmail or Notifications in Email to have the phone alert you to new messages.
- Choose a specific ringtone for the account in Gmail by touching Select Ringtone, below Notifications. In the Email program, choose Notifications and then Select Ringtone.
- Specify whether the phone vibrates upon the receipt of new email by choosing Vibrate.
- The ringtone and vibration options are available only when the Email Notifications option is selected.

11

Out on the Web

In This Chapter

- Looking at a web page on your phone
- Browsing around the web
- Bookmarking pages
- Working with multiple browser windows
- Searching the web
- Sending a link to a friend
- Downloading stuff from the web
- Changing the home page

The web wasn't designed to be viewed on a cell phone. That's akin to seeing China through the porthole on a ship. You'll never really get respect for what you're looking at, thanks to the tiny screen. Sure, the Droid X2 has a high-resolution, super-dooper screen, but it's still smaller than what you see on a computer. Even so, you can browse the web using your phone, which means that you can browse the web anywhere you go.

Although using the web is probably very familiar to you, using it on a cell phone might not be. Consider this chapter a quick brush up on the art and practicality of surfing the web on your Droid X2.

- If possible, activate the Droid X2 Wi-Fi connection before you venture out on the web. Although you can use the phone's cellular data connection, the Wi-Fi connection is *far* faster. See Chapter 19 for more information.
- The Droid X2 has apps for Gmail, social networking (Facebook, Twitter, and so on), YouTube, and potentially other popular locations or activities on the web. I highly recommend using those applications on the phone, as opposed to visiting the web sites using the phone's browser.

Behold the Web Page

You access the World Wide Web on your phone by using an app called Browser. It's found on the App screen, though it probably exists on the Home screen as well. Opening that app begins your cell phone web adventure.

Looking at the web

Just like on a computer, when you open the Browser app on your Droid X2, you'll see a home screen, such as the Google screen shown in Figure 11-1.

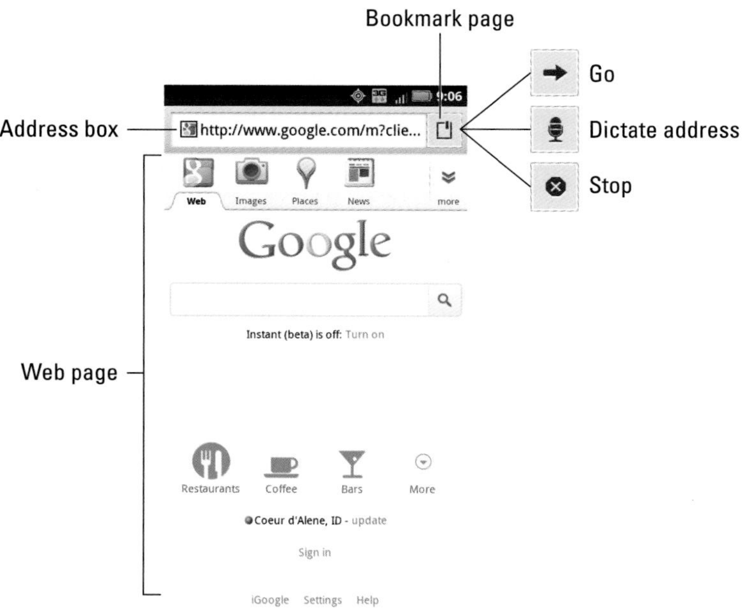

Figure 11-1: The Browser app at the Google home page.

Not every page you look at on the web shows up as cleanly as Google. To help you better see things on web pages that don't show up as nicely, try some of these tricks:

- Pan the web page by dragging your finger across the touchscreen. You can pan up, down, left, and right.
- Double-touch the screen to zoom in or zoom out.

- Pinch the screen to zoom out, or spread two fingers to zoom in.
- Tilt the phone to its side to read a web page in landscape mode. Then you can spread or double-tap the touch screen to make teensy text more readable.

Visiting a web page

To visit a web page, type its address into the Address box (refer to Figure 11-1). You can also type a search word, if you don't know the exact address of a web page. You can touch the Go button to search the web or visit a specific web page.

If you don't see the Address box, swipe your finger so that you can see the top of the web page, where the Address box lurks.

You click links on a page by using your finger on the touchscreen.

- To reload a web page, press the Menu soft button and choose the Refresh command. Refreshing updates web pages that change often, and the command can be used also to reload a web page that may not have completely loaded the first time.
- To stop a web page from loading, touch the Stop button that appears to the right of the Address box (refer to Figure 11-1).

Browsing back and forth

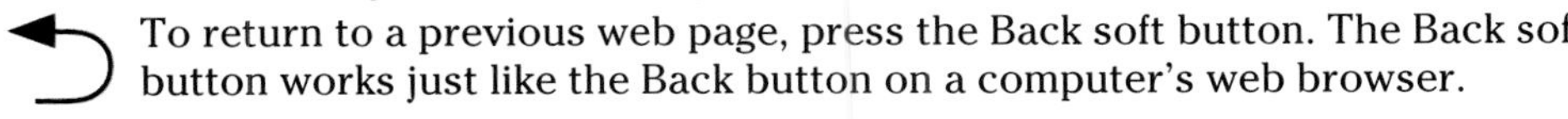

To return to a previous web page, press the Back soft button. The Back soft button works just like the Back button on a computer's web browser.

To go forward, press the Menu soft button and choose the Forward command.

To review the long-term history of your web browsing adventures, follow these steps:

1. **Press the Menu soft button.**
2. **Choose Bookmarks.**
3. **At the top of the Bookmarks page, choose History.**

To view a page you visited weeks or months ago, you can choose a web page from the History list.

To clear the History list, press the Menu soft button while viewing the History list and choose the Clear History command.

Using bookmarks

Bookmarks are those electronic breadcrumbs you can drop as you wander the web. Need to revisit a web site? Just look up its bookmark. This advice assumes, of course, that you bother to create (I prefer *drop*) a bookmark when you first visit the site. Here's how to drop a bookmark:

1. **Visit the web page you want to bookmark.**
2. **Touch the Bookmarks button, found at the top of the Browser window.**

   (Refer to Figure 11-1 to see the location of the Bookmarks button.) After pressing the button, you see the Bookmarks screen, shown in Figure 11-2. The screen lists your bookmarks, showing web site thumbnail previews.

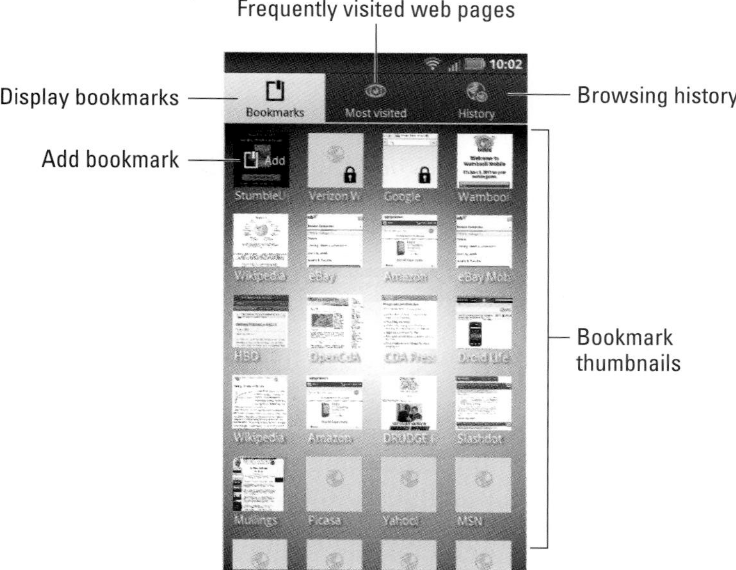

Figure 11-2: Adding a bookmark.

3. **Touch the Add button.**

   The Add button appears in the upper-left square on the Bookmarks screen (refer to Figure 11-2). It has the name of the site or page you're bookmarking just below the square.

4. **If necessary, edit the bookmark name.**

   The bookmark is given the web page name, which might be kind of long. I usually edit the name to something shorter that can fit into the thumbnail squares.

5. **Touch OK.**

After the bookmark is set, it appears in the list of bookmarks, usually at the end. You can swipe the list downward to see the bookmarks and all their fun thumbnails.

When you tilt the phone sideways, you'll see larger web page thumbnails displayed in a long chain, which you can swipe left and right.

Another way to add a bookmark is to touch the Most Visited tab at the top of the Bookmarks screen (refer to Figure 11-2). That screen lists web pages you visit most often. To add one of those pages, long-press the thumbnail and choose the command Add Bookmark.

- Remove a bookmark by long-pressing its thumbnail on the Bookmarks screen. Choose the command Delete Bookmark. Touch the OK button to confirm.
- Bookmarked web sites can also be placed on the Home screen: Long-press the bookmark thumbnail and choose the command Add Shortcut to Home.
- You can switch between thumbnail and list views for your bookmarks: When viewing the Bookmarks screen, press the Menu soft button and choose the List View command to switch to list view. To return to thumbnail view, press the Menu soft button and choose Thumbnail View.

- You can obtain the MyBookmarks app at the Android Market. The app can import your Internet Explorer, Firefox, and Chrome bookmarks from your Windows computer into the Droid X2. See Chapter 18 for more information on the Android Market.
- Refer to Chapter 4 for information on editing text on the Droid X2.

Managing multiple web page windows

Because the Browser app sports more than one window, you can have multiple web pages open at a time on your Droid X2. You have several ways to summon another browser window:

- *To open a link in another window,* long-press the link. Choose the command Open in New Window from the menu that appears.
- *To open a bookmark in a new window,* long-press the bookmark and choose the command Open in New Window.
- *To open a blank browser window,* press the Menu soft button and choose New Window.

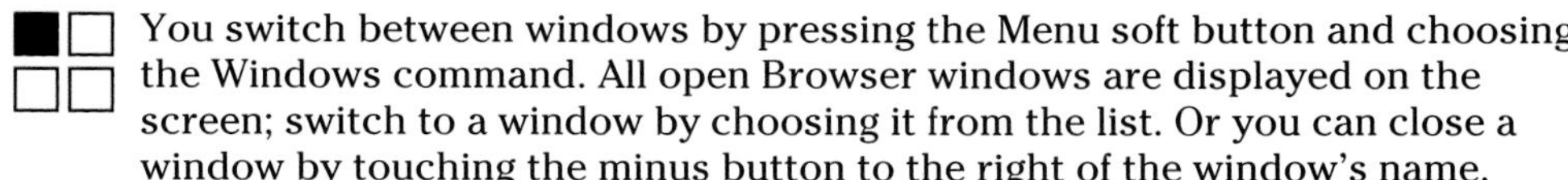

You switch between windows by pressing the Menu soft button and choosing the Windows command. All open Browser windows are displayed on the screen; switch to a window by choosing it from the list. Or you can close a window by touching the minus button to the right of the window's name.

New windows open using the home page that's set for the Browser application. See the section "Setting a home page," later in this chapter, for information.

Searching the web

The handiest way to find things on the web is to use the Google widget, found floating on the main Home screen, and shown in Figure 11-3. Use the Google widget to type something to search for, or touch the Microphone button to dictate what you want to find on the Internet.

Figure 11-3: The Google widget.

To search for something any time you're viewing a web page in the Browser app, press the Search soft button. Type the search term into the box. You can choose from a suggestions list, or touch the Go button to complete the search using the Google search engine.

To find text on the web page you're looking at, as opposed to searching the entire Internet, follow these steps:

1. **Visit the web page where you want to find a specific tidbit o' text.**
2. **Press the Menu soft button.**
3. **Choose the More command.**
4. **Choose Find on Page.**
5. **Type the text you're searching for.**

6. **Use the left- or right-arrow button to locate that text on the page — backward or forward, respectively.**

   The found text appears highlighted in green.

7. **Touch the X button when you're done searching.**

When the text isn't found, nothing is highlighted on the page and you see *0 matches* below the search text box.

See Chapter 22 for more information on widgets, such as the Google widget.

Sharing a page

The Droid X2 lets you easily share information you find on your phone. With regard to the web pages you visit, you can easily share links and bookmarks. Follow these steps:

1. **Long-press the link or bookmark you want to share.**
2. **Choose the command Share Link.**

   A pop-up menu of places to share appears, looking similar to Figure 11-4. The variety and number of items on the Share Via menu depends on the applications installed on your phone.

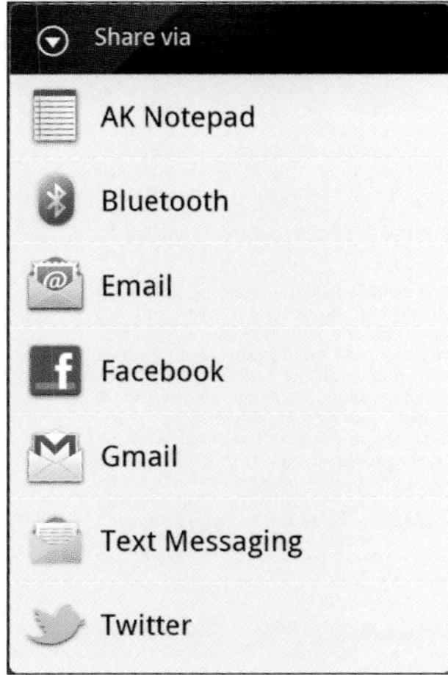

Figure 11-4: Options for sharing a web page.

3. **Choose a method to share the link.**

   For example, choose Email to send the link by mail, or Text Messaging to share via a text message.

4. **Do whatever happens next.**

   Whatever happens next depends on how you're sharing the link.

Most likely, whatever happens next opens another application, where you can complete the process. Refer to various parts of this book for the specifics.

The Perils and Joys of Downloading

One of the most abused words in all computerdom is *download*. People don't understand what it means. It's definitely not a synonym for *transfer* or *copy,* though that's how I hear it used most often.

For the sake of the Droid X2, a *download* is a transfer of information from another location to your phone. When you send something from the phone, you're *uploading* it. There. Now the nerd in me feels much better.

You can download information from a web page into your phone. It doesn't work exactly like downloading does for a computer, which is why I wrote this section.

- There's no need to download program files to your Droid X2. If you want new software, you can obtain it from the Android Market, covered in Chapter 18.

- When the phone is downloading information, the Downloading notification appears and animates while the file is being downloaded. You can also pull down the notifications to check the download's progress as a percentage.

Grabbing an image from a web page

The simplest thing to download is an image from a web page. It's cinchy: Long-press the image. You see a pop-up menu appear, from which you choose the command Save Image.

- The image is copied and stored on your Droid X2 specifically, in the Gallery's My Library folder.
- Refer to Chapter 15 for information on the Gallery.

- Technically, the image is stored on the phone's microSD card. You can read about storage on the microSD card in Chapter 20.

Downloading a file

When a link opens a document on a web page, such as a Microsoft Word document or a PDF (Adobe Acrobat) file, you can download that information to your phone. Simply long-press the download link and choose the command Save Link from the menu that appears.

You can view the link by referring to the Download History screen. See the next section.

Reviewing your downloads

After you download information, you can view it by perusing the Download History screen, shown in Figure 11-5. That screen normally appears right after you download anything, or you can summon it at any time while using the Browser app by pressing the Menu soft button, choosing the More command, and then choosing Downloads.

The stuff you download is viewed by using special apps on your phone, such as the QuickOffice app, which can view Microsoft Office files as well as PDF documents. Don't fret the process: Simply choose the item you download from the Download History screen and you can then see it on your phone.

Well, of course, some things that you can download you cannot view. When that happens, you see an appropriately rude error message.

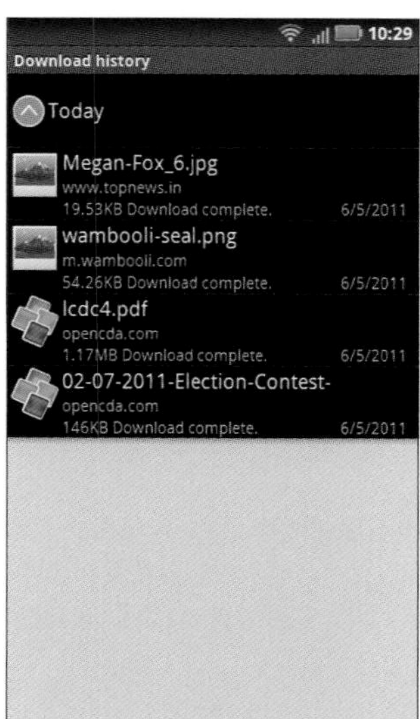

Figure 11-5: The Download History screen.

Web Controls and Settings

More options and settings and controls exist for the Browser program than just about every other program I've used on the Droid X2. It's complex. Rather than bore you with every dangdoodle detail, I thought I'd present just a few of the options worthy of your attention.

Setting a home page

The *home page* is the first page you see when you start the Browser application, and it's the first page that's loaded when you fire up a blank window. To set your home page, heed these instructions:

1. **Browse to the page you want to set as the home page.**
2. **Press the Menu soft button.**
3. **Choose More, then choose Settings.**

   A massive list of options and settings appears.
4. **Choose Set Home Page.**

   You see a Set Home Page box, where you can type the home page address. Because you obeyed Step 1, you don't need to type that address right now.
5. **Touch the Use Current Page button.**
6. **Touch OK.**

   The home page is set.

Unless you've already set a new home page, the Droid X2 comes configured with the Google search page as your home page.

If you want your home page to be blank (not set to any particular web page), set the name of the home page (refer to Step 5) to `about:blank`. That's the word *about,* a colon, and then the word *blank,* with no period at the end and no spaces in the middle. I prefer a blank home page because it's the fastest web page to load. It's also the web page with the most accurate information.

Changing the way the web looks

REMEMBER

You can do a few things to improve the way the web looks on your phone. First and foremost, don't forget that you can orient the phone horizontally to see a wide view on any web page.

From the Settings screen, you can also adjust the text size used to display a web page. Heed these steps:

1. **Press the Menu soft button.**
2. **Choose More, then choose Settings.**
3. **Choose Text Size.**
4. **Select a better size from the menu.**

   For example, try Large or Huge.
5. **Press the Back soft button to return to the web page screen.**

I don't make any age-related comments about text size at this time, and especially at this point in my life.

Setting privacy and security options

With regard to security, my advice is always to be smart and think before doing anything questionable on the web. Use common sense. One of the most effective ways that the Bad Guys win is by using *human engineering* to try to trick you into doing something you normally wouldn't do, such as click a link to see a cute animation or a racy picture of a celebrity or politician. As long as you use your noggin, you should be safe.

As far as the phone's settings go, most of the security options are already enabled for you, including the blocking of pop-up windows (which normally spew ads).

If web page cookies concern you, you can clear them from the Settings window. Follow Step 1 in the preceding section and choose the option Clear All Cookie Data. Touch the OK button to confirm.

You can also use the command Clear Form Data and ensure that the option Remember Forum Data doesn't have a check mark by it. These two settings prevent any text you've input on a web page from being summoned automatically by someone who may steal your phone.

You might be concerned about various warnings regarding location data. What these messages mean is that the phone can take advantage of your location on planet earth (using the Droid X2 GPS or satellite position system) to help locate businesses and people near you. I see no security problem in leaving that feature on, though you can disable location services from the Browser's Settings screen: Remove the check mark by Enable Location. You can also choose the item Clear Location Access to wipe out any information saved in the phone and used by certain web pages.

See the earlier section "Browsing back and forth" for steps on clearing your web browsing history.

12

A Social Networking Butterfly

In This Chapter

- Accessing your social networking accounts
- Updating your status
- Sharing photos on Facebook
- Using the Facebook app
- Setting up a Twitter client
- Accessing other social networking sites

There was a belief that the Internet would isolate people and keep us alone in our homes and away from human contact. Bah! The Internet is the most social hub the world has seen since the Tower of Babel. The whole idea of social networking has taken over the information superhighway. Being online and well-connected is now the pinnacle of social success.

The locus for your digital social life on the Droid X2 is an app named Social Networking. Sure, other social networking apps are available, and this chapter covers a few of them, but the Social Networking app is a central location from which you can master and control your online social self.

Social Networking Accounts

The Social Networking app lets you access accounts from Facebook, LinkedIn, MySpace, and Twitter all in one spot. You get things set up by telling the Droid X2 about your social networking accounts.

- The Social Networking app may be updated in the future to add more types of accounts.
- Even if your social networking site lacks access through the Social Networking app, you can use an individual app for just about any type of social networking hub. Later sections in this chapter discuss a few of those apps.

Adding a social networking account

When you start the Social Networking app for the first time, the only thing you'll see is the Add a Social Network button. Obviously, the app is trying to tell you something: You need to add some social networking accounts.

I recommend first setting up your social networking accounts on the web, preferably using a computer. That way, you have a full screen and keyboard to help you create the accounts and get things configured.

After setting up an account using a computer, and getting a login ID and password for that social networking site, it's time to set things up on your phone. Obey these steps:

1. **From the Home screen, press the Menu soft button.**
2. **Choose Settings.**
3. **Choose Manage Accounts.**
4. **Touch the Add Account button, found at the bottom of the screen.**
5. **Choose the social networking site where you already have setup an account.**

   For example, if you have a Facebook account, choose Facebook. If you have a Twitter account, choose Twitter.
6. **Type the account login ID or your email address, whichever is required to access your account on the social networking site.**

   You may need to type only the first part of your email address; if you see a menu with your email address listed, choose it.
7. **Type the account's password, and then touch the Done button or press the Back soft button.**

   Either button dismisses the onscreen keyboard.
8. **Touch the Next button.**

   The Social Networking app configures and adds your account to its inventory.
9. **Touch the Done button.**

Repeat these steps to add additional social networking accounts to the Social Networking app's inventory. When you're done, you can press the Home soft button to return to the Home screen.

The Droid X2 is updated immediately with your social networking site information. See the section "Your Digital Social Life" for information on using the Social Networking app to conduct your digital social life.

Managing your social networking accounts

When you get all huffy and change your online social life, you'll need to update your account information in the Social Networking app. For example, if you finally make good and quit MySpace, you can remove that account. Or maybe you clicked a bad link on Facebook and need to update your account's password. Those account management chores are handled by following these steps:

1. **Start the Social Networking app.**

   It's found on the Apps screen, along with all the other apps on your phone.

2. **Press the Menu soft button.**
3. **Choose Manage Accounts.**

   All the accounts associated with the Droid X2 appear in the My Accounts list. Even your Google account is listed, though it's not officially a social networking app.

You can do with the accounts:

- **Update your password:** To change your password, choose an account from the list and type in a new password. Touch the OK button when you're done.
- **Remove an account:** To remove an account, choose it from the list and touch the Remove Account button. Touch the Yes button to confirm.
- **Add an account:** Refer to the preceding section for information on adding a new account.

You use the Social Networking app to update your password, not to change it. Change the password using the social networking site on the web, preferably by using a computer. After making the change, you'll need to update the account information on your phone.

Your Digital Social Life

The whole point of social networking is to be social. The whole benefit to being on the Internet is that you don't have to wear proper social clothing. Of course, when you're out and about with your phone, proper clothing is necessary. Other necessary things for social networking with the Social Networking app are covered in this section.

Finding out what's going on

When you start the Social Networking app, you'll see a list of status updates, news, and tweets from your social networking pals, similar to what's shown in Figure 12-1. Tiny icons flag the various social networking sites from which the information is pulled, as illustrated in the figure.

To see only information intended for you, touch the Me button at the top of the screen, as shown in Figure 12-1. Or you can restrict the display to certain sites by touching the Services button (refer to Figure 12-1) and then selecting which social networking site you want to view.

When you want to see all the services again, touch the Services button again and choose All Services from the Select menu.

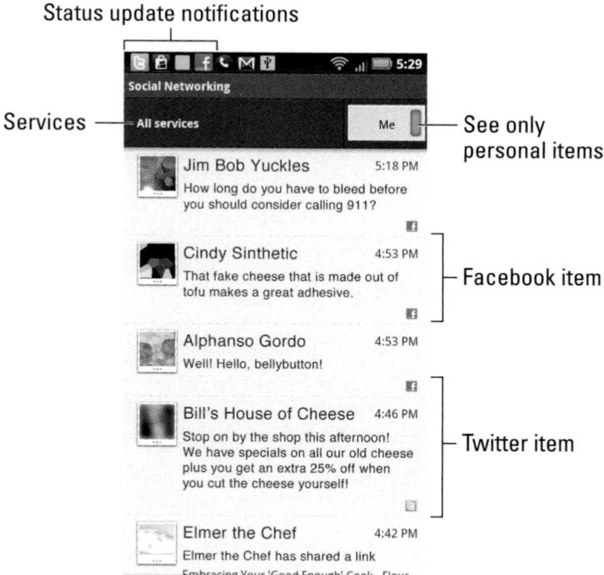

Figure 12-1: Social networking updates.

Touching an entry displays more details, such as comments, links, or images. For example, if you want to "like" an item in Facebook, touch that item to see the details. Touch the Like button on the details screen to like the post, or touch the Add Comment button to express your opinion.

Updates to your social networking sites are flagged by notification icons, as illustrated in Figure 12-1. Choose the notification icon, as described in Chapter 3, to see what's up.

Setting your status

There's no point in doing the social network thing if you're not going to be social. With the Social Networking app, sharing the most intimate details of your life with the entire online universe is as simple as it is potentially embarrassing. In the Social Networking app, follow these steps:

1. **Press the Menu soft button.**
2. **Choose Set Status.**

   The Set Your Status screen appears, as shown in Figure 12-2, with your current status on all your social networking sites. The status you set is posted to the sites you specify.

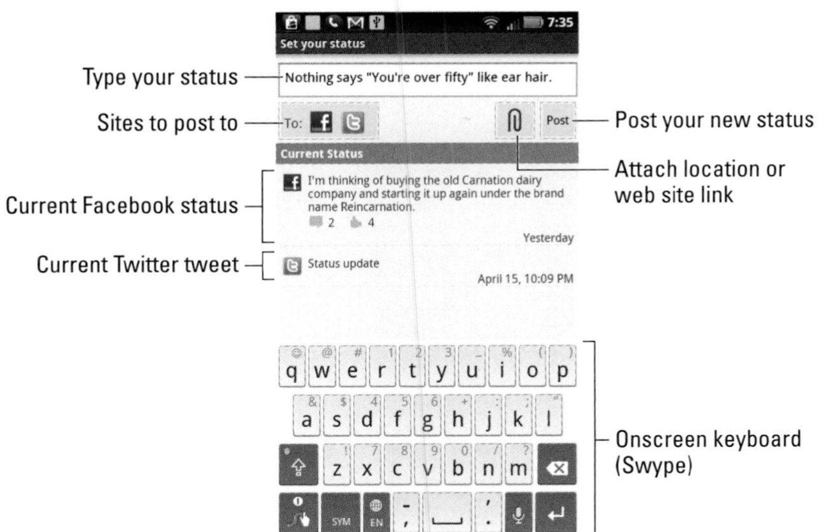

Figure 12-2: Sharing your status.

3. **Use the onscreen keyboard to type in a new status.**

   When posting to Twitter, only the first 140 characters of your status appear.

4. **Touch the To field (refer to Figure 12-2) to specify to which social networks you want to post.**

   The icons in the To field show which services are currently selected.

5. **Touch the paperclip icon to attach your current location or a web page link.**

   If you choose Web Page, you'll see a list of the last several web sites you've been to; there is no need to copy-and-paste a web page link.

6. **Touch the Post button to send your merry message on its way.**

Your social networking status is updated immediately on whichever sites you selected. The next screen displays your status in the Social Networking app.

- When posting to Facebook, your status explains that you posted "via DROID." That's a clue to others that you used your phone to set your status.
- A Social Networking widget on the Home screen reflects your current status. It's preinstalled on the first Home screen panel to the left of the main Home screen.
- There is no way to unpost a status using the Social Networking app. For that kind of magic, I recommend visiting the social networking site on a computer.

Uploading a picture

You can't directly send a picture to your social networking sites using the Social Networking app. Instead, I recommend that you take the picture and then visit the Gallery, as described in Chapter 15. You can then share the picture by following these steps:

1. **View the image you want to share.**

2. **Choose the Share command from the bottom of the screen.**

   The icon is shown in the margin.

3. **From the Select An Action menu, choose Photo Share.**

   As this book goes to press, the Photo Share command works only with the Facebook site.

4. **Replace the image's long, cryptic name with a more appropriate description.**

   The name shown is the image's filename as it's stored on the Droid X2. Long-press that name to select it, then type something new.

5. **Touch the Send button to upload the image and its description to Facebook.**

Uploading an image in this manner is more a function of the Gallery app than the Social Networking app. See Chapter 15 for more information on how to use the Gallery app, as well as other ways to share your images.

Also see later sections in this chapter, which cover uploading images using the Facebook and Twitter apps.

Other Social Networking Apps

The Social Networking app is handy but limiting. For example, you can't use it to find new friends or follow new twits, er, tweets. For those activities, you'll need to obtain and use more specific social networking apps on your phone.

Using the Facebook app

To get access to more popular Facebook features than the Social Networking app provides for, I recommend that you download the Facebook for Android app. You can scan the QR code shown in the margin, or you can visit the Android Market to search for the Facebook app, as described in Chapter 18.

The main Facebook screen is shown in Figure 12-3. You can use that interface to do most of the Facebook things you can do on the web, including upload a photo or keep your status up to date wherever you go with your Droid X2.

After installing the Facebook for Android app, accept the licensing agreements and sign in. You need to sign in even if you've already configured Facebook for the Social Networking app; they are two separate apps.

Set your Facebook status by touching the Status button, labeled in Figure 12-3.

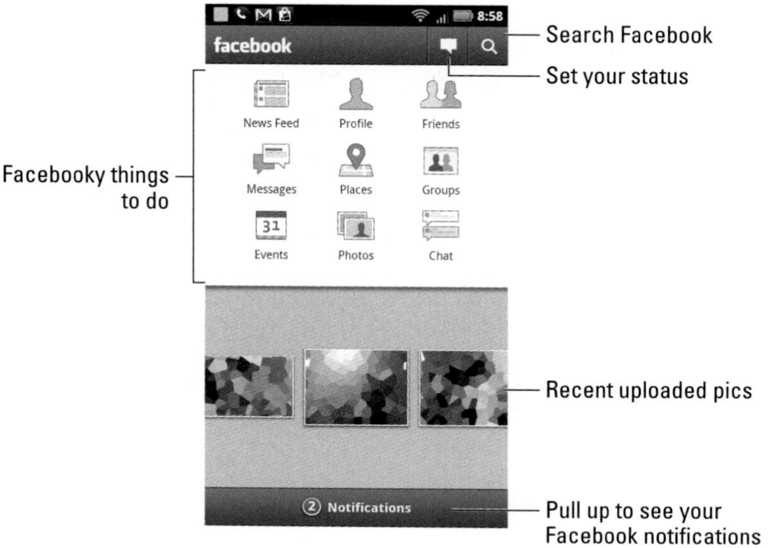

Figure 12-3: Facebook on your phone.

To take a picture with the Facebook app, touch the Camera icon that appears to the left of the text box where you type your status. You get to decide whether to upload a picture you've already taken from the Gallery or choose the Capture a Photo command to take a picture immediately.

After you take the picture, touch the Done button. Add a caption, then touch the Upload button to send the picture to Facebook.

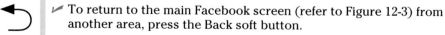

- Choose the News Feed item to status updates, newly added photos, and other information from your Facebook friends.
- Choose Photos to review your Facebook photo albums.
- Choose Profile to review your personal Facebook page, your status updates, and whatever else you're wasting your time doing on Facebook.
-  To return to the main Facebook screen (refer to Figure 12-3) from another area, press the Back soft button.
- To sign out of Facebook on your phone, touch the Menu soft button when viewing the main Facebook screen and choose the Logout command. Touch the Yes button to confirm.

Tweeting to other twits

The Twitter social networking site proves the hypothesis that everyone will be famous on the Internet for 140 characters or fewer.

Like Facebook, Twitter is used to share your existence with others or simply to follow what others are up to or thinking. It sates some people's craving for attention and provides the bricks that pave the road to fame — or so I hear. I'm not a big Twitter fan, but your phone is capable of letting you *tweet* from wherever you are.

The Twitter application provides an excellent interface to many Twitter tasks. You can search for it at the Android Market or use your phone to scan the QR code in the margin. Chapter 18 offers more information on installing new apps for the Droid X2.

After installing the app, sign in. You'll eventually see the Twitter app's main interface, where you can read the tweets from the people you're following.

To tweet, touch the New Tweet icon, shown in the margin. Use the New Tweet screen to send text, upload an image from the Gallery, or take a picture.

- They say that of all the people who have accounts on Twitter, only a small portion of them actively use the service.
- A message posted on Twitter is a *tweet.*
- You can post messages on Twitter or follow others who post messages.

Exploring other social networking opportunities

The web is brimming with new social networking phenomenon. My guess is that each of them is trying to de-throne Facebook as the king of the social networking sites. Good luck with that.

Despite the fact that Facebook and Twitter capture a lot of media attention, other popular social networking sites are out there, such as

- Google Buzz
- LinkedIn
- Meebo
- MySpace

These sites may have special Android apps you can install on your Droid X2, such as the MySpace Mobile app for MySpace.

As with Facebook and Twitter, you should always configure an account using a computer and then set up options on your phone.

After adding some social networking apps, you may see them appear on various Share menus on the Droid X2. Use the Share menus to help you share media files with your online social networking pals.

Part IV

O What Your Phone Can Do!

In this part . . .

I suppose this part of the book would be a lot thinner if I could list only those things that the Droid X2 can't do. For example, the Droid X can't slice vegetables. I've tried using the Droid X2 as a tennis racquet but the balls go all over. And forget about ironing your clothes with the Droid X2, even when the battery gets hot. No, it's better that I just give in and write about all the amazing non-phone things your phone can do.

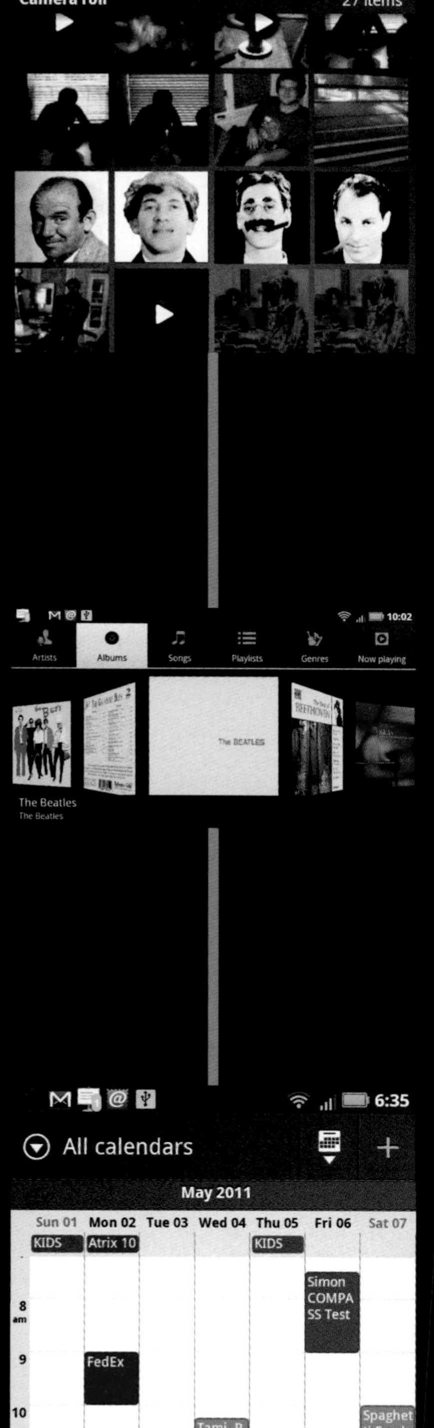

13 Fun with Maps and Navigation

In This Chapter

- Exploring your world with Maps
- Viewing optional map features
- Searching for people and places
- Finding a restaurant
- Getting to your location
- Using the phone as a navigator
- Adding a navigation Home screen shortcut

The rude imp shouted at me, "Get lost!" I just laughed and showed him my Droid X2. I remarked that by using the Maps app, the phone's amazing technology could be used with geosynchronous satellites to pinpoint my exact location on the planet. Further, thanks to the Maps app's amazing searching capabilities, I could not only never be lost but could instantly find my way to whatever location I desired.

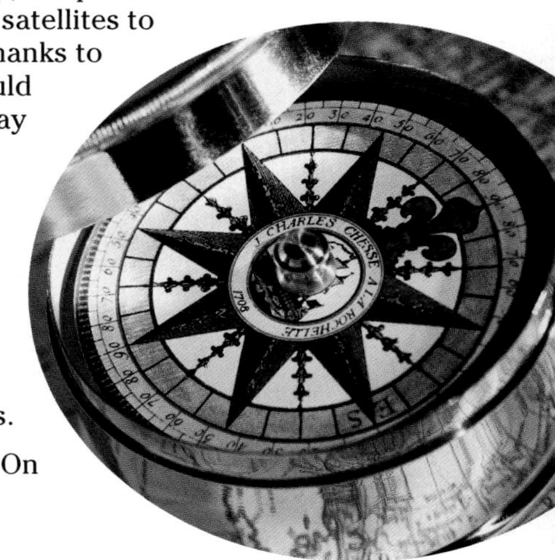

I wanted to say more, but the imp muttered something rude and smoldered off. Rather than lose my train of thought, I sat down and wrote this chapter.

- The Droid X2 uses GPS, the global positioning system. It's the same technology used by car navigation toys as well as handheld GPS gizmos.

- When the Droid X2 is using the GPS, the GPS Is On status icon appears.

Basic Map

Your location, as well as the location of things near and far, is found on the Droid X2 by using the Maps app. Good news: You run no risk of improperly folding the Maps app. Better news: The Maps app charts the entire country, including freeways, highways, roads, streets, avenues, drives, bike paths, addresses, businesses, and points of interest.

Using the Maps app

You start the Maps app by choosing Maps from the Apps screen. If you're starting the app for the first time, you can read its What's New screen; touch the OK button to continue.

The Droid X2 communicates with global positioning system (GPS) satellites to hone in on your current location. (See the sidebar "Activate your locations!") You see that location on a map, similar to Figure 13-1. The position is accurate to within a given range, as shown by the blue circle.

Figure 13-1: An address and your location on a map.

Here are some fun things you can do when viewing the basic street map:

- **Zoom in:** To make the map larger (to move it closer), touch the Zoom In button, double-tap the screen, or spread your fingers on the touchscreen.
- **Zoom out:** To make the map smaller (to see more), touch the Zoom Out button, double-tap the screen, or pinch your fingers on the touchscreen.
- **Pan and scroll:** To see what's to the left or right or at the top or bottom of the map, drag your finger on the touchscreen; the map scrolls in the direction you drag your finger.
- **Rotate:** Using two fingers, rotate the map clockwise or counterclockwise. Touch the Compass Pointer (shown in Figure 13-1) to reorient the map with north at the top of the screen.

- **Perspective:** Tap the Location button to switch to perspective view, where the map is shown at an angle. Touch the Perspective button again to return to a flat-map view or, if that doesn't work, touch the Compass Pointer.

The closer you zoom in to the map, the more detail you see, such as street names, address block numbers, businesses and other sites — but no tiny people.

- A blue triangle in the Maps app shows in which general direction the phone is pointing.
- The blue triangle may not show up if there is some sort of interference with the phone's compass. For example, in Figure 13-1, you see a blue dot, which means the compass direction is currently unavailable.
- Perspective view can be entered for only your current location.

Adding layers

You add or remove information from the Maps app by applying or removing layers. A layer can add detail, information, or other fun features to the basic street map, such as the satellite view shown in Figure 13-2.

The key to accessing the layers is to touch the Layers button, labeled in Figure 13-2. Choose an option from the Layers menu to add that information to the Map's app display.

You can add another layer by choosing it from the Layers menu, but keep in mind that some layers obscure others. For example, the Terrain layer overlays the Satellite layer, so that you see only the Terrain layer.

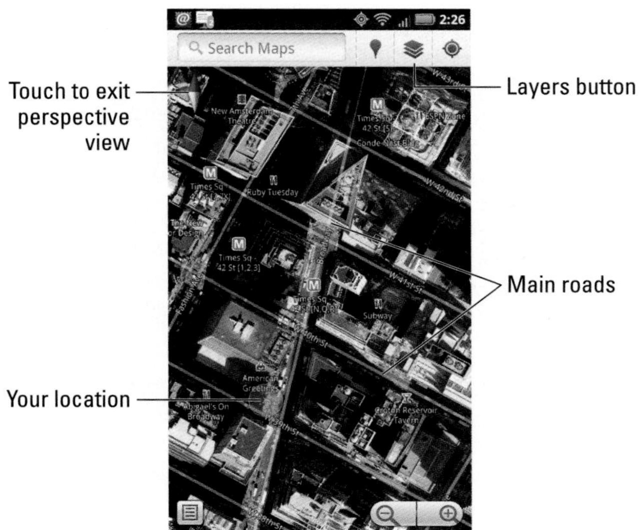

Figure 13-2: The satellite layer.

To remove a layer, choose it from the Layers menu; any active layer appears with a green check mark to its right. To return to street view, remove all the layers.

- When all you want is a virtual compass, similar to the one you lost as a kid, you can get the Compass app from the Android Market. See Chapter 18 for more information on the Android Market.
- Most of the features found on the Layers menu originated in Google Labs. To see new features that may be added to the Maps app in the future, visit Google Labs by pressing the Menu soft button in the Maps app. Choose More and then Labs to pour over potential new features.

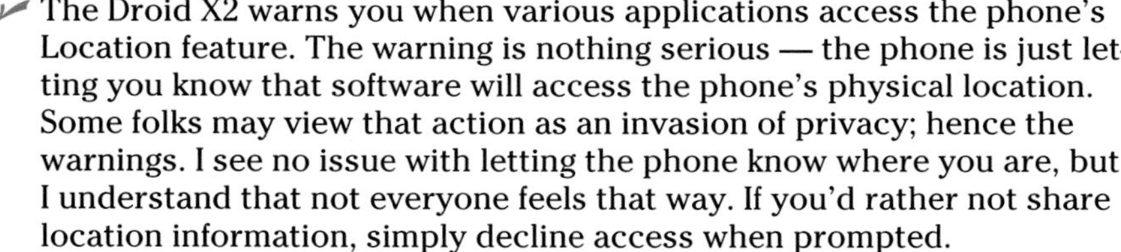

- The Droid X2 warns you when various applications access the phone's Location feature. The warning is nothing serious — the phone is just letting you know that software will access the phone's physical location. Some folks may view that action as an invasion of privacy; hence the warnings. I see no issue with letting the phone know where you are, but I understand that not everyone feels that way. If you'd rather not share location information, simply decline access when prompted.

Activate your locations!

The Maps app works best when you activate all of the Droid X2's location technology. I recommend that you turn on three settings. From the Home screen, press the Menu soft button, choose Settings, and then choose Location & Security. In the Location and Security Settings, ensure that green check marks are next to these items:

- **Google Location Services:** This setting allows software access to your location using Google technology.
- **Standalone GPS Services:** This setting allows your phone to access the GPS satellites, but it's not that accurate.
- **VZW Location Services:** This setting allows the phone to use signals from the Verizon cell towers to triangulate your position and refine the data received from GPS Services.

Further, you can activate the phone's Wi-Fi for even more exact location information. See Chapter 19 for information on turning on the Droid X2's Wi-Fi.

Find Things

The true power of the Maps app lies in its powerful searching capability. You use the app to locate where you are and where nearby things are, to search for people or businesses, and to find out how to get there. Maps is one of my favorite apps on the Droid X2. This section explains how all that stuff works without getting you lost.

Finding out where you are

The Maps app shows your location as a blue dot or compass arrow on the screen. But *where* is that? I mean, if you need to phone a tow truck, you can't just say, "I'm the blue triangle on the orange slab by the green thing."

Well, you *can* say that, but it probably won't do any good.

To find your current street address, or any street address, long-press a location on the Maps screen. Up pops a bubble, similar to the one shown in Figure 13-3, giving your approximate address.

If you touch the address bubble (refer to Figure 13-3), you see a screen full of interesting things you can do, as shown in Figure 13-4.

Figure 13-3: Finding an address.

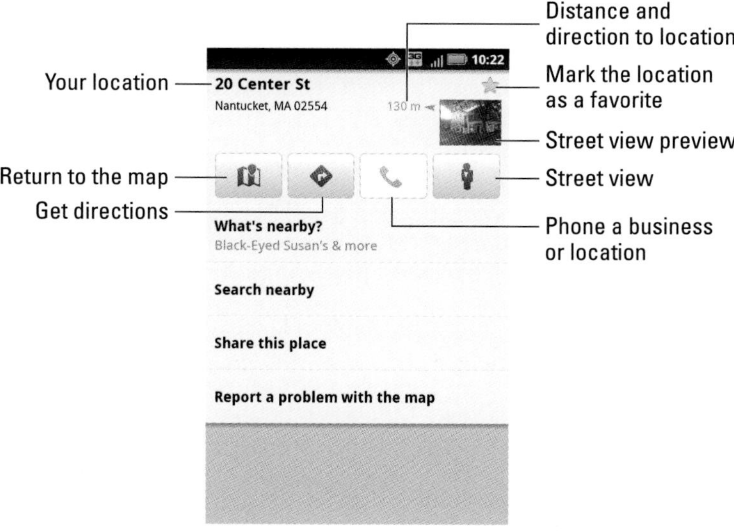

Figure 13-4: Things to do with a location.

The What's Nearby command displays a list of nearby businesses or points of interest, some of them shown on the screen (refer to Figure 13-4) and others available by touching the What's Nearby command.

Choose the Search Nearby item to use the Search command to locate businesses, people, or points of interest near the given location.

The Report a Problem command doesn't connect you with the police; instead, it's used to send information back to Google regarding an improper address or another map malfunction.

What's *really* fun to play with is the Street View command (when it's available). Choosing this option displays the location from a 360-degree perspective. In street view, you can browse a locale, pan and tilt, or zoom in on details to familiarize yourself with an area, for example — whether you're familiarizing yourself with a location or planning a burglary.

Press the Back soft button to return to regular map view from street view.

Locating people and places

The Maps app can help you find places in the real world, just like the Browser app helps you find places on the Internet. Both operations work basically the same:

Open the Maps app and press the Search soft button. You can type a variety of terms into the Search box, as explained next.

Look for a specific addresses

To locate an address, type it into the Search box; for example:

> 1600 Pennsylvania Ave., Washington, D.C. 20006

Touch the Search button on the onscreen keyboard, and that location is then shown on the map. The next step is getting directions, which you can read about in the later section "Getting directions."

- You don't need to type the entire address. Often times, all you need is the street number and street name and then either the city name or zip code.
- If you omit the city name or zip code, the Droid X2 looks for the closest matching address near your current location.

Look for a type of business, a restaurant, or a point of interest

You may not know an address, but you know when you crave sushi or Tex-Mex or perhaps Indian food. Maybe you need a hotel or gas station. To find a business entity or a point of interest, type its name in the Search box; for example:

> Movie theater

This command flags movie theaters on the current Maps screen or nearby.

Specify your current location, as described earlier in this chapter, to find locations near you. Otherwise, the Maps app looks for places near the area you see on the screen.

Or, you can be specific and look for businesses near a certain location by specifying the city name, district, or zip code, such as

> Coffee 02554

After typing this command and touching the Search button, you see a smattering of coffee huts and restaurants found in downtown Nantucket, similar to the what's shown in Figure 13-5.

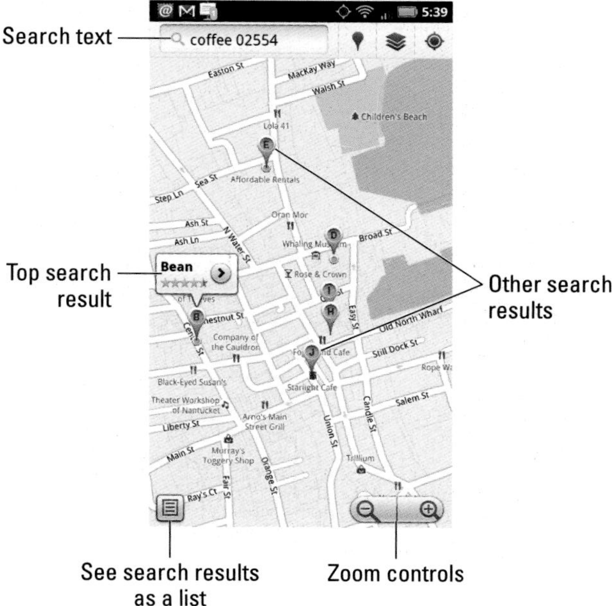

Figure 13-5: Search results for coffee in Nantucket.

To see more information about a result, touch its cartoon bubble, such as the one for the Bean in Figure 13-5. The screen that appears offers more information, plus perhaps even a web address and phone number. You can touch the Directions button (refer to Figure 13-4) to get directions; see the later section "Getting directions."

- Each letter or dot on the screen represents a search result (refer to Figure 13-5).
- Use the zoom controls or spread your fingers to zoom in to the map.
- You can create a contact for the location, keeping it as a part of your Contacts list: After touching the location balloon, touch the More button and choose the command Add As a Contact. The contact is created using data known about the business, including its location and phone number and even a web page address — if that information is available.

Find interesting places

Maybe you don't know what you're looking for. Maybe you're like my teenage sons, who stand in front of the open refrigerator, waiting for the sandwich fairy to hand them a snack. The Maps app features a sort of "I don't know what I want but I want something" fairy. It's the Places command.

Touch the Places button (refer to Figure 13-1) to see the Places screen. It shows categories of places near you: restaurants, coffee, bars, hotels, attractions, and more. Touch an item to see matching locations in your vicinity.

You can also use the Places app to directly visit the Places screen. You'll find the Places app on the Apps screen.

Look for a contact's location

You can home in on where your contacts are located by using the map. This trick works when you've specified an address for the contact — either home or work or another location. If so, the Droid X2 can easily help you find that location or even give you directions.

The secret to finding a contact's location is the little postcard icon by the contact's address, shown in the margin. Anytime you see that icon, you can touch it to view that location by using the Maps app.

The Droid X2 Copilot

Finding something is only half the job. The other half is getting there. The Droid X2 is ever-ready, thanks to the various direction and navigation features nestled in the Maps app.

Getting directions

One command associated with locations on the map is Get Directions. Here's how to use it:

1. **Touch a location's cartoon bubble displayed by an address, a contact, or a business or from the result of a map search.**
2. **Touch the Directions button.**

   The menu has three options. See the next section for information on the Navigation options. You want the Get Directions item.

3. **Choose Get Directions.**

   You see the directions listed, as shown in Figure 13-6. The Maps app has already chosen your current location (shown as My Location in the figure) as the starting point and the location you searched for or are viewing on the map as the destination.

You can follow the directions on the screen or touch the Map button (refer to Figure 13-6) to see the path you need to take as illustrated on the map. Zoom in or out to see more or less detail.

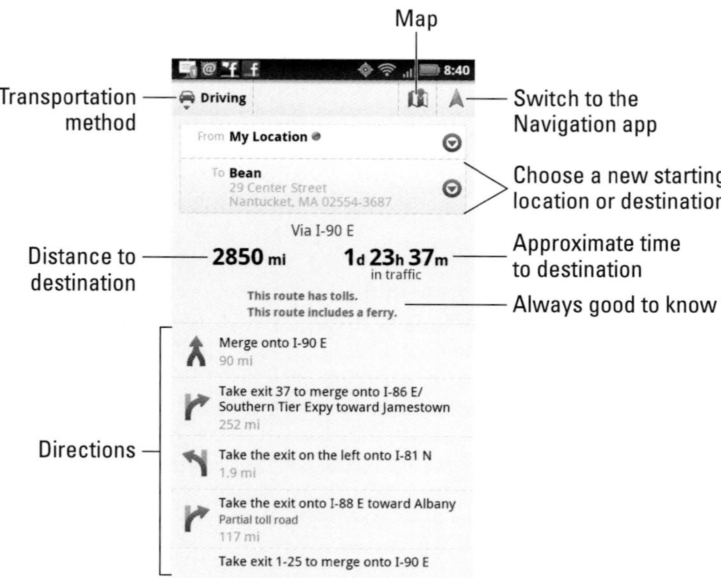

Figure 13-6: Going from here to there.

- To receive vocal directions, touch the Navigation button or just read the next section.
- Touch the From or To field to change the point of origin or the destination, though I admit that it's easier to simply start over.
- The Transportation Method button (refer to Figure 13-6) displays a menu from which you can choose a different way to travel, such as on foot, by bicycle, or via public transportation (transit).
- In Figure 13-6, the Maps app notes that toll roads are on the route specified. As you travel, you can choose alternative, non-toll routes if available. You'll be prompted to switch routes during navigation; see the next section.
- The Maps app may not give you the perfect directions, but for places you've never been, it's a great tool.

Navigating to your destination

Lists are so 20th century. I don't know why anyone would bother, especially when the Droid X2 features a digital copilot in the form of voice navigation.

To navigate your way to a destination, choose the Navigation option from any list of directions. Or touch the Navigation button (labeled in Figure 13-6). You can also enter the Navigation app directly by choosing it from the Apps screen, though then you must type (or speak) your destination, so it's just easier to start in the Maps app.

In navigation mode, the Droid X2 displays an interactive map that shows your current location and turn-by-turn directions for reaching your destination. A digital voice tells you how far to go and when to turn, for example, and gives you other nagging advice — just like a backseat driver, albeit an accurate one.

After choosing Navigation, sit back and have the phone dictate your directions. You can simply listen, or just glance at the phone for an update of where you're heading.

To stop Navigation, press the Menu soft button and choose the Exit Navigation command.

- To remove the navigation route from the screen, exit navigation and return to the Maps app. Press the Menu soft button and choose the Clear Map command.
- When you tire of hearing the navigation voice, press the Menu soft button and choose the Mute command.

- I refer to the navigation voice as *Gertrude*.
- You can press the Menu soft button while navigating and choose Route Info to see an overview of your journey.

- When viewing the Route Info screen, touch the Gears button to see a handy pop-up menu. From that menu, you can choose options to modify the route so that you avoid highways or avoid toll roads.
- The neat thing about Navigation is that whenever you screw up, a new course is immediately calculated.

- In navigation mode, the Droid X2 consumes a lot of battery power. I highly recommend that you plug the phone into your car's power adapter ("cigarette lighter") for the duration of the trip.

Adding a navigation shortcut to the Home screen

When you visit certain places often — such as the parole office — you can save yourself the time you would spend repeatedly inputting navigation information, by creating a navigation shortcut on the Home screen. Here's how:

1. **Long-press a blank part of the Home screen.**
2. **From the pop-up menu, choose Shortcuts.**
3. **Choose Directions & Navigation.**
4. **Type a contact name, an address, a destination, or a business in the text box.**

   As you type, suggestions appear in a list. You can choose a suggestion to save yourself some typing.
5. **Choose a traveling method.**

   Your options are car, public transportation, bicycle, and on foot.
6. **Scroll down a bit to type a shortcut name.**
7. **Choose an icon for the shortcut.**
8. **Touch the Save button.**

   The Navigation shortcut is placed on the Home screen.

To use the shortcut, simply touch it on the Home screen. Instantly, the Maps app starts and enters navigation mode, steering you from wherever you are to the location referenced by the shortcut.

See Chapter 22 for additional information on creating Home screen shortcuts.

14

Smile and Say "Cheese"

In This Chapter

- Taking a still picture
- Turning on the flash
- Setting image resolution
- Choosing photo-taking options
- Shooting video with the phone
- Changing video resolution

To an alien observing human culture, it would be obvious to suppose that the purpose of photography is to deliver a cultured dairy product to eager people standing still and grinning. Truly, it would amaze me if, while standing under a hot sun with the Chesapeake Bay in the background, a camera actually dispensed some tangy Dubliner or Gruyère.

Of course, saying "Cheese" when having your picture taken has more to do with *cheese* the word than cheese the food. That's because the long sound in *cheese* supposedly positions the human mouth into a smile, making it look as though everyone in the photograph is having the best time. That isn't a worry for you because you will have read this chapter and understand how to use your Droid X2 as a camera in a deft and practical manner, thereby keeping your subjects content without the need for some Gouda or Brie.

The Droid X2 Has a Camera

Before I became a computer nerd, I was a photographer. I had my own darkroom, and I was even crazy enough to develop color slides. As a photographer, I can tell you that the potential for taking pictures is always there. The problem is that you often don't have your camera with you or you're out of film. The Droid X2 solves both problems.

As a resident of the 21st century, you most likely always be chained to your cell phone. Consider it a bonus that the cell phone can double as a camera. It may not be perfect, but it's handy — especially for those times you see a UFO and no one else will ever believe you without a picture as proof.

Taking a picture

To use your Droid X2 phone as a camera, you need to know that the back of the phone holds the lens. To take a picture, you need to hold the phone away from your face, which I hear is hell to do when you wear bifocals. Before doing that, start the Camera app, which may be found on the Home screen and can always be found on the Apps screen.

After starting the Camera app, you see the main Camera screen, as illustrated in Figure 14-1. The controls shown in the figure eventually disappear, leaving the full screen to preview the image.

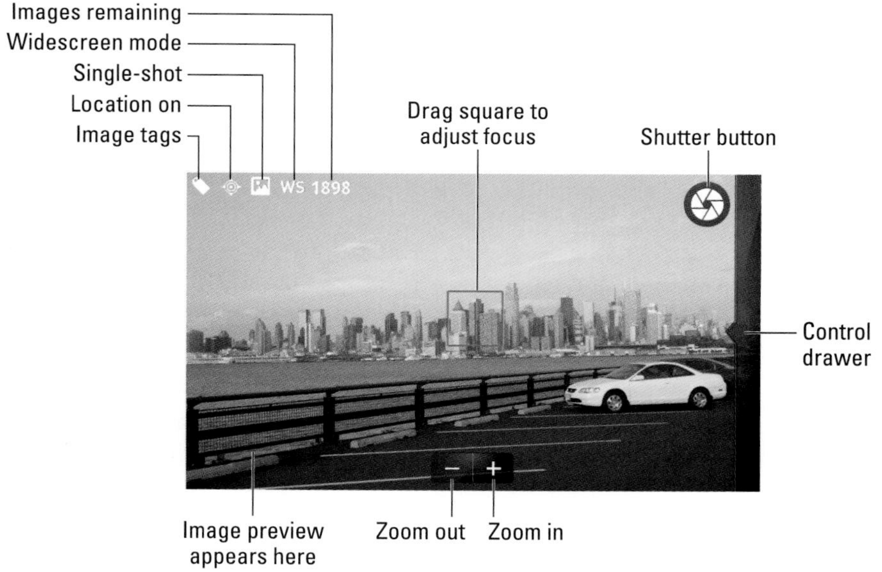

Figure 14-1: Your phone as a camera.

To take a picture, point the camera at the subject and touch the Shutter button (labeled in Figure 14-1). On the original Droid X, you can use the phone's physical shutter button as well.

After you touch the Shutter button, the camera will focus, you may hear a mechanical shutter sound play, and the flash may go off. The image you just took appears briefly on the screen for your review. Otherwise, to preview the image, touch the little icon that appears in the lower-left corner of the screen, as shown in Figure 14-1.

- To delete an image right after you snap the picture, touch the image preview that appears in the lower-left corner of the screen. When the image appears, touch the Menu button (shown in the margin) and choose the Delete command. Touch the OK button to confirm. Press the Back soft button to return to the Camera app.
- The camera focuses automatically, though you can drag the focus square around the touchscreen to specifically adjust the focus (refer to Figure 14-1).
- You can zoom in or out by using the onscreen controls (Figure 14-1) or by pressing Volume up or Volume down, respectively. The zoom is a *digital zoom*, so the image is magnified. (In an optical zoom, you adjust the camera's lens.)
- If the onscreen controls disappear, touch the screen again to bring them back.
- The phone can be used as a camera in either landscape or portrait orientation, though the phone's controls and gizmos are always presented in landscape format (refer to Figure 14-1).
- You can take as many pictures with your Droid X2 as you like, as long as you don't run out of storage for them on the phone's internal storage or microSD card.

- If your pictures appear blurry, ensure that the camera lens on the back of the Droid X2 isn't dirty.
- You can use the Gallery to preview your pictures, manage images, and delete the ones you don't want. See Chapter 15 for more information about the Gallery.
- The Droid X2 not only takes a picture but also keeps track of where you were located on planet earth when you took the picture. See Chapter 15 for information on reviewing a photograph's location.

- The Droid X2 stores pictures in the JPEG image file format (with the JPG filename extension). Images are stored in the dcim/Camera folder on the phone's internal storage (Droid X2) or on the microSD card (original Droid X).

Setting the flash

The camera on the Droid X2 sports three flash settings, as shown in Table 14-1.

Table 14-1 Droid X2 camera flash settings

Setting	Icon	Description
Auto		The flash activates during low-light situations but not when it's bright out
On		The flash always activates
Off		The flash never activates, even in low-light situations

To change or check the flash setting, touch the control drawer on the Camera app screen, as shown in Figure 14-1. The drawer slides out, and you can confirm the current flash setting by looking at the Flash command. Choose the Flash command to change the setting.

A good time to turn on the flash is when taking pictures of people or objects in front of something bright, such as Aunt Carol holding her prize-winning peach cobbler in front of a forest fire.

Changing the resolution

A picture's resolution describes how many pixels, or dots, are in the image. The more dots, the better the image looks and prints. But lower resolution images mean you can store more images on the phone, and they look fine for uploading to Facebook or sending via email.

To set or check the Droid X2 camera's resolution, heed these steps while using the Camera app:

1. **Press the Menu soft button and choose the Settings command.**
2. **Choose Picture Resolution.**
3. **Select a resolution from the list.**
4. **Press the Back soft button to return to the Camera app.**

The camera's resolution appears in a cryptic manner on the screen, illustrated in Figure 14-1. WS stands for the widescreen mode. Otherwise you'll see the setting as 1MP, 3MP, 5MP, or 8MP, which indicates the image's size in *megapixels*.

- There is no reason to take images at the highest resolution if you intend to upload them to the Internet. Choosing the 1MP resolution is fine for social networking and web page images.
- The smaller the resolution, the more images you can store inside the phone.
- The WS mode snaps pictures at a widescreen ratio, similar to a widescreen monitor or TV (16:9 aspect ratio). The resolution is approximately 5MP.

- MP stands for *megapixel*. It's a measurement of the amount of information stored in an image. One megapixel is approximately one million pixels, or individual dots that compose an image.

Taking a panoramic shot

One of the Droid X2 camera's modes allows you to crunch several images into a single, panoramic shot. It's a great way to capture wide vistas or family portraits where not everyone likes each other. Obey these steps:

1. **Start the Camera app.**
2. **Press the Menu soft button and choose Picture Modes.**
3. **Choose Panorama.**
4. **Hold your arms steady.**

   Pivot on your feet as you scan around you to compose the panoramic image.
5. **Touch the Shutter button.**

   You'll see an indicator at the bottom left of the screen that helps you orient the camera in relation to the previous image.
6. **Pivot slightly to your right (or left, but you must continue in the same direction).**

   As you move the camera, the indicator adjusts to your new position. The next image in the panorama is snapped automatically. All you need to do is keep moving.
7. **Keep moving as subsequent shots are taken, or touch the Stop button to finish the panorama.**

   After the last image is snapped, wait while the image is assembled.

The Camera app sticks each of the shots together, creating a wide panoramic image. The image is previewed, similar to all other pictures you take, and is available for viewing in the Gallery app. See Chapter 15.

Setting the image's location

The Droid X2 not only takes a picture, it also keeps track of where you're located when you took the picture — providing that you've turned on that option. The feature is called Auto Location Tag, and here's how to ensure that it's on:

1. **While using the Camera app, press the Menu soft button.**
2. **Choose Tags.**
3. **Check that the box next to Auto Location Tag has a green check mark.**

   If not, touch the gray box to put a check mark there.

Not everyone is comfortable with the phone recording a picture's location, so you can turn off the option. Just repeat the preceding steps, but in Step 3 remove the green check mark by touching the box.

See Chapter 15 for information on reviewing a photograph's location.

Adjusting the camera

Your Droid X2 is more phone than camera — still, it has various camera adjustments you can make. Two such adjustments are found by touching the control drawer (labeled in Figure 14-1) and choosing either the Scenes or Effects item:

- **Scenes:** Choosing this item lets you configure the camera for taking certain types of pictures. After touching the Scenes button, swipe the options left or right. The options affect the type of picture you're taking, such as Sports for quick-action shots, Night Portrait for low-light situations, Macro for close-ups, and other settings. The Auto scene directs the camera to choose the best settings by guessing randomly.
- **Effects:** Add special visual effects by touching the Effects option and then swiping left or right. A preview window shows you how the chosen effect changes the way things appear.

Another way to change how the camera works is to press the Menu soft button and choose the Picture Modes command. The three modes are Single-Shot, Panorama, and Multi-Shot. Single-Shot is the camera's normal mode of operation. Panorama is covered earlier in this chapter. The Multi-Shot mode directs the camera to take six pictures in a row after you press the shutter button.

Don't forget to restore the Picture Mode command to Single-Shot after you use one of the special modes.

You Ought to Be on Video

When the action is hot, when you need to capture more than a moment (and maybe the sounds), you switch the Droid X2 camera into video capture mode. Doing so may not turn you into the next Quentin Tarantino, because I hear he uses an iPhone to make his films.

Recording video

Video chores on the Droid X2 are handled by the Camcorder app, found on the Apps screen. You can also enter Video mode from the Camera app: Touch the Control Drawer and choose the Switch To command.

The Camcorder app is illustrated in Figure 14-2. It looks amazingly similar to the Camera app, probably because they're pretty much the same app.

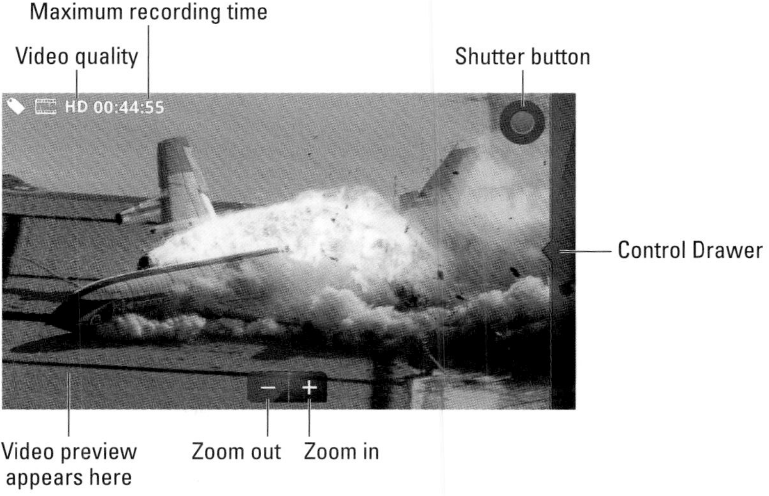

Figure 14-2: Your phone is a video camera.

Start shooting the video by pressing the Shutter button (labeled in Figure 14-2) — the same button you use to take a picture.

When recording, the Shutter button changes to a Stop button; touch the Stop button when you're done recording.

Recorded video is saved in the phone's storage: the internal storage for the Droid X2 and the microSD card for the original Droid X. You can immediately watch the video you just shot by touching the Previous Video button, not shown in Figure 14-2.

- While the phone is recording, a Mute button appears on the touchscreen. Use it to mute the sound.
- In addition to the zoom controls on the screen, you can use the Volume button to zoom in or out as you record video.
- See the next section for more information on previewing a recently shot video.
- Chapter 15 covers the Gallery app, used to view and manage videos stored on your phone. Directions are also found in Chapter 15 for uploading your video to YouTube.
- Hold the phone steady! The camera still works when you whip around the phone, but wild gyrations render the video unwatchable.
- The length of your video depends on its resolution (see the next section) as well as the storage available on your phone. The maximum recording time is shown on the screen before you shoot (refer to Figure 14-2). While you record, elapsed time appears.

- The video is stored on the Droid X2 using the Third Generation Partnership Project video file format. The video files are located in the dcim/Camera folder, and have the 3GP filename extension.

Setting video mode and resolution

For shooting video on the Droid X2, you have two modes: normal video and video message. The video message mode is especially designed for quick upload to the Internet or attachment to a MMS (multimedia text message).

To set video message mode, press the Menu soft button and choose Video Message. If you see the command Normal Video, the camera is already in video message mode.

When you choose normal video mode, you can set the video's resolution by following these steps in the Camera app:

1. **Press the Menu soft button and choose Settings.**
2. **Choose Video Resolution.**
3. **Choose a resolution from the Video Resolution menu.**

   You have four choices, ranging in quality and size from High Definition (720p) down to QVGA.
4. **Press the Back soft button to return to the Camcorder app.**

The High Definition resolution isn't always your best choice. It occupies a lot of storage, and the output looks good only on high-resolution digital devices. For Internet video, a lower resolution is preferable.

- Choosing the video message mode overrides any selection you've made from the Video Resolution menu.
- In addition to setting the video mode, you can apply visual effects to the video by touching the control drawer and choosing the Effects command.
- The Light command on the control drawer controls the camera's LED flash, turning it on for better video recording in low-light situations. Turning on the LED flash, however, drains the phone's battery more quickly.

15

The Digital Photo Album

In This Chapter

- Viewing images and videos stored on your phone
- Finding an image's location
- Editing an image
- Sharing an image on the Internet
- Sending an image by email
- Printing an image at a local developer
- Publishing a video on YouTube

There's no point in stuffing all those pictures and videos into your Droid X2 unless you have a way to view and enjoy them later. The images — whether synchronized from your computer, downloaded from the Internet, or taken with the phone's camera — can all be viewed using an app called Gallery. That's the good news.

The bad news is that the Gallery app for the Droid X2 is insanely stupid. The Gallery app for the original Droid X doesn't suffer from inanity, but the newer version on the Droid X2 is completely bereft of intelligence and simplicity. This chapter shows you how to deal with the Droid X2's limited Gallery app, but you'll probably be happier using something else.

- Future updates to the Droid X2 might include a newer, better version of the Gallery app — if you're lucky.

- An excellent replacement app for the Droid X2's insipid Gallery app is QuickPic. You can obtain QuickPic at the Android Market by scanning the QR code in the margin. See Chapter 18 for more information on the Market.
- This chapter does not cover using QuickPic specifically.

A Gallery of Images

Gone are the days of carrying around photos in your wallet. As long as you keep your Droid X2 with you, you'll be able to use the Gallery app to view pictures and enjoy videos you've taken. Plus you can shove the phone in someone else's face and force them to enjoy your pictures too!

Perusing the Gallery

To access images and videos stored on your Droid X2, you start the Gallery app, which you can find on the Apps screen. The Gallery's main screen is shown in Figure 15-1, where both the Droid X2 and original Droid X versions of the Gallery are shown.

The Camera Roll item lists all the media taken by the Droid X2 and stored inside the phone. Choosing that item displays a list of all the pictures and videos you snapped with the camera.

To see all the media stored on the phone, choose the My Library item for the Droid X2. For the original Droid X, choose All Photos or All Videos to see pictures or videos, respectively.

Figure 15-1: The Gallery's main screen.

You can choose the My Library item on the Droid X2 Gallery to see your media organized into piles, or albums, similar to the way the original Droid X Gallery works: Touch the Menu button at the top of the screen and choose the item Album from the My Library menu.

When you open a category, such as the camera roll, you'll see all the images displayed either in a grid or one after the other. The grid view shows up when you hold the phone vertically; when you hold the phone horizontally, you see the pictures one after the other. Figure 15-2 shows both views.

Vertical orientation

Horizontal orientation

Figure 15-2: Viewing an album.

To view an image or a video, touch it with your finger. The image appears in full size on the screen, and you can tilt the phone to the left to see the image in another orientation.

You can view more images by swiping your finger left and right.

Videos appear with the Play Button icon, shown in the margin. Touching the icon plays the video.

To return to the main category in the Gallery, press the Back soft button.

Finding an image location on a map

In addition to snapping a picture, the Droid X2 also saves the location where you took the picture. That information is obtained from the phone's GPS, the same tool used to find your location on a map. In fact, you can use the information saved with a picture to see exactly where the picture was taken.

For example, Figure 15-3 shows the location where I took the image shown in Chapter 14, in Figure 14-1. That location was saved by the phone's GPS technology and is available as part of the picture's data.

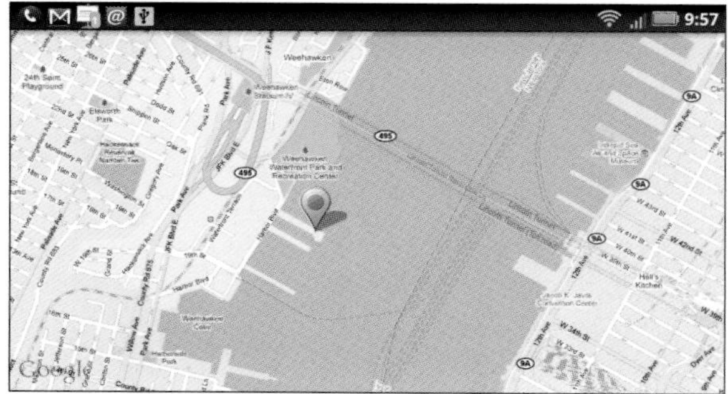

Figure 15-3: A picture's location.

To see where you've taken a picture, follow these steps for the Droid X2 Gallery:

1. **View the image in the Gallery.**
2. **Press the Menu soft button.**
3. **Choose More, then Map.**

Follow these steps for the original Droid X version of the Gallery:

1. **Touch the screen to bring up the on-screen controls.**
2. **Touch the Menu button on the screen (shown in the margin).**
3. **Choose Picture Info.**
4. **Choose the Location item.**

Not every image has location information. In some cases, the Droid X2 cannot read the GPS to store the information. When that happens, location information is unavailable.

Working with pictures

The original Droid X features a Menu button in place of the Comments button shown in Figure 15-4. That Comments button is used when viewing your online photos, specifically those shared on a social networking site.

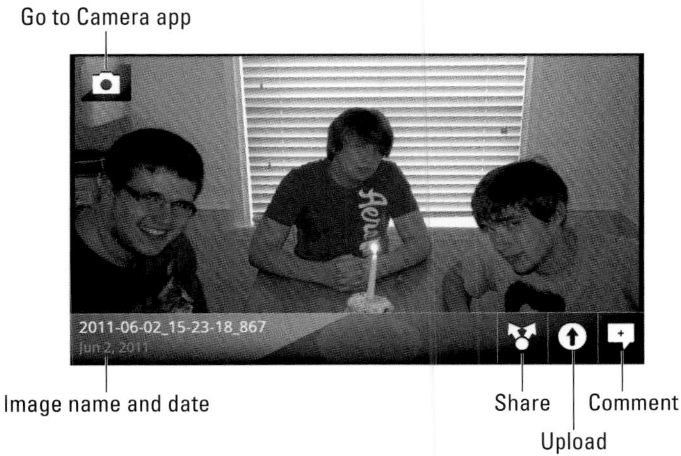

Figure 15-4: Onscreen controls for messing with an image.

Although the Gallery isn't a full-on image-editing program, you can still do a few useful things with an image:

- **Share an image:** Touch the Share button to send the image elsewhere on the Internet or in a text message. See the next section "Share Your Pics and Vids with the World" for details.
- **Delete an image:** On the Droid X2, press the Menu soft button and choose the Delete command to remove the image you're viewing. On the original Droid X, touch the Menu button on the screen and choose the Delete command. You're prompted before the image is removed; touch the OK button to delete the image.
- **Use an image for a contact or as wallpaper:** Touch the Menu soft button (Droid X2) or the Menu button on the screen (Droid X) and choose the Set As command to apply the image you're viewing to a contact or to set that image as the Home screen wallpaper (background).
- **Rotate left, rotate right:** Press the Menu soft button or the Menu button on the screen, choose the Edit command, and then choose Rotate. Use the circle control on the touchscreen to reorient the image. Touch the Apply or Save button when you're pleased with the results.

- **Crop an image:** On the Droid X2, press the Menu soft button, choose Edit, then Advanced Editing. Touch the Crop icon at the bottom of the screen. (On the original Droid X, touch the screen and then the Menu button. Choose Edit, Advanced Editing, then Crop.) Drag your finger to adjust the cropping rectangle's size and location. Touch the Apply button to crop the image.

Some images cannot be edited, such as images brought in from social networking sites and online photo-sharing albums.

Share Your Pics and Vids with the World

Why hide your artistic genius? Yes, there is a place beyond your phone where you can share your images and videos. It's a vast place, populated by just about everyone these days. It's called the Internet. The Droid X2 lets you easily share stuff from the Gallery with folks on the Internet, as well as other locations as described in this section.

Refer to Chapter 20 for information on synchronizing and sharing information between the Droid X2 and your computer.

Using the Share commands

Occasionally, you stumble across the Share command when working with photos and videos in the Gallery. That command is used to distribute images and videos from your Droid X2 to your pals on the Internet — and beyond.

The menu that appears when you choose the Share command contains various options for sharing media. The number and variety of items you find on that menu depend upon which software you have installed on your Droid X2, which Internet services you belong to, and which type of media is being shared.

The following sections describe some of the media items you can choose from the menu and how the media is shared.

Photo Share and Video Share

The Photo Share and Video Share items work with social networking sites as well as any photo-sharing or hosting sites. You must set up your account on the Droid X2 for these options to work: Use the My Accounts app on the Apps screen to add a social networking or photo-sharing site. Once configured, you choose the Photo Share or Video Share command, choose a site to send the image to, optionally add a comment, and then upload the image to that site.

See Chapter 12 for more information on social networking with the Droid X2.

Email and Gmail

Choosing Email or Gmail for sharing sends the media files from your Droid X2 as a message attachment. Fill in the To, Subject, and Message text boxes as necessary. Touch the Send button to send the media.

- You may not be able to send video files as email attachments, probably because some video files are humongous. They would not only take too long to send but also might be too big for the recipient's inbox.
- As an alternative to sending large video files, consider uploading them to YouTube. See the later section "Uploading a video to YouTube."

Picasa

Perhaps the sanest way to share photos is to upload them to Google's Picasa photo-sharing site. Heck, you probably already have a Picasa account synced with your phone, so this option is perhaps the easiest and most obvious to use. Here's how it works:

1. **View a picture in the Gallery.**
2. **Choose Picasa from the menu that appears after you touch the Share command.**
3. **Type a caption.**
4. **Optionally, choose your Google account (if you have more than one).**
5. **Choose a Picasa album.**

   You may need to scroll up the top part of the screen a bit to see the Album item if it's hidden behind the onscreen keyboard.
6. **Touch the Upload button to send the images.**

Because Picasa may automatically sync images with your Droid X2, you can end up with two copies of the image on the phone. If so, you can delete the non-Picasa version of the image from its original gallery.

- Picasa is for sharing images only, not video.
- Your Google account automatically comes with access to Picasa. If you haven't yet set things up, visit `picasaweb.google.com` to get started.
- Using your computer, you can share images stored on the Picasa web site by clicking the Share button found above each photo album.
- To make a Picasa album public, choose the Edit⇨Album Properties command, found just above the album. Choose Public from the pop-up menu, by the Share command in the Edit Album Information window.

Print to Retail

Here's a crazy idea: Connect your phone to a local photo developer, such as Costco, and have it send your images electronically so that they can be printed. After choosing the Print to Retail option, you can do exactly that: The Droid X2 uses its GPS powers to locate a printer near you. You can then fill in the various forms to have your pictures sent and printed.

Text Messaging

Media can be attached to a text message, which then becomes the famous MMS that I write about in Chapter 9. After choosing the Text Messaging sharing option, input the contact name or phone number to which you want to send the media. Optionally, type a brief message. Touch the Send button to send the message.

- Some images and videos may be too large to send as multimedia text messages.
- The Droid X2 may prompt you to resize an image in order to send it as an MMS message.
- Not every cell phone has the capability to receive multimedia text messages.

YouTube

The YouTube sharing option appears when you've chosen to share a video from the Gallery. See the section, "Uploading a video to YouTube."

Downloaded apps

Some apps you've obtained at the Android Market may have the capability to share media. For example, Facebook, Twitter, Dropbox, as well as other apps may appear on the Share menu. Choose the app from the list, then follow the directions on screen to share your media.

Uploading a video to YouTube

The best way to share a video is to upload it to YouTube. As a Google account holder, you also have a YouTube account. You can use the YouTube app on the Droid X2 along with your account to upload your phone's videos to the Internet, where everyone can see them and make rude comments about them. Here's how:

1. **Activate the Wi-Fi connection for your Droid X2.**

   The best — the only — way to upload a video is to turn on the Wi-Fi connection, which is oodles faster than using the cell phone digital network. See Chapter 19 for information on how to turn on the Wi-Fi connection.

2. **From the Apps screen, choose the Gallery app.**
3. **View the video you want to upload.**

   Or simply have the video displayed on the screen.

4. **Touch the Share button.**

   Refer to Figure 15-4 for its location; touch the screen if you don't see the button.

5. **Choose YouTube.**
6. **Type the video's title.**
7. **Touch the More Details button.**
8. **Optionally, type a description, specify whether to make the video public or private, add tags, or change other settings.**
9. **Touch the Upload button.**

   You return to the Gallery while the video is being uploaded. It continues to upload, even if the phone falls asleep.

To view your video, open the YouTube app in the Apps screen, press the Menu soft button, and choose the My Channel command. If necessary, choose your Google account from the pop-up list. Your video should appear in the My Videos list. If not, choose All My Videos and you'll find it there.

You can share your video by sending its YouTube web page link to your pals. I confess that using a computer for this operation is easier than using your phone: Log in to YouTube on a computer to view your video. Use the Share button that appears near the video to share it via email or Facebook or other methods.

- YouTube often takes a while to process a video after it's uploaded. Allow a few minutes to pass (longer for larger videos) before the video becomes available for viewing.
- Wi-Fi access drains battery power, so don't forget to turn it off when you no longer need it after uploading your video.
- *Upload* is the official term to describe sending a file from your phone to the Internet.
- See Chapter 17 for more information on using YouTube on your Droid X2.

16

The Droid Is Alive with the Sound of Music

In This Chapter

- Listening to music on your Droid X2
- Enjoying a tune
- Moving music from your computer to your phone
- Purchasing music
- Organizing your tunes into playlists
- Making a new playlist
- Using your phone as an FM radio

The Droid X2 helps lighten your gizmo inventory by reducing the number of 21st century gadgets you must carry with you. One of those gadgets you no longer need to tote around is the MP3 player, or portable digital music player. You don't need one of those things anymore because your Droid X2, which sometimes pretends to be a phone, can also play music. You can transfer music from your computer, buy tunes on the Internet, and even use your phone as a radio.

Music, Music, Music!

Your Droid X2 is ready to entertain you with music whenever you want to hear it. Simply plug in the headphones, summon the Music app, and choose tunes to match your mood. It's truly blissful — well, until someone calls you and the Droid X2 ceases being a musical instrument and returns to being the ball-and-chain of the modern digital era.

Browsing your music library

Music Headquarters on your phone is the app named, oddly enough, Music. You can start the app by touching its icon found on the Apps screen. Soon, you discover the main Music browsing screen, shown in Figure 16-1.

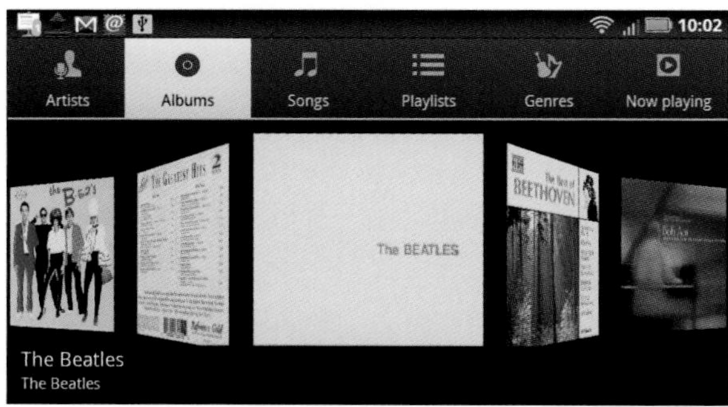

Figure 16-1: The Music library.

All music stored on your phone can be viewed in several categories:

- **Artists:** Songs are listed by recording artist or group. Choose Artist to see the list of artists. Then choose an artist to see his or her albums. Choosing an album displays the songs for that album. Some artists may have only one song, not in a particular album.
- **Albums:** Songs are organized by album. Choose an album to list its songs.
- **Songs:** All songs are listed alphabetically.
- **Playlists:** Only songs you've organized into playlists are listed by their playlist names. Choose a playlist name to view songs organized in that playlist. The section "Organize Your Music," later in this chapter, discusses playlists.
- **Genres:** Tunes are organized by their theme, such as classical, rock, irritating, and so on.
- **Now Playing:** This item isn't a category but rather a quick link to the currently playing (or paused) song. When the phone is held in a vertical orientation, this item appears at the bottom of the screen.

These categories are merely ways that the music is organized, ways to make the music easier to find when you know an artist's name but not an album title or when you want to hear a song but don't know who recorded it.

- Music is stored on the Droid X2's internal storage as well as on the microSD card. For the original Droid X, music is stored on the microSD card.
- The size of the phone's storage limits the total amount of music you can keep on your phone. Also, consider that pictures and videos on your phone horn in on some of the space that can be used to store music.
- See the later section "More Music for Your Phone" for information on getting music into your phone.
- Album artwork generally appears on imported music as well as on music you purchase online. If an album doesn't have artwork, it cannot be added or updated manually.
- When the Droid X2 can't recognize an artist, it uses the title *Unknown Artist*. That happens with music you copy manually to the Droid X2. Music that you purchase, or import or synchronize with a computer, generally retains the artist and album information. (Well, the information is retained as long as it was supplied on the computer or another original source.)

Playing a tune

To listen to music on the Droid X2, you first find a song in the library, as described in the preceding section, and then you touch the song title. The song plays in another window, shown in Figure 16-2.

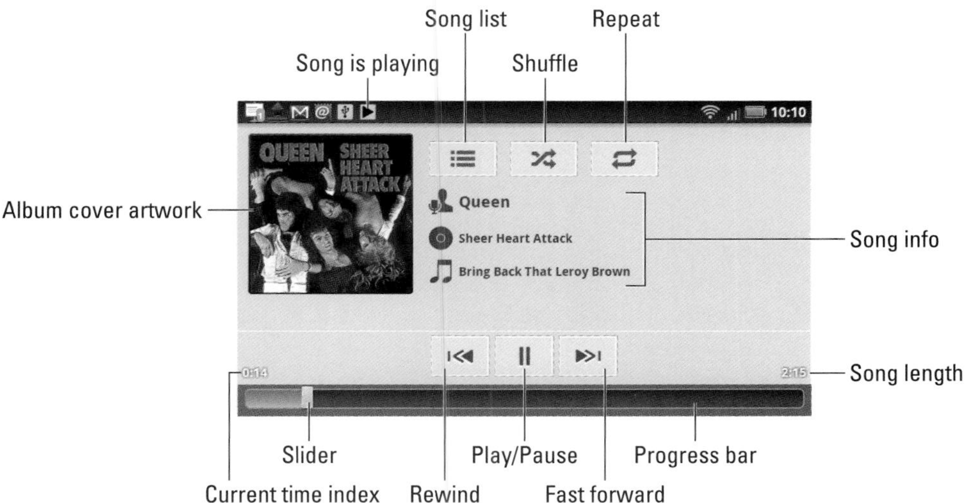

Figure 16-2: A song is playing.

While the song is playing, you're free to do anything else with the phone. In fact, the song continues to play even if the phone goes to sleep.

After the song is done playing, the next song in the list plays. Touch the Song list button (labeled in Figure 16-2) to review the songs in the list.

The next song doesn't play if you have the Shuffle button activated (refer to Figure 16-2). In that case, the phone randomizes the songs in the list, so who knows which one is next?

The next song also might not play if you have the Repeat option on: The three repeat settings are illustrated in Table 16-1, along with the Shuffle settings. To change settings, simply touch either the Shuffle or Repeat button.

Table 16-1 Shuffle and Repeat Button Icons

Icon	*Setting*	*When You Touch the Icon*
	Shuffle Is Off	Songs play one after the other
	Shuffle Is On	Songs are played in random order
	Repeat Is Off	Songs don't repeat
	Repeat All Songs	All songs in the list play over and over
	Repeat Current Song	The same song plays over and over

To stop the song from playing, touch the Pause button (refer to Figure 16-2).

When music plays on the phone, a notification icon appears, as shown in the margin. Use that notification to quickly summon the Music app to see which song is playing, or to pause the song.

Information about the current song playing appears also on the phone's lock screen. In fact, if you touch that notification, you can control the music without unlocking the phone.

- Volume is set by using the Volume switch on the side of the phone: Up is louder, down is quieter.
- When you're browsing your music library, you may see a green Play icon, similar to the one in the margin. That icon flags any song that's playing or paused.
- Determining which song plays next depends on how you chose the song that's playing. If you choose a song by artist, all songs from that artist play, one after the other. When you choose a song by album, that album plays. Choosing a song from the entire song list causes all songs in the phone to play.
- To choose which songs play after each other, create a playlist. See the section "Organize Your Music," later in this chapter.
- After the last song in the list plays, the phone stops playing songs — unless you have Repeat on, in which case the list plays again.

More Music for Your Phone

Odds are good that your Droid X2 came with no music preinstalled. However, some resellers preinstall a smattering of tunes, which merely lets you know how out of touch they are musically. Regardless, you can add music to your phone in a number of ways, as covered in this section.

Stealing music from your computer

Your computer is the equivalent of the 20th-century stereo system — a combination tuner, amplifier, and turntable, plus all your records and CDs. If you've already copied your music collection to your computer, or if you use your computer as your main music storage system, you can share that music with the Droid X2.

In Windows, you can use a music jukebox program, such as Windows Media Player, to synchronize music between your phone and the PC. Here's how it works:

1. **Connect the Droid X2 to the PC using the supplied USB cable.**
2. **On your Droid X2, pull down the USB notification, choose the item Windows Media Sync, and touch the OK button.**

3. **On your PC, start Windows Media Player.**

   You can use most any media program, or jukebox. These steps are specific to Version 12 of Windows Media Player, though they're similar to the steps you take in any media-playing program.

4. **If necessary, click the Sync tab in Windows Media Player.**

   The Droid X2 appears in the Sync list on the right side of Windows Media Player, as shown in Figure 16-3.

5. **Drag to the sync area (on the right side of the screen) the music you want to transfer to the Droid X2 (refer to Figure 16-3).**
6. **Click the Start Sync button to transfer the music to the Droid X2.**
7. **Close Windows Media Player when you're done transferring music.**

   Or you can keep it open — whatever.

8. **Unmount the Droid X2 from the PC's storage system.**

   Refer to Chapter 20 for specific unmounting instructions, also known as turning off USB storage.

When you have a Macintosh or detest Windows Media Player, use the doubleTwist program to synchronize music between your Droid X2 and your computer. Refer to the section about synchronizing with doubleTwist in Chapter 20 for more information.

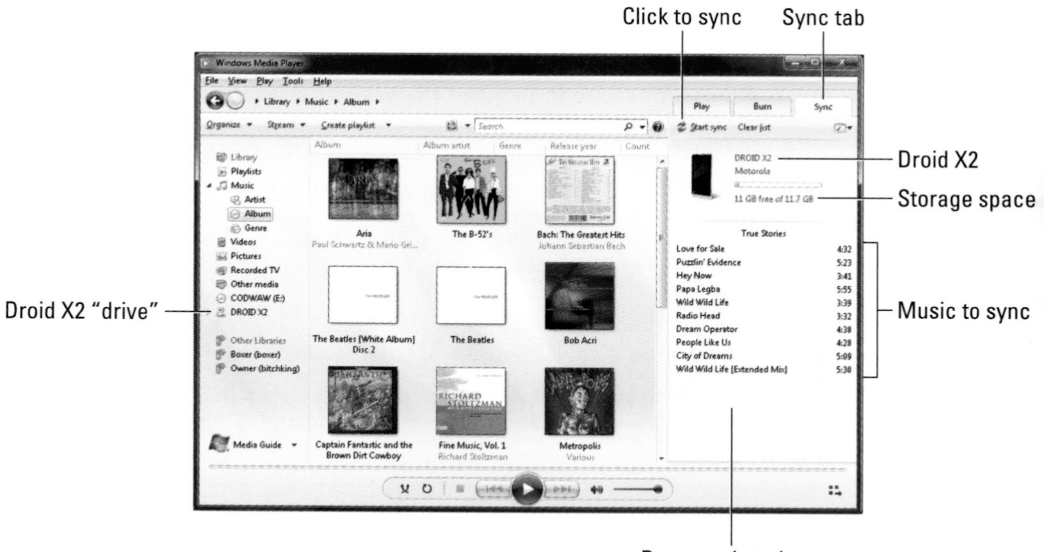

Figure 16-3: Windows Media Player meets Droid X2.

- The Droid X2 can store only so much music! Don't be overzealous when copying over your tunes. In Windows Media Player, a capacity thermometer thing (labeled in Figure 16-3) shows you how much storage space is used and how much is available on your phone. Pay heed to that indicator!
- You cannot use iTunes to synchronize music with the Droid X2.

- Okay, I lied in the preceding point: You *can* synchronize music using iTunes but only when you install the iTunes Agent program on your PC. You then need to configure the iTunes Agent program to use your Droid X2 with iTunes. After you do that, iTunes recognizes the Droid X2 and lets you synchronize your music. Yes, it's technical; hence the icon in the margin.
- The Droid X2 cannot access its storage (music, photos, contacts) while it's mounted to a computer for music syncing. You'll be able to access that information after you unmount the phone from the computer.

Buying music at the Amazon MP3 store

You don't have the music on your computer. You don't even have the CD to *burn* into your computer! You can't jam an old CD into the Droid X2! At this point, a normal person would begin to panic, but because you have this book, you will instead visit the Amazon MP3 store to buy the music you need for your phone.

Before running through the steps, you must have an Amazon account. If you don't have one set up, use your computer to visit `www.amazon.com` and create one. You also need to keep a credit card on file for the account, which makes purchasing music with the Droid X2 work O so well.

Follow these steps to buy music for your phone:

1. **Ensure that you're using a Wi-Fi or high-speed digital network connection.**

   Activating the phone's Wi-Fi is described in Chapter 19.

2. **From the Apps screen, choose the Amazon MP3 app.**

   The Amazon MP3 app connects you with the online Amazon music store, where you can search or browse for tunes to preview and purchase for your Droid X2.

   The Amazon MP3 store presents you with two options for purchasing music: Store and Player. The Store option is where you buy music to download to your phone. The Player option, which I don't cover here, lets you save your music on the Internet, where you can play it from any device connected to the Internet.

3. **Touch the Store button.**

4. **Touch the Search button to begin your music quest.**

   Or you can browse by top-selling songs and albums, new releases, or browse by category.

5. **Type some search words, such as an album name, a song title, or an artist name.**

6. **Touch a result.**

   If the result is an album, you see the contents of the album. Otherwise, an audio preview plays.

7. **When the result is an album, choose a song in the album to hear the preview.**

   Touch the song again to stop the preview.

8. **To purchase the song, touch the big button with the amount in it.**

   Some buttons say Free, for free songs. Touching the button changes the price into the word *Buy*.

9. **Touch the word *BUY*.**

10. **If necessary, accept the license agreement.**

    This step happens the first time you buy something from the Amazon MP3 store.

11. **Log in to your Amazon.com account: Type your account name or email address and password.**

    Your purchase is registered, account authorized, and download started. If they aren't, touch the Retry button to try again.

12. **Wait while the music downloads.**

    Well, actually, you don't have to wait: The music continues to download while you do other things on the phone.

No notification icon appears when the song or album has finished downloading. Notice, however, that the MP3 Store downloading icon vanishes from the notification part of the screen. It's your clue that the new music is in the phone and ready for your ears.

- Amazon emails you a bill for your purchase. That's your purchase record, so I advise you to be a good accountant and print it and then input it into your bookkeeping program or personal finance program at once!
- You can review your Amazon MP3 store purchases in the MP3 Store app by pressing the Menu soft button and choosing the Downloads command.

Organize Your Music

A *playlist* is a collection of tunes you create. You build the list by combining songs from one album or artist or another — whatever music you have on your phone. You can then listen to the playlist and hear the music you want to hear. That's how to organize music on your Droid X2.

Reviewing your playlists

Any playlists you've already created, or that have been preset on the Droid X2, appear under the Playlists heading on the Music app's main screen. Touching the Playlists heading displays playlists, similar to the ones shown in Figure 16-4.

To listen to a playlist, long-press the playlist name and choose the Play command from the menu that appears.

You can also touch a playlist name to open the playlist and review the songs listed. Then choose any song in the list to start listening to that song.

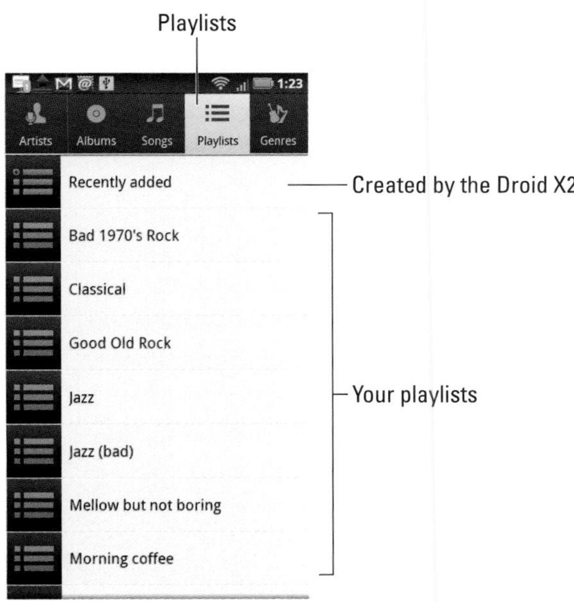

Figure 16-4: Playlists on the Droid X2.

A playlist is a helpful way to organize music when a song's information may not have been completely imported into the Droid X2. For example, if you're like me, you probably have a lot of songs by "Unknown Artist." The quick way to remedy that situation is to name a playlist after the artist and then add those unknown songs to the playlist. The next section describes how it's done.

Creating a playlist

The Droid X2 ships with one playlist already set up for you, the Recently Added playlist, shown in Figure 16-4. That playlist contains all the songs you've purchased for or imported to your phone. Obviously having more playlists would be a good idea.

Playlists aren't created from scratch on the Droid X2. Instead, you must choose a song and then add it to a new playlist. Follow these steps:

1. **Long-press the song you want to use to start a new playlist.**

   Use the Music app to locate the song. You don't have to play the song; just locate its name on the screen.

2. **Choose Add to Playlist.**
3. **Choose New from the Add to Playlist menu.**
4. **Type the playlist name.**

   Erase whatever silly text already appears in the input field. Type or dictate a new, better playlist name.

5. **Touch the Save button.**

   The new playlist is created and the song you were playing (refer to Step 1) is added to the playlist.

A new playlist has only one song. That's not much of a playlist, unless, of course, the song is by the Grateful Dead. To add more songs to a playlist, follow these steps:

1. **Long-press the song you want to add to the playlist.**
2. **Choose Add to Playlist.**
3. **Choose an existing playlist.**

   You may have to scroll down the list to see all your playlists.

You can continue adding songs to as many playlists as you like. Adding songs to a playlist doesn't noticeably affect the phone's storage capacity.

- Songs in a playlist can be rearranged: Use the tab on the far left end of the song's title in the list to drag the song up or down.
- To remove a song from a playlist, long-touch the song in the playlist and choose the command Remove from Playlist. Removing a song from a playlist doesn't delete the song from your phone. (See the next section for information on deleting songs from the Music library.)
- To delete a playlist, long-press its name in the list of playlists. Choose the Delete command. Although the playlist is removed, none of the songs in the playlist are deleted.

Deleting music

To purge unwanted music from your Droid X2, follow these brief, painless steps:

1. **Long-press the music that offends you.**

   It can be an album, a song, or even an artist.

2. **Choose Delete.**

   A warning message appears.

3. **Touch the OK button.**

   The music is gone.

As the warning says, the music is deleted permanently from the phone's storage. You free up storage space, but you cannot recover any music you delete. If you want the song back, you have to reinstall it, sync it, or buy it again, as described elsewhere in this chapter.

Your Phone Is a Radio

With the proper software installed on your Droid X2, you don't have to worry about buying or carrying around the right music with you. That's because your phone can also be used as a radio. Think about it: The same technology that kids once carried around with them as *portable transistor radios* in the 1960s can be part of your 21st-century phone. What will they think of next?

Listening to FM radio

The Droid X2 ships with an app named FMPlayer. It magically pulls radio signals from the air and puts them into your ear. Kids: That's the only way Mom and Dad listened to music back when we were teenagers.

Start using the FMPlayer app by first plugging a headset into your Droid X2. (If you forget, the app bugs you about it.) Then choose the FMPlayer app from the Apps screen.

The first time you use the FMPlayer app, you're prompted to scan available stations: Touch the Yes button do to so. The Droid X2 scans all FM frequencies and makes a note of which are active.

After the initial scan, you can use the FMPlayer app to listen to broadcast FM radio on your phone. The app's interface is shown in Figure 16-5. Use the controls as illustrated in the figure to change stations or scan for new stations.

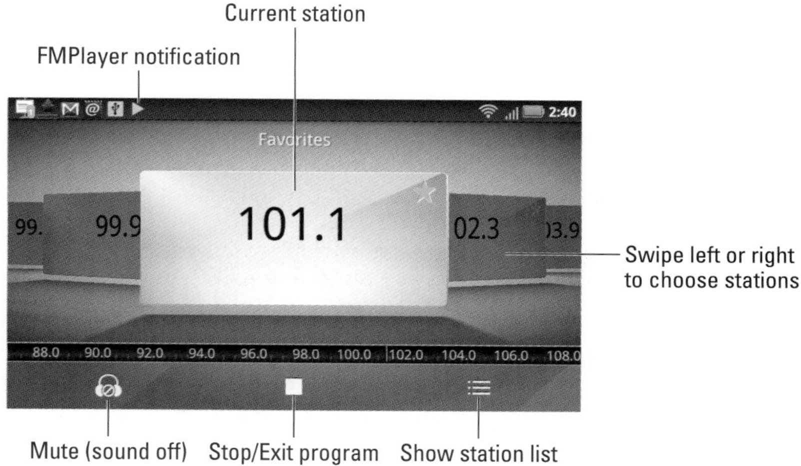

Figure 16-5: Listening to the radio on your phone.

You're free to leave the FMPlayer app and do other things while listening to music. To return to the FMPlayer, choose the app's notification icon labeled in Figure 16-5.

It's possible to listen to the FMPlayer app over the Droid's speakers: Press the Menu soft button and choose the Switch to Speaker command.

To quit the FMPlayer app, touch the Stop button (refer to Figure 16-5).

The FMPlayer app uses the headset as an antenna. If you unplug the headset, the FMPlayer app closes.

Streaming music from the Internet

Although they're not broadcast radio stations, some sources on the Internet — *Internet radio* — play music. You can listen to this Internet music using the Slacker Personal Radio app that comes with your Droid X2.

Start Slacker from the Apps screen. You need to create an account, if you don't already have one. Otherwise, log in to your account. Then peruse the various stations available. From that point on, Slacker works just like listening to a portable radio.

Beyond Slacker, you can get other apps available for your Droid X2 for listening to music as though the phone were a radio:

- Pandora Radio
- StreamFurious

Pandora Radio lets you select music based on your mood and customizes what you listen to according to your feedback. The app works like the Internet site `www.pandora.com`, in case you're familiar with it.

StreamFurious streams music from various radio stations on the Internet. Although not as customizable as Pandora, it uses less bandwidth.

Both apps are available at the Android Market. They're free, though a paid, Pro version of StreamFurious exists.

See Chapter 18 for more information about the Android Market.

17

Various and Sundry Apps

In This Chapter

- Setting alarms
- Using the Droid X2 as a calculator
- Using the Calendar
- Checking your schedule
- Adding an event
- Playing games
- Searching for videos on YouTube

The Droid X2 comes packaged with a plethora of practical *apps* — tiny programs that can help you and your phone get through your day. These apps can replace other gizmos you would normally carry with you, such as a watch, datebook, or television set. They can provide useful information or offer diverse entertainment. It's all part of the grand scheme of cramming your entire digital life into a teeny little box.

It's an Alarm Clock

The Droid X2 keeps constant and accurate track of the time, which is displayed at the top of the Home screen and also when you first wake up the phone. When you'd rather have the phone wake you up, you can take advantage of the Alarm & Timer app.

Start the Alarm & Timer app by choosing its icon from the Apps screen. The alarm clock is shown in Figure 17-1. You can change the clock image, so the clock you see on your phone may look different from Figure 17-1.

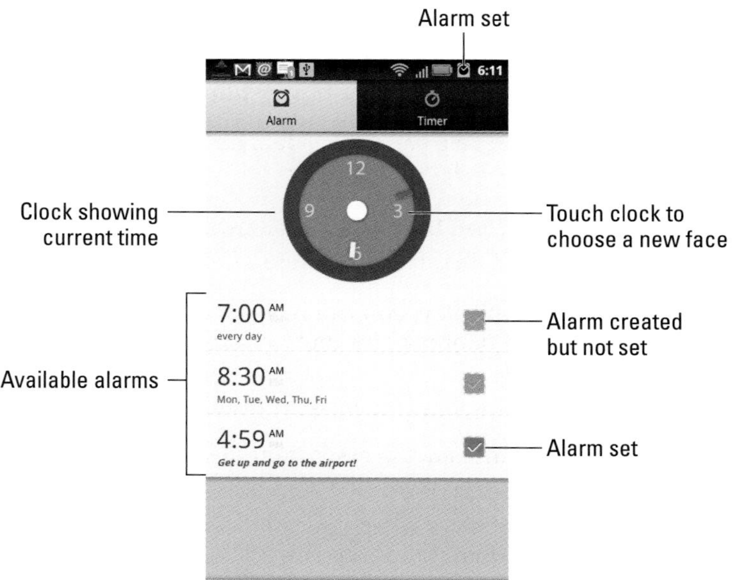

Figure 17-1: The clock.

If you see an alarm you want to set, touch the gray square (refer to Figure 17-1) to set that alarm. A green check mark in a square indicates that an alarm is set.

To create your own alarm, follow these steps while using the Alarm Clock app:

1. **Press the Menu soft button and then choose Add Alarm.**
2. **Choose the Name item to type or dictate a label for the alarm.**

   In Figure 17-1, the bottom alarm is named *Get up and go to the airport!* It's one of my favorite alarms.
3. **Choose Time, set the alarm time, and then touch the Set button.**

   Use the gizmo to set the hour and minute and specify AM or PM.
4. **Touch the Sound button to choose a ringtone for the alarm — something suitably annoying.**
5. **Specify whether the phone vibrates by placing a check mark (or removing one) next to the Vibrate option.**

6. **Choose whether the alarm repeats.**

   Choose which days of the week you want the alarm to sound.

7. **Touch the Done button to create the alarm.**

   The alarm appears in a list on the main alarm clock screen, along with any other available alarms.

Alarms must be set or else they will not trigger. To set an alarm, place a check mark in the gray box (refer to Figure 17-1).

- For a larger time display, you can add a Clock widget to the Home screen. Refer to Chapter 22 for more information about widgets on the Home screen.
- Turning off an alarm doesn't delete the alarm.
- To remove an alarm, long-press it from the list and choose the option Delete Alarm from the menu. Touch the OK button to confirm.
- The alarm doesn't work when you turn off the phone. The alarm does work, however, when the phone is sleeping.
- A notification icon appears when an alarm is set, as shown in Figure 17-1. Another notification appears when an alarm has gone off but has been ignored.
- So tell me: Do alarms go *off* or do they go *on*?

It's a Calculator

The Calculator is perhaps the oldest of all traditional cell phone apps. It's probably also the least confusing and frustrating app to use, at least on the Droid X2.

Start the Calculator app by choosing its icon from the Apps screen. The Calculator appears, as shown in Figure 17-2.

- You can swipe the screen to the left to see a panel of strange, advanced mathematical operations you'll probably never use.
- I use the Calculator most often to determine the tip at a restaurant. It takes me almost as long to use the Calculator as it does for smarty-pants Barbara to do the 15 percent calculation in her head.

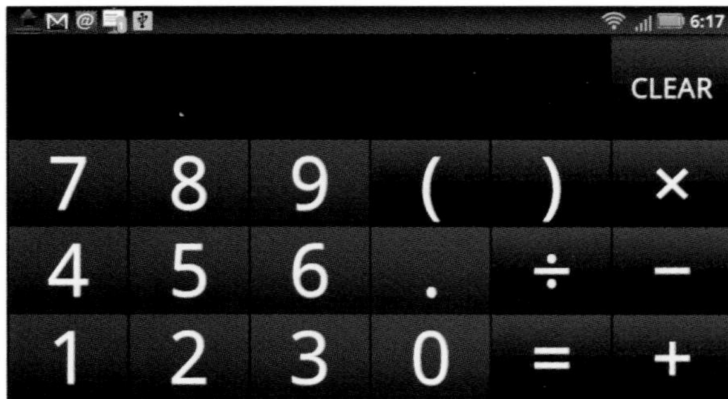

Figure 17-2: The Calculator.

It's a Date Book

Some people have a datebook. Others might write down appointments on business cards or on their palms. These methods can be effective, but they pale in comparison to the power of using your Droid X2 as your calendar and date keeper. Your phone can easily serve as a reminder of obligations due or delights to come. It all happens thanks to Google Calendar and the Calendar app on your phone.

If all you need is a to-do list, check out the Tasks app, found on the Apps screen. It offers a simple interface for creating tasks, honey-do lists, and reminders.

Understanding the Calendar

The Droid X2 takes advantage of a feature on the Internet named Google Calendar. If you have a Google account (and I'm certain that you do), you already have a Google Calendar. You can visit the Google Calendar by using your computer to go to `calendar.google.com`.

If necessary, log in using your Google account. You can use Google Calendar to keep track of dates or meetings or whatever else occupies your time. You can also use your phone to do the same thing, thanks to the Calendar app.

- I recommend that you use the Calendar app on your phone to access Google Calendar. It's a better way to access your schedule on the Droid X2 than using the Browser app to get to Google Calendar on the Web.
- The Droid X2 comes with a Calendar widget for the Home screen. You might find it already lurking on the first Home screen panel to the left of the primary Home screen. See Chapter 22 for details on using widgets on the Home screen.

Browsing dates

To see your schedule or upcoming important events, or just to know which day of the month it is, summon the Calendar app. Touch the Launcher button at the bottom of the Home screen to display a list of all apps on the phone; choose the one named Calendar.

The first screen you see is most likely the monthly calendar view, shown in Figure 17-3. The calendar looks like a typical monthly calendar, with the month and year at the top. Scheduled appointments appear as colored highlights on various days.

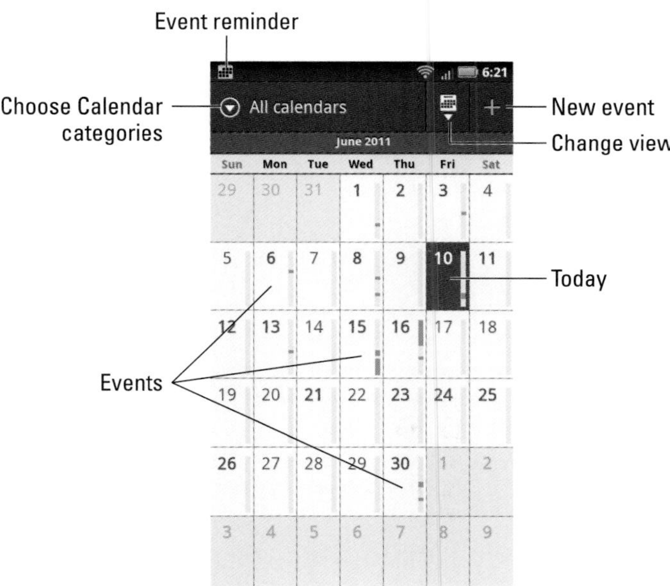

Figure 17-3: The calendar's month view.

Use the Change View button (labeled in Figure 17-3) to view your appointments by week or day. You can choose the Agenda item from the Change View menu to see your appointments in a list format.

Figure 17-4 shows both week and day views in the Calendar app. In both views, you can see the color coding used to identify different calendar categories. The categories are chosen from the All Calendars menu (labeled in Figure 17-3).

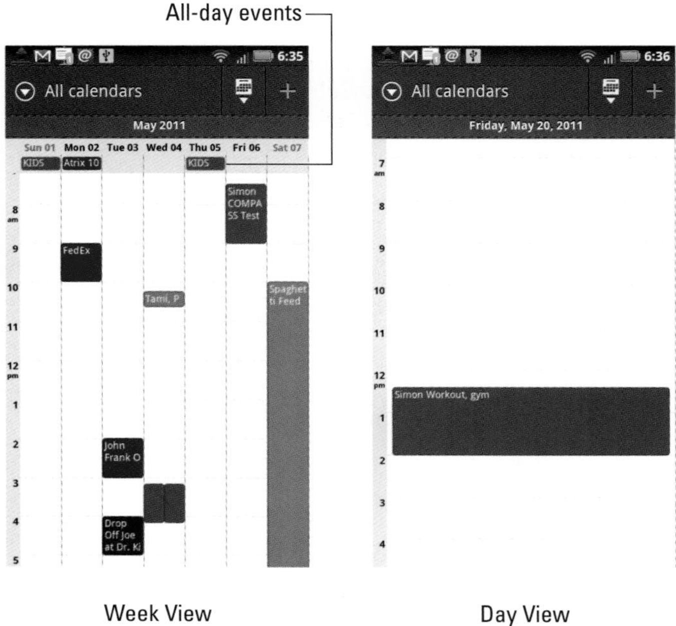

Figure 17-4: The calendar's week and day views.

You can return to the month view at any time by touching the Change View button and choosing Month.

- Use month view to see an overview of what's going on, but use week or day view to see your appointments.
- I check week view at the start of the week to remind me of what's coming up.
- Use your finger to flick the week and day views up or down to see your entire schedule, from midnight to midnight.
- Navigate the days, weeks, or months by flicking the screen with your finger. Months scroll up and down; weeks and days scroll from left to right.
- To see the current day on the calendar, press the Menu soft button and choose Go to Date. The current date is shown in the Go to Date menu, so just touch the Go button.

Reviewing your schedule

To see more detail about an event, touch it. When you're using month view, touch the date with the event on it and then choose the event from day view. Details about the event appear similarly to the ones shown in Figure 17-5.

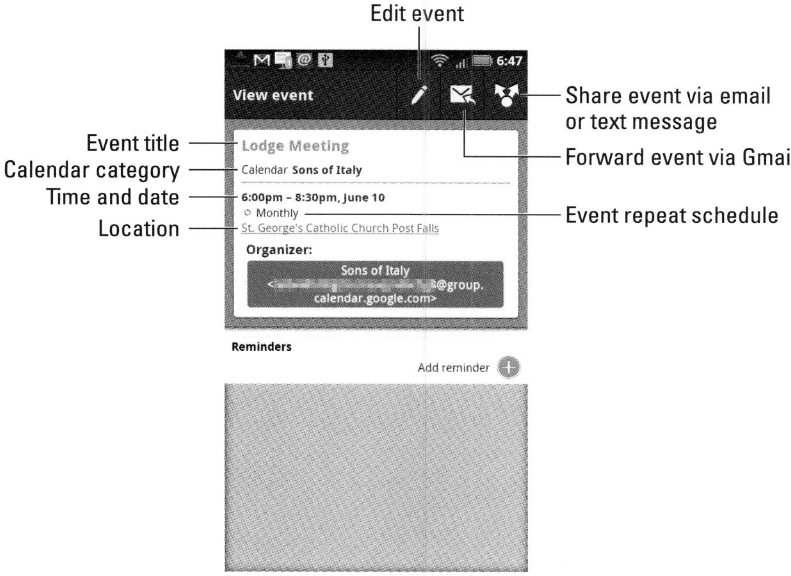

Figure 17-5: Event details.

To see all upcoming events, choose Agenda from the Change View button (refer to Figure 17-3). Rather than list a traditional calendar, the agenda screen lists only those dates with events and the events themselves.

As with the events in the non-agenda views, simply touch an event to see more details (refer to Figure 17-5).

- Not every event has the level of detail shown in Figure 17-5. The minimum amount of information necessary for an event is a name and the date and time.
- If you touch the event on the calendar too long — if you do a long-press — choose the item View Event from the menu.

- Touching a location, as shown in Figure 17-5, conjures up the Maps app, where you'll see the event's location on the map. From there it's easy to get directions, as described in Chapter 13.

Making a new event

The key to making the calendar work is to add events: appointments, things to do, meetings, or full-day events such as birthdays and volcano eruptions. To create a new event, follow these steps in the Calendar app:

1. **Select the day for the event.**

   Use month or week view and touch the day of the new event.

   To save time, use day view and touch the hour at which the event starts.

2. **Touch the New Event button.**

   Refer to Figure 17-3 for its location.

3. **Choose the event Calendar category.**

   Categories are best set up on the Internet using a computer. Basically, they let you organize your events by category and color. Also, you can show or hide individual calendar categories when you have a particularly busy schedule.

4. **Type the event subject.**

   For example, type `Colonoscopy`.

5. **Use the controls by Start to set the starting date and time.**

6. **Use the controls by End to set the ending date and time.**

   When events last all day, like when your mother-in-law visits for an hour, simply touch the All Day button found beneath the End time. All-day events appear at the top of the day when the calendar is shown in week view (refer to Figure 17-4).

   At this point, you've entered the minimum amount of information for creating an event. Any details you add are okay but not necessary.

7. **Optionally, touch the Where field to enter a location.**

   The location can be used by the Maps app to help you get to your appointment. My theory is that you should specify a location as if you're typing something to search for on the map. See Chapter 13 for more information on the Maps app.

8. **Optionally, set or dismiss a reminder.**

   Reminders are nice, but if you forget about them they can be annoying. For example, if you forget to remove the reminder for an all-day event, the phone will make a noise at 15 minutes to midnight. Don't ask how long it took me to figure that out.

9. **Touch the Save button.**

   The Calendar app creates the event.

You can change an event at any time: Simply touch the Edit Event button when viewing the event; refer to Figure 17-5.

To remove an event, long-press it in the week or day view. Choose the Delete Event command. Touch the OK button to confirm.

- The Repetition menu, found at the bottom of the Create Event screen, helps you to create repeating events, such as weekly or monthly meetings, anniversaries, and birthdays.

- Reminders can be set so that the phone alerts you before an event takes place. The alert can take several forms: a notification icon (shown in the margin), an audio alert, or a vibrating alert.
- To deal with an event notification, pull down the notifications and choose the event. You can touch the Dismiss All button to remove event alerts.
- Alerts sounds for events are set by pressing the Menu soft button in the Calendar app and choosing the Settings command. Use the Select Ringtone option to choose an audio alert. Use the Vibrate option to control whether the phone vibrates to alert you of an impending event.

It's a Game Machine

One of the best uses of a smartphone, for all its seriousness and technology, is to play games. I'm not talking about the silly arcade games (though I admit that they're fun). No, I'm talking about some serious portable gaming.

To whet your appetite, the Droid X2 comes with a small taste of what the device can do in regard to gaming. It's the NFS Shift app, which is a car-racing game, shown in Figure 17-6.

Figure 17-6: Games on the Droid X2.

NFS Shift uses the phone's accelerometer to steer a high-speed race car around various racing tracks from all over the globe. The game also plays stereotypical rock music, which either makes the action more exciting or merely irritates you.

If you want to continue playing NFS Shift, you have to buy it. The program lets you know how much it costs after you complete your first free race.

Of course, gaming isn't limited to NFS Shift. Many games — arcade, action, and puzzle — are to be found in the Android Market. See Chapter 18.

It's a YouTube Player

YouTube is the Internet phenomenon that proves Andy Warhol right: In the future, everyone will be famous for 15 minutes. Or in the case of YouTube, they'll be famous on the Internet for the duration of a maximum 15-minute video. That's because YouTube is *the* place on the Internet for anyone and everyone to share their video creations.

To view the mayhem on YouTube, or to contribute something yourself, start the YouTube app. Like all apps on the Droid X2, it can be found on the Apps screen. The YouTube app is shown in Figure 17-7.

To view a video, touch its name or icon in the list. To see more videos, press the Menu soft button and choose Home or Browse.

To search for a video, press the Search soft button. Type or dictate what you want to search for, and then peruse the results.

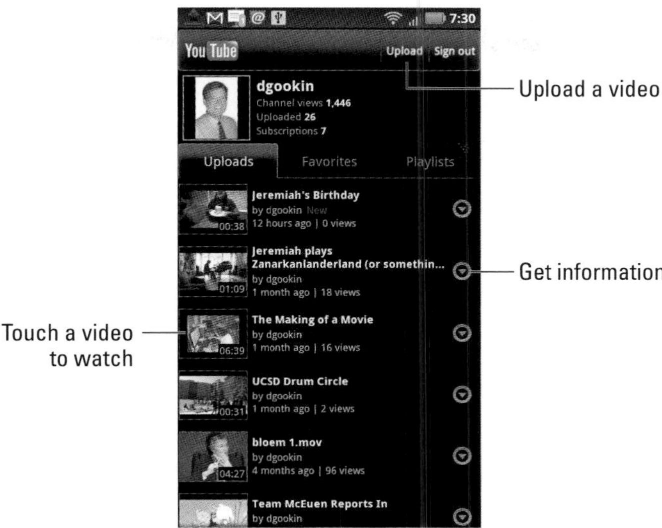

Figure 17-7: YouTube on the Droid X2.

Videos in the YouTube app play best in landscape mode, so tilt your phone to the left to see the videos in their proper orientation. The videos take up the entire screen; touch the screen to see the onscreen video controls.

Press the Back soft button to return to the main YouTube app after watching a video or if you tire of a video and need to return to the main screen out of boredom.

- Use the YouTube app to view YouTube videos, rather than use the Browser app to visit the YouTube web site.
- Not all YouTube videos are available for viewing on mobile devices.
- Press the Menu soft button and choose My Channel to view your own videos or upload new videos.
- You can touch the Upload button (refer to Figure 17-6) to shoot and then immediately send a video to YouTube. Refer to Chapter 15 for information on recording video with your Droid X2.

18

Even More Apps at the Android Market

In This Chapter

- Using the Market app
- Searching for apps
- Downloading a free app
- Getting a paid app
- Reviewing apps you've downloaded
- Deleting apps
- Maintaining apps
- Building app groups

Your phone isn't limited to the paltry assortment of apps available on the Home screen or even all the apps available on the Apps screen. No, the potential of the Droid X2 can be fully exploited by more than 200,000 apps, the bulk of which are free or so cheap they could be considered free. The place to find those apps is a digital shopping mall called the Android Market.

- Because the Droid X2 uses the Android operating system, it can run nearly all applications written for Android.
- You can be assured that all apps that appear in the Android Market on your phone can be used with the Droid X2. There's no way that you can download or buy something that's incompatible with your phone.
- App is short for *application*. It's another word for *software,* which is another word for a program that runs on a computer or on a mobile device, such as your Droid X2 phone.

Welcome to the Market

Shopping for new software for your Droid X2 can be done anywhere that you and your phone just happen to be. You don't even need to know what kind of software you want; like many a mindless ambling shopper, you can browse until the touchscreen is blurry with your fingerprints.

- You obtain software from the Market by *downloading* it into your phone. That file transfer works best at top speeds; therefore:
- I highly recommend that you connect to a Wi-Fi network if you plan to purchase software at the Android Market. See Chapter 19 for details on connecting the Droid X2 to a Wi-Fi network.

Visiting the Market

New apps await delivery into your phone, like animated vegetables shouting, "Pick me! Pick me!" To get to them, open the Market icon, which can be found on the primary Home screen or accessed from the Apps screen.

After opening the Market app, you see the main screen, similar to the one shown in Figure 18-1. You can browse for apps, games, or special apps from Verizon by touching the appropriate doodad, as shown in the figure.

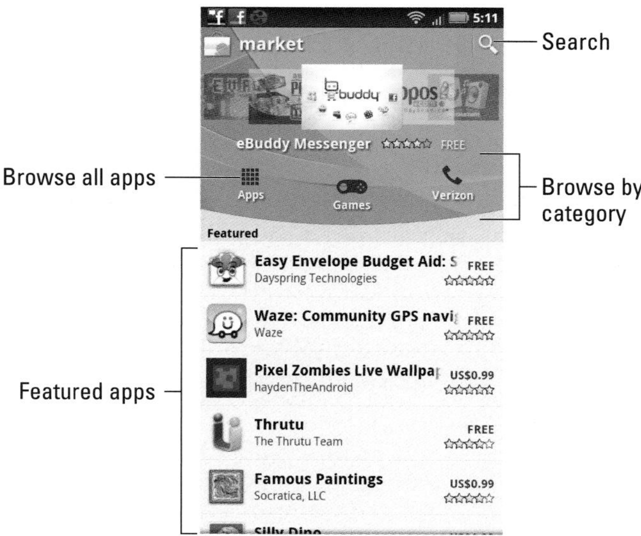

Figure 18-1: Android Market.

Find apps by browsing the lists: Choose Apps (refer to Figure 18-1). Then choose a specific category to browse. You can sort apps by their popularity, their price (paid or free), and their introduction date (recent apps).

When you know an app's name or an app's category or even what the app does, searching for the app works fastest: Touch the Search button at the top of the Market screen (refer to Figure 18-1). Type all or part of the app's name or perhaps a description. Touch the Search button to begin your search.

To see more information about an app, touch it. Touching the app doesn't buy it but instead displays a more detailed description, screen shots, and comments, plus links to see additional apps or contact the developer.

- The first time you enter the Android Market, you have to accept the terms of service; touch the Accept button.
- Pay attention to an app's ratings. Ratings are added by people who use the apps, like you and me. Having more stars is better. You can see additional information, including individual user reviews, by choosing the app.
- In addition to getting apps, you can download widgets for the Home screen as well as wallpapers for the Droid X2. Just search the Android Market for *widget* or *live wallpaper.*
- See Chapter 22 for more information on widgets and live wallpapers.

Getting a free app

After you locate an app you want, the next step is to download it. Follow these steps to obtain a free app from the Android Market:

1. **If possible, activate the phone's Wi-Fi connection.**

   Downloads complete much faster over the Wi-Fi connection than over the digital cellular connection. See Chapter 19 for information on connecting your Droid X2 phone to a Wi-Fi network.

2. **Open the Market app.**
3. **Locate the app you want and open its description.**

   Refer to the preceding section for details.

4. **Touch the Free button.**

   It's found at the top of the screen, below the word *Install.*

   After touching the Free button, you're alerted to any services that the app uses. The alert isn't a warning, and it doesn't mean anything bad. It's just that the app is being honest with you about what it does on your phone.

5. **Touch the OK button to begin the download.**

   The download continues while you do other things on your phone.

   After the download is successful and the app has been installed, the phone's status bar shows a new icon, as shown in the margin. That's the Successful Install notification.

6. **Pull down the notifications.**

   See Chapter 3 for details, in case you've never pulled down notifications.

7. **Choose the app from the list of notifications.**

   The app is listed by its app name, with the text *Successfully Installed* below it.

At this point, what happens next depends on the app you've downloaded. For example, you may have to agree to a license agreement. If so, touch the I Agree button. Additional setup may involve signing in to an account or creating a profile, for example.

After the initial setup is complete, or if no setup is necessary, you can start using the app.

- Don't forget to turn off Wi-Fi after downloading your app; Wi-Fi is a drain on the phone's battery.
- The new app's icon is placed on the Apps screen, along with all the other apps on the Droid X2.
- You can also place a shortcut icon for the app on the Home screen. See Chapter 22.
- The Android market has many wonderful apps you can download. Chapter 26 lists some that I recommend, all of which are free.

Buying an app

Some great free apps are available, but many of the apps you dearly want probably cost money. It's not a lot of money, especially compared to the price of computer software. In fact, it seems odd to sit and stew over whether paying 99 cents for a game is "worth it."

I recommend that you download a free app first, to familiarize yourself with the process. See the preceding section.

When you're ready to pay for an app, follow these steps:

1. **Activate the phone's Wi-Fi connection.**
2. **Open the Market app.**
3. **Browse or search for the app you want, and choose the app to display its description.**

   Review the app's price.
4. **Touch the price button, found below the word *Buy*.**
5. **Touch the OK button.**

   If you don't have a Google Checkout account, you're prompted to set one up. Follow the directions on the screen.
6. **Choose the payment method.**

   If you choose to add a new credit card, you're required to fill in all information about the card, including the billing address.
7. **Touch the Buy Now button.**

   The Buy Now button lists the app's price.

   After you touch the Buy button, the app is downloaded. You can wait or do something else with the phone while the app is downloading.

The app may require additional setup steps, confirmation information, or other options.

After it's installed, the app can be accessed from the Apps screen, just like all other apps available on your Droid X2.

Eventually, you receive an email message from Google Checkout, confirming your purchase. The message explains how you can get a refund from your purchase within 24 hours. The section "Removing downloaded apps," later in this chapter, discusses how it's done.

Some apps are developed overseas, which means you're buying them using U.S. dollars at an exchange rate. That explains the unusual pricing on various apps. Your credit card is charged an exchange fee for the purchase; usually it's only a few pennies.

Be sure to disable the phone's Wi-Fi after downloading the app, because Wi-Fi is a drain on the phone's battery.

Manage Your Applications

The Market is not only where you buy apps — it's also the place you return to for performing app management. That task includes reviewing apps you've downloaded, updating apps, organizing apps, and removing apps you no longer want or that you severely hate.

Reviewing your downloaded apps

If you're like me, and if I'm like anyone, you probably sport a whole host of apps on your Droid X2. It's kind of fun to download new software and give your phone new capabilities. To review the apps you've acquired, follow these steps:

1. **Start the Market app.**
2. **Press the Menu soft button.**
3. **Choose My Apps.**
4. **Scroll your downloaded apps.**

The list of downloaded apps should look similar to the one shown in Figure 18-2.

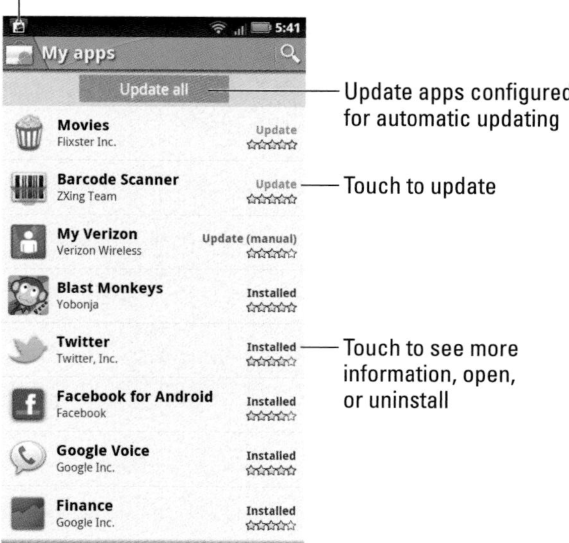

Figure 18-2: Apps downloaded for the Droid X2.

Besides reviewing the list, you can do two things with an installed app: Update it or remove it. The following two sections describe how each operation is done.

- You can also review downloaded apps from the Apps screen: Touch the Group menu on the Apps screen and touch the Downloaded icon. To return to the all apps view, touch the Group button and choose All Apps.
- The Downloads list is accurate in that it represents apps you've downloaded. Some apps in the list, however, might not be installed on your Droid X2: They were downloaded, installed, and then removed. To review all apps installed on the phone, see the section "Controlling your apps," later in this chapter.

Updating an app

One nice thing about using the Android Market to get new software is that the Market also notifies you of new versions of the programs you download. Whenever a new version of any app is available, you see the Updates Available notification icon, shown in the margin.

Locate apps that need updating by pulling down the phone's notifications and choosing Updates Available. Or you can visit the Downloads list, as described in the preceding section.

To update an app, obey these steps:

1. **Turn on the phone's Wi-Fi access, if it's available.**

   Updates are downloaded from the Internet, which means the faster your phone can connect, the more quickly the updates are made.

2. **Open the Market app.**
3. **Press the Menu soft button and choose My Apps.**
4. **If you see the Update All button, touch it.**

   Touching the Update All button (refer to Figure 18-2) updates all the apps you've configured for automatic updating.

5. **If you don't see the Update All button or your app must be updated individually:**

   a. **Choose the app that needs updating.**

      Refer to Figure 18-2 for an example of apps that are flagged for updating or apps that demand a manual update.

b. **On the app's description screen, put a green check mark by the Allow Automatic Updating item.**

c. **Touch the Update button.**

   Or touch the Update All button — yes, apps you configure to be automatically updated can be updated in one fell swoop (as was done in Step 4).

6. **Touch OK to proceed with the upgrade.**
7. **Touch the OK button to heed the warning.**

   The update means that an entirely new version of the app is downloaded and installed, which replaces the installed version. That's okay.

8. **If prompted, read about the services that the app uses on your phone and then touch the OK button.**

   The update is downloaded.

You're free to do other things with the phone while the update is downloading. When downloading is complete, the Successful Install notification appears, as shown in the margin. You can then start using your updated app or continue applying updates by repeating the steps in this section.

Removing downloaded apps

You might want to remove installed software for a few reasons. The first, most odiously, is that you just don't like a program or it does something so hideously annoying that you find removal of the app to be emotionally satisfying. The second is that you have a better program that does the same thing. The third reason is to free up a modicum of storage on the phone's internal storage area or microSD card.

Whatever the reason, removing an app from your Droid X2 works like this:

1. **Start the Market app.**
2. **Press the Menu soft button and choose My Apps.**

   You'll see a list of all the apps you've downloaded into your phone, similar to what's shown in Figure 18-2.

3. **Touch the app that offends you.**
4. **Touch the Uninstall button.**
5. **Touch the OK button to confirm.**

   The app is removed.

6. **Fill in the survey to specify why you removed the app.**

   Be honest, or be as honest as you can given the short list of reasons.

7. **Touch OK.**

   The app is gone!

The app continues to appear on the Downloads list even after it's been removed. After all, you downloaded it once. That doesn't mean the app is still installed.

- In most cases, if you uninstall a paid app before 24 hours has passed, your credit card or account is fully refunded.
- You can always reinstall paid apps that you've uninstalled. You aren't charged twice for doing so.

Controlling your apps

The Droid X2 has a technical place where you can review and manage all apps you've installed on your phone. To visit that place, follow these steps:

1. **At the Home screen, press the Menu soft button.**
2. **Choose Settings, then choose Applications.**
3. **Choose Manage Applications.**

   A complete list of all applications installed on your phone is displayed. Unlike the My Apps list in the Market app, only installed applications appear.

4. **Touch an application name.**

   An application Info screen appears, showing lots of trivia about the app.

Among the trivia you'll find several useful buttons, including:

- **Force Stop:** Touch this button to halt a program run amok. For example, I had to stop an older Android app that continually made noise and offered no option to exit.
- **Uninstall:** Touch the Uninstall button to remove the app, which is another way to accomplish the same steps described in the preceding section.
- **Share:** Touch the Share button to send a text or email message to a friend. In the message is a link the recipient can use to install the app on their phone.

Or you can just press the Back soft button when you're done being baffled by the information.

Creating app groups

You can organize your apps on the Droid X2 in three ways. The first way is to place frequently used apps on the Home screen. That technique is covered in Chapter 22, but it has its limitations. The second way is not to organize your apps at all. That duty is handled by the Apps screen, which lists all the apps in your phone.

The third way is to create app groups on the Apps screen. Heed these steps:

1. **Touch the Launcher to display the Apps screen.**
2. **Touch the Groups button and choose New Group.**
3. **Name the group.**

   For example, name the Group games, as shown in Figure 18-3, to create a group that holds all the games on your phone.
4. **Choose an appropriate icon from the icons menu (refer to Figure 18-3).**

   I like the happy face icon for my games group.
5. **Touch the Save button.**

   The group is created, but it's empty. The next step is to add apps to the group.
6. **Touch the green plus button.**

   The Select Apps menu appears. It lists all the apps installed on your phone.
7. **Scroll through the list of apps, placing a green check mark by the apps you want to add to your group.**

   The apps are not moved; only a copy of the app (a shortcut or alias) is placed into your new group.
8. **Touch the OK button when you're done adding apps.**

   The group is created, filled with apps, and appears on the screen.

You can redisplay all apps by choosing the All Apps command from the Group menu. Or you can choose any other group from the Groups menu, or create even more groups to further organize your apps.

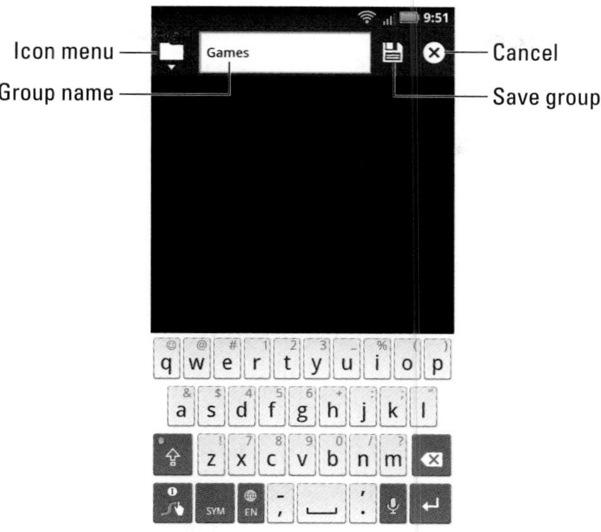

Figure 18-3: Creating an apps group.

You can edit or remove the group by long-pressing it on the Groups menu. You can even add the group to the Home screen as a shortcut, which is yet another way to organize your apps.

Part V
Specifics and Particulars

In this part . . .

Some things you can do with your phone don't quite fall into the category of making phone calls or any of the several amazing things that the Droid X2 is capable of doing. These things include some configuration items, customization, getting the phone to talk with a computer and share information, as well as the more mundane topics of maintenance and troubleshooting. Those tasks may not be as sexy as sharing your Facebook status while you're standing in line at Starbucks (and I'm kind of tired of that), but they're necessary and covered in this part of the book.

19

No Wires, Ever!

In This Chapter

- Understanding wireless networking
- Using Wi-Fi on the Droid X2
- Connecting to a Wi-Fi network
- Setting up a 3G mobile hotspot
- Sharing the Internet connection
- Using a Bluetooth headset

Call me a fool, but the more wires that come out of something, the less likely that something is truly portable. Verily, the ultimate mobile device wouldn't have any wires at all. Oh, sure: Maybe a wire to charge the thing or transfer files, but even in those cases, nifty wireless ways can perform various tasks.

The Droid X2 can live a nearly wireless existence. After charging the device, you're free to wander out and about, all while communicating with other gizmos without the horrid fashion faux pas of an ugly wire. The phone can use the digital cellular network, Wi-Fi, or Bluetooth to make its wireless connections. This chapter shows you the ropes, er, well, the lack-of ropes.

Wireless Networking

Although you can't see it, wireless communication is going on all around. No need to duck — the wireless signals are intercepted only by items such as cell phones and laptop computers. The Droid X2 uses those signals to let you talk on the phone and communicate over the Internet and other networks.

Understanding the digital network

You pay your cellular provider a handsome fee every month. That fee comes in two chunks. One chunk is the telephone service. The second chunk is the data service, which is how the Droid X2 gets on the Internet. That system is called the cellular data network.

The Droid X2 can communicate with several types of cellular data networks, but you'll see only two status icons to represent them:

- **3G:** The *third generation* of wide-area data networks is several times faster than the previous generation of data networks. 3G networks also provide for talking and sending data at the same time, though such a feature may not be enabled by the cellular carrier.
- **1X:** The slower data connection comes in several technical flavors, but only one icon appears on the phone's status bar. The 1X network is actually the second generation of cellular data technology. It's a lot slower than 3G, but it's better than nothing.

Your phone always uses the best network available. So, if the 3G network is within reach, it's the network the Droid X2 uses for Internet communications. Otherwise, a 1X network is chosen.

- Accessing the digital cellular network isn't free. Your Droid X2 most likely has some form of subscription plan for a certain quantity of data. When you exceed that quantity, the costs can become prohibitive.
- See Chapter 21 for information on how to avoid cellular data overcharges when taking your Droid X2 out and about.

Turning on Wi-Fi

Wi-Fi is the same wireless networking standard used by computers for communicating with each other and the Internet. To make Wi-Fi work on your Droid X2 requires two steps. First, you must activate Wi-Fi, by turning on the phone's wireless radio. The second step is to connect to a specific wireless network.

Follow these steps to activate Wi-Fi on your Droid X2:

1. **At the Home screen, press the Menu soft button.**
2. **Choose Settings.**
3. **Choose Wireless & Networks.**
4. **Choose Wi-Fi.**

   A green check mark appears by the Wi-Fi option, indicating that the phone's Wi-Fi radio is now activated.

Turning on the Wi-Fi radio is only half the process. The next step is to connect the Droid X2 to a Wi-Fi network, which is covered in the next section.

From the And-Now-He-Tells-Us Department, you can quickly activate the phone's Wi-Fi radio by touching the Wi-Fi Power Control widget, shown in Figure 19-1. The Power Control widget is preinstalled on the second Home screen panel to the left of the main panel. Touch the Wi-Fi button and the Droid X2 turns on its Wi-Fi capabilities.

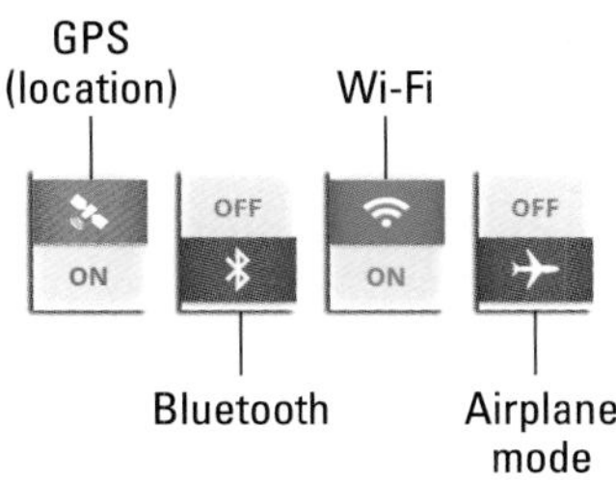

Figure 19-1: The Power Control widget.

To turn off Wi-Fi, repeat the steps in this section. Doing so turns off the phone's Wi-Fi access, disconnecting you from any networks.

- Using Wi-Fi to connect to the Internet doesn't incur data usage charges.
- Yes, the Wi-Fi radio is called a radio even though it's not a music-playing type of radio.
- The Wi-Fi radio places an extra drain on the battery, but it's truly negligible. If you want to save a modicum of juice, especially if you're out and about and don't plan to be near a Wi-Fi access point for any length of time, turn off the Wi-Fi radio as described in this section.

Accessing a Wi-Fi network

After activating the Droid X2's Wi-Fi radio, you can connect to an available wireless network. For networks you've already set up, the connection happens automatically. Otherwise you'll need to set things up. Heed these steps:

1. **Press the Menu soft button while viewing the Home screen.**
2. **Choose Settings.**
3. **Choose Wireless & Networks.**

4. **Choose Wi-Fi Settings.**

   You see a list of Wi-Fi networks displayed, as shown in Figure 19-2. If no wireless network is displayed, you're sort of out of luck regarding wireless access from your current location.

5. **Choose a wireless network from the list.**

   In Figure 19-2, I chose the Imperial Wambooli network, which is my office network.

6. **If required, type the network password.**

   Touch the Password text box to see the onscreen keyboard.

7. **Touch the Connect button.**

   You should be immediately connected to the network. If not, try the password again.

When the Droid X2 is connected, you see the Wi-Fi status icon atop the touchscreen. That icon means that the phone's Wi-Fi is on, connected, and communicating with a Wi-Fi network.

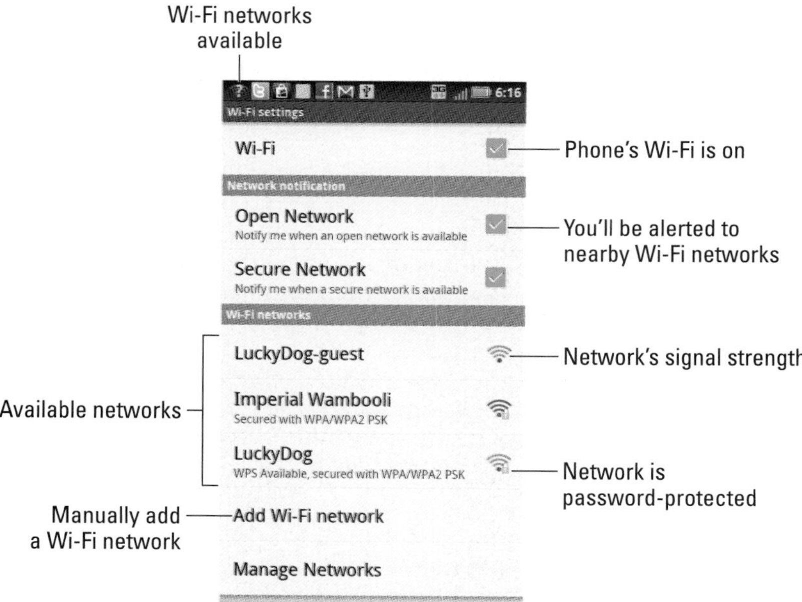

Figure 19-2: Hunting down a wireless network.

Some wireless networks don't broadcast their names, which adds security but also makes accessing them more difficult. In those cases, choose the Add Wi-Fi Network command (refer to Figure 19-2) to manually add the network. You need to input the network name, or *SSID,* and the type of security. You also need the password, if one is used. You can obtain this information from the guy with the pierced nose who sold you coffee or from whoever is in charge of the wireless network at your location.

- Not every wireless network has a password.
- Some public networks are open to anyone, but you have to use the Browser app to get on the web and find a login page that lets you access the network: Simply browse to any page on the Internet and the login page shows up.
- The phone automatically remembers any Wi-Fi network it's connected to as well as that network password.
- To disconnect from a Wi-Fi network, simply turn off Wi-Fi on the phone. See the preceding section.
- A Wi-Fi network is faster than the 3G cellular data network, so it makes sense to connect with Wi-Fi whenever you can.

- Unlike a cellular data network, a Wi-Fi network's broadcast signal goes only so far. My advice is to use Wi-Fi when you plan to remain in one location for a while. If you wander too far, your phone loses the signal and is disconnected.

Share the Connection

You and your Droid X2 can get on the Internet anywhere you receive a digital cellular signal. But pity the poor laptop that sits there, seething with jealousy.

Well, laptop, be jealous no more! You can easily share your Droid X2's digital cellular signal in one of two ways. The first is to create a mobile hotspot, which allows any Wi-Fi enabled gizmo to access the Internet through your phone. The second is a direct connection between your phone and some other device, which is a concept called *tethering.*

Creating a mobile hotspot

You can direct the Droid X2 to share its cellular data network connection with as many as eight other devices. Those devices connect wirelessly with your phone, accessing a shared 3G network. The process is referred to as *creating a mobile, wireless hotspot*, though no fire is involved.

To set up a 3G mobile hotspot with your Droid X2, heed these steps:

1. **Turn off the Wi-Fi radio.**

   There's no point in creating a Wi-Fi hotspot if one is already available.

2. **From the Apps screen, open the Mobile Hotspot icon.**

   You may see text describing the process. If so, dismiss the text.

3. **Touch the box to place a green check mark by Mobile Wi-Fi Hotspot.**

   A warning message appears, recommending that you plug your Droid X2 into a power source because the mobile hotspot feature sucks down a lot of battery juice.

4. **Touch the OK button to dismiss the warning.**

   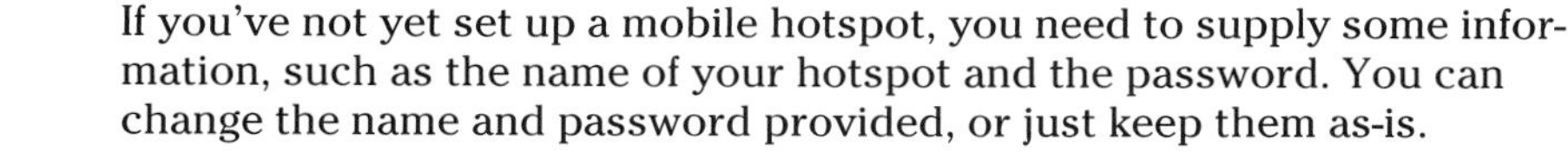

   If you've not yet set up a mobile hotspot, you need to supply some information, such as the name of your hotspot and the password. You can change the name and password provided, or just keep them as-is.

   Make a note of the password. You'll need it to log in to the mobile hotspot.

5. **Touch the OK or Save button to save your settings and start the hotspot.**

   You're done.

When the 3G hotspot is active, you see the Tethering or Hotspot Active notification icon, as shown in the margin. You can then access the hotspot using any computer or mobile device that has Wi-Fi capabilities.

To turn off the 3G hotspot, open the Mobile Hotspot app and remove the green check mark.

- The range for the mobile hotspot is about 30 feet.
- Data usage fees apply when you use the mobile hotspot. Those charges can add up quickly, especially with several of your friends access the Internet through your phone's mobile hotspot.
- Don't forget to turn off the mobile hotspot when you're done using it.

Tethering the Internet connection

A more private, intimate way to share the Droid X2's digital cellular connection is to connect the phone directly to a computer and activate the tethering feature.

Yes: I am fully aware that tethering goes against the wireless theme of this chapter. Still, it remains a solid way to provide Internet access to another gizmo, such as a laptop or desktop computer. Follow these steps to setup Internet tethering on your Droid X2:

1. **Connect the phone to another device by using the USB cable.**
2. **On the Droid X2, at the Home screen, press the Menu soft button.**
3. **Choose Settings.**
4. **Choose Wireless & Networks.**
5. **Choose Tethering & Mobile Hotspot.**
6. **Touch the box to place a green check mark by the item USB Tethering.**

   Internet tethering is activated.

The other device should instantly recognize the Droid X2's network access. Further configuration may be required, which depends on the device using the tethered connection. For example, you may be prompted on the PC to locate and install software for the Droid X2. Do so: Accept the installation of new software when prompted by Windows.

When tethering is activated on the Droid X2, a Tethering notification icon appears. The icon looks nearly the same as the standard USB connection icon. In fact, your clue that USB tethering is active is that you'll see *two* USB notification icons.

- There is no need to disable the Wi-Fi radio to activate USB tethering on the Droid X2.
- Sharing the digital network connection incurs data usage charges against your cellular data plan. Be careful with your data usage when you're sharing a connection.

Bluetooth Gizmos

One type of computer network you can confuse yourself with is Bluetooth. It has nothing to do with the color blue or any dental problems. *Bluetooth* is simply a wireless protocol for communication between two or more gizmos.

For your Droid X2, the primary Bluetooth peripheral you'll consider using is one of those ear-clingy earphones. There's far more to Bluetooth, however, than walking around looking like you have a stapler stuck to your ear.

Activating Bluetooth

You must turn on the phone's Bluetooth networking before you can use one of those Borg-earpiece implants and join the ranks of walking nerds. Here's how to turn on Bluetooth for the Droid X2:

1. **At the Home screen, press the Menu soft button.**
2. **Choose Settings.**
3. **Choose Wireless & Networks.**
4. **Choose Bluetooth.**

   Note that if a little green check mark appears by the Bluetooth option, Bluetooth is already on.

You can also turn on Bluetooth by using the Power Control widget (refer to Figure 19-1). Just touch the Bluetooth button to turn it on.

To turn off Bluetooth, repeat the steps in this section.

- When Bluetooth is on, the Bluetooth status icon appears, as shown in the margin.
- Activating Bluetooth on the Droid X2 can quickly drain the battery. Be mindful to use Bluetooth only when necessary, and remember to turn it off when you're done.

Using a Bluetooth headset

To make the Bluetooth connection between the Droid X2 and a set of those "I'm so cool" earphones, you need to *pair* the devices. That way, the Droid X2 picks up only your earphone and not anyone else's.

To pair the phone with a headset, follow these steps:

1. **Ensure that Bluetooth is on.**
2. **Turn on the Bluetooth headset.**
3. **At the Home screen, press the Menu soft button and choose Settings.**
4. **Choose Wireless & Networks.**
5. **Choose Bluetooth Settings.**

   The Bluetooth Settings screen appears.
6. **Choose Scan for Devices.**
7. **If necessary, press the main button on the Bluetooth gizmo.**

   The main button is the one you use to answer the phone. You may have to press and hold the button.

   Eventually, the device should appear on the screen, or you'll see its code number.

8. **Choose the device.**
9. **If necessary, input the device's passcode.**

   It's usually a four-digit number, and quite often it's simply 1234.

And now, the device is connected. You can stick it in your ear and press its main answer button when the phone rings.

After you've answered the call (by pressing the main answer button on the earphone), you can chat away. The Call-in-Progress notification icon is blue for a Bluetooth call, as shown in the margin.

If you tire of using the Bluetooth headset, you can touch the Bluetooth button on the touchscreen to use the Droid X2 speaker and microphone. (Refer to Figure 5-2, in Chapter 5, for the location of the Bluetooth button.)

- You can turn on or off the Bluetooth earphone after it's been paired. As long as Bluetooth is on, the Droid X2 instantly recognizes the earphone when you turn it on.

- The Bluetooth status icon changes when a device is paired. The new icon is shown in the margin.
- You can unpair a device by locating it on the Bluetooth Settings screen. Long-press the device and choose the Disconnect or Disconnect & Unpair commands.
- Don't forget to turn off the earpiece when you're done with it. The earpiece has a battery, and it continues to drain when you forget to turn the thing off.

20

Connect, Store, Share

In This Chapter

- Getting the phone and the computer to talk
- Mounting the phone as computer storage
- Synchronizing media
- Copying files between the phone and computer
- Understanding phone storage
- Connecting the Droid X2 to an HDMI monitor
- Sharing files with DNLA

Welcome to the chapter that betrays the notion that the Droid X2 is a wireless and portable device. Most of the time, it is. At times, however, it's practical and even necessary to hook up your phone to various physical devices, such as a computer or a large-screen monitor. The reasons for making the connections vary, as do the methods. All that stuff can be confusing, so I wrote this chapter to make the process easier. Also, I get a thrill when I type the acronym USB.

The USB Connection

The most direct way to mate a Droid X2 with a computer is by using a USB cable. Coincidentally, a USB cable came with the phone. It's a match made in heaven, but like many matches it often doesn't work smoothly. Rather than hire a counselor to get the phone and computer on speaking terms, I offer you some good USB connection advice in this section.

Connecting the phone to the computer

Communication between your computer and the Droid X2 works faster when both devices are physically connected. That connection happens by using the USB cable: The cable's A end plugs into the computer. The other end, known as a micro-USB connector, plugs into the Droid X2's left flank.

The connectors cannot be plugged in either backward or upside down. That's good.

When the Droid X2 is connected via USB cable to a computer, you'll see the USB connection notification icon appear. Refer to the next section for what you can do with that notification to configure the USB connection.

- If you don't have a USB cable for your phone, you can buy one at any computer- or office-supply store. Get a USB-A-male-to-micro-USB cable.

- A lot of activities take place when you first connect the Droid X2 to a Windows PC. Notifications pop up about new software that's installed, or you may see the AutoPlay dialog box prompting you to install software. Do so.

Configuring the USB connection

Upon successful connection of your Droid X2 to a computer, you have the option of configuring the USB connection. You have several choices, as shown in Figure 20-1.

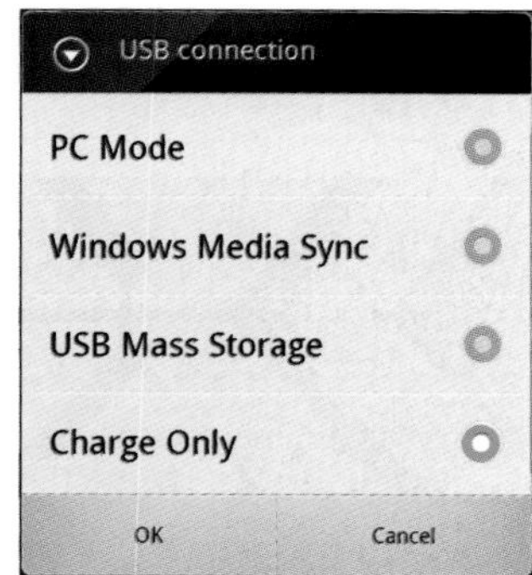

Figure 20-1: The USB connection menu.

To see the USB Connection menu, pull down the notifications and choose USB Connection. Select an item from the menu and touch the OK button. Here is what each item means:

- **PC Mode:** Don't use this option.
- **Windows Media Sync:** This option is used on a Windows PC to treat the phone as a media device, similar to a camera or MP3 music player. It's ideal for synchronizing files.
- **USB Mass Storage:** When this option is chosen, the computer treats the phone like a removable storage device, such as a USB thumb drive or media card.
- **Charge Only:** Use this option when you want to only charge the phone and not have it communicate with the computer at all.

When in doubt, choose the Charge Only option. I write about using the other options elsewhere in this chapter.

- After choosing the Windows Media Sync or USB Mass Storage option, you will see an AutoPlay dialog box on your Windows PC. You can choose how to deal with the phone using that dialog box by choosing an item such as Open Folder to View Files or Windows Media Player. Or just close the dialog box.

- When in doubt about which USB connection mode to choose, I recommend selecting the USB Mass Storage option.
- On a Macintosh, use either the Charge Only or USB Mass Storage option for connecting the phone. The Mac may not recognize the Droid X2 PC Mode or Windows Media Sync setting.
- When you're done accessing information on the Droid X2, you should properly unmount the phone from your computer system. See the next section.
- Another advantage of connecting your phone to your computer is that the phone charges itself as long as it's plugged in. It charges even when it's turned off, but the computer must be on for the phone to charge.

- You cannot access the phone's microSD card while the Droid X2 is mounted into a computer storage system. Items such as your music and photos are unavailable until you disconnect the phone from the computer or choose the Charge Only setting for the USB connection.
- No matter which USB connection option you've chosen, the phone's battery charges when it's connected to a computer's USB port — as long as the computer is turned on, of course.

Disconnecting the phone from the computer

When you're using any USB connection option other than Charge Only, it's important that you properly disconnect the phone from the computer. Never just yank out the USB cable. Never! Never! Never! Doing so can damage the phone's storage, which is a Bad Thing. Instead, follow these steps to do things properly:

1. **Close whichever programs or windows are accessing the Droid X2 from the computer.**
2. **Properly unmount the phone from the computer's storage system.**

   On a PC, locate the phone's icon in the Computer or My Computer window. Right-click that icon and choose the Eject or Safely Remove command.

   On a Macintosh, drag the phone's storage icon to the Trash.
3. **On the Droid X2, pull down the notifications.**
4. **Choose USB Connection.**
5. **Choose Charge Only.**
6. **Touch the OK button to confirm.**

   The phone's storage is unmounted and can no longer be accessed from your computer.
7. **If necessary, unplug the USB cable.**

If you choose to keep the phone connected to the computer, the phone continues to charge. (Only when the computer is off does the phone not charge.) Otherwise, the computer and phone have ended their little tête-à-tête and you and the phone are free again to wander the earth.

Synchronize Your Stuff

The synchronizing process involves hooking up your Droid X2 to a computer and then swapping music, pictures, and other information back and forth. That process can be done automatically by using special software, or it can be done manually. The manual method is not pleasant but often necessary.

- See Chapter 15 for information on swapping pictures between your Droid X2 and your computer or the Internet.
- Synchronizing music between your phone and computer is covered in Chapter 16.

Synchronizing with doubleTwist

One of the most popular ways to move information between your Droid X2 and a computer is to use the third-party utility doubleTwist. This amazing program is free, and it's available at `www.doubletwist.com`.

doubleTwist isn't an Android app. You use it on your computer, either a PC or a Macintosh. It lets you easily synchronize picture, music, videos, and web page subscriptions between your computer's media libraries and any portable device, such as the Droid X2. Additionally, doubleTwist gives you the ability to search the Android Market and obtain new apps for your phone.

To use doubleTwist, connect your phone to your computer as described earlier in this chapter. Ensure that USB sharing is on; *mount* the microSD card as a USB Mass Storage device. Start the doubleTwist program if it doesn't start by itself. The simple doubleTwist interface is illustrated in Figure 20-2.

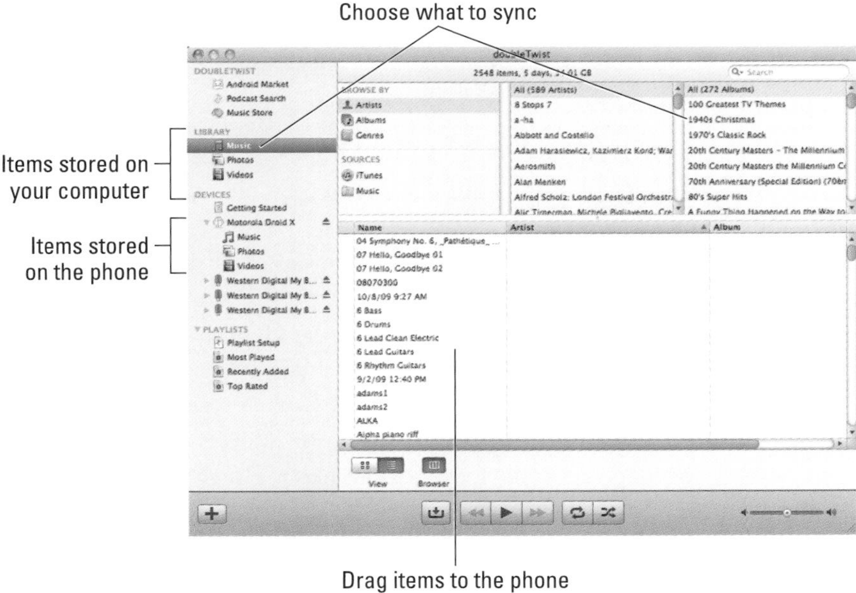

Figure 20-2: The doubleTwist synchronization utility.

The way I use doubleTwist is to drag and drop media from my computer to the Droid X2 or the other way around. Use the program's interface to browse for media, as shown in Figure 20-2.

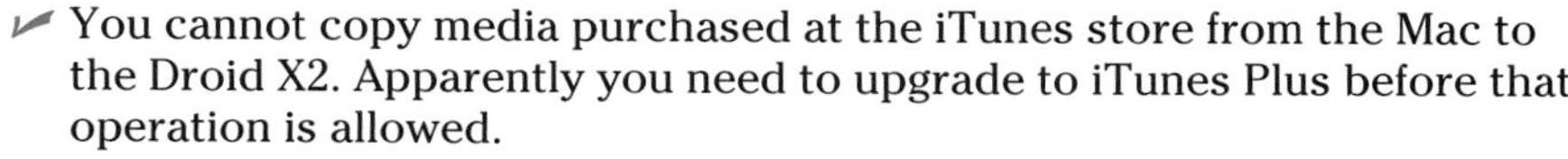

- You cannot copy media purchased at the iTunes store from the Mac to the Droid X2. Apparently you need to upgrade to iTunes Plus before that operation is allowed.

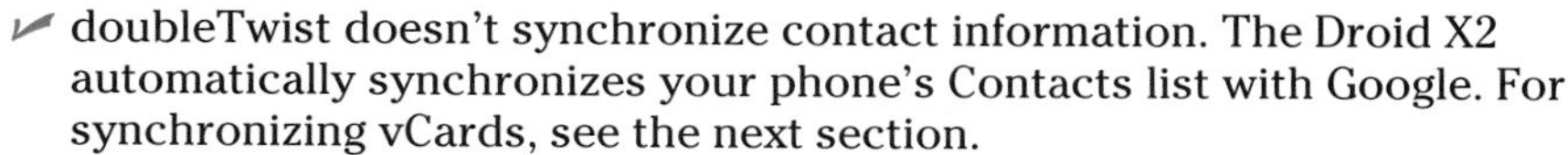

- doubleTwist doesn't synchronize contact information. The Droid X2 automatically synchronizes your phone's Contacts list with Google. For synchronizing vCards, see the next section.

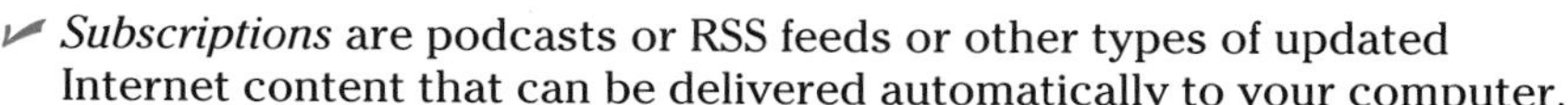

- *Subscriptions* are podcasts or RSS feeds or other types of updated Internet content that can be delivered automatically to your computer.

Doing a manual sync

When you can't get software on your computer to synchronize automatically, you'll have to end up doing the old manual connection. Yes, it can be complex. And bothersome. And boring. But it's often the only way to get some information out of the Droid X2 and on to a computer, or vice versa.

Follow these steps to copy files between your computer to the Droid X2:

1. **Connect the Droid X2 to the computer by using the USB cable.**
2. **Choose the USB Mass Storage option for the USB connection.**

   Specific directions are offered earlier in this chapter.

3a. **On a PC, in the AutoPlay dialog box, choose the option Open Folder to View Files.**

   The option might also read Open Device to View Files.

   You see a folder window appear, which looks like any other folder in Windows. The difference is that the files and folders in that window are on the Droid X2, not on your computer.

3b. **On a Macintosh, open the Removable Drive icon that appears.**

   The Droid X2 is assigned a generic, removable drive icon when it's mounted on a Macintosh. Most likely, it's given the name *NONAME.*

4. **Open a folder window on your computer.**

   Open either the folder from which you're copying files to the Droid X2, or the folder that will receive files from the Droid X2. For example, the Documents folder.

   If you're copying files from the phone to your computer, use the Pictures folder for pictures and videos and use the Documents folder for everything else.

5. **Drag the file icons from one folder window to the other to copy them between the phone and computer.**

   Use Figure 20-3 as your guide.

6. **When you're done, properly unmount the Droid X2 from your computer's storage system and disconnect the USB cable.**

   You must eject the Droid X2's storage icon from the Macintosh computer before you can turn off USB storage on the phone.

Any files you've copied to the phone are now stored on the Droid X2's microSD card. What you do with them next depends on the reason you copied the files: to view pictures, use the Gallery, import vCards, use the Contacts app, listen to music, or use the Music Player, for example.

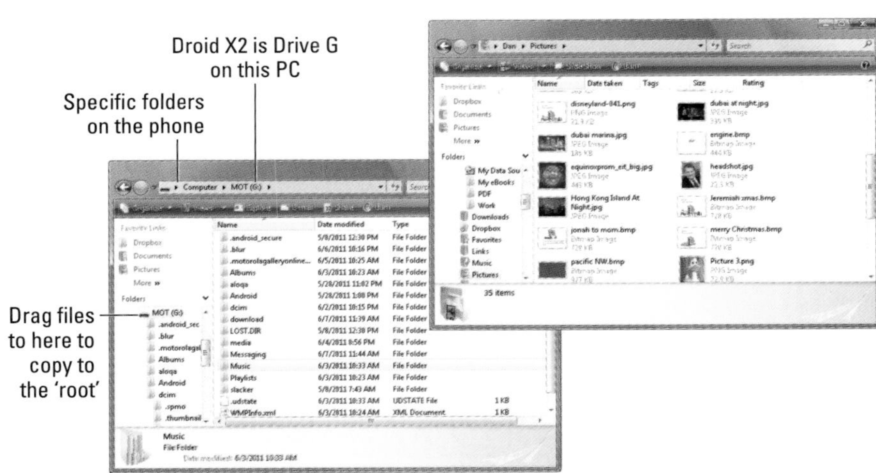

Figure 20-3: Copying files to the Droid X2.

- Files you've downloaded on the Droid X2 are stored in the Download folder.
- Pictures and videos on the Droid X2 are stored in the dcim/Camera folder.
- Music on the Droid X2 is stored in the Music folder, organized by artist.

- Quite a few files can be found in the *root folder,* the main folder on the Droid X2's microSD card, which you see when the phone is mounted into your computer's storage system and you open its folder.
- The Droid X2 mounts as *two* storage devices: the microSD card and then the phone's internal storage. All the good stuff is most likely on the internal storage. You can tell the difference between the two storage areas because the internal storage on the Droid X2 shows a lot of folders (refer to Figure 20-3); the microSD card doesn't have as many folders.
- The original Droid X mounts only the microSD card.

- A good understanding of basic file operations is necessary to get the most from transferring file between your computer and the phone. Those basic operations include copying, moving, renaming, and deleting. A familiarity with the concept of folders is also helpful. A doctorate in entanglement theory is optional.

Phone Storage Stuff

Information stored on your phone (pictures, videos, music) is kept in two places: On the removable microSD card and on the phone's internal storage. That's about all you need to know, though if you're willing to explore the concept further — including the scary proposition of file management on a cell phone — keep reading.

Generally speaking, you use specific apps to access the stuff stored on your phone. For example, you use the Gallery app to view pictures or the Music app to listen to tunes. Beyond that, you can employ some nerdy apps to see where stuff on the Droid X2 really dwells.

The first app, which is the least scary, is the Downloads app. That app displays the Downloads screen, which is used to review those files you've downloaded from the Internet (via the web or an email attachment) to your phone.

Alas, the Downloads app exists only on the original Droid X phone. To see your downloads on the Droid X2 (as well as the original Droid X), open the Browser app: press the Menu soft button and choose More, then Downloads.

The second app — which is scary because it's a file management app and those apps aren't that friendly — is the Files app. It works like this:

1. **Start the Files app.**

   It's found on the Apps screen.

2. **Choose which storage device to examine: Internal Phone Storage or SD Card.**

   Choose the option Internal Phone Storage on the Droid X2. The original Droid X lacks the Internal Phone Storage option, so choose SD Card.

3. **Browse through the files just as you would on a computer.**

   If you're familiar with computer file management, you'll be right at home amidst the folder and file icons. Touch a folder icon to open it and see what subfolders and files dwell inside. Touch a file icon to preview it — if that's possible.

4. **To manage a file or folder, long-press it.**

   A menu appears where you can perform typical file management operations: delete, rename, copy, move, and so on.

You can press the Home soft button when you're done being frightened by file management in the Files app.

Another option available for browsing files is titled Shared Folders. Basically, that option lets you access file servers over the Internet or your local network to browse shared folders. If that sentence makes any sense, give it a try! Otherwise, you can safely avoid choosing the Shared Folders option.

Viewing Your Media Elsewhere

The Droid X2 has the capability to project its media — pictures, video, and music — onto other devices. It's not the easiest thing to do, but the phone is capable of doing it.

Making the HDMI connection

It's possible to connect the Droid X2 to a large-screen monitor. That capability sates your big screen desires for playing Angry Birds without totally losing the phone's capability to easily slip into your pocket. The trick is to connect the phone to an HDMI monitor or television set.

Well, that's not really the trick. The trick is to fork out the money for the expensive HDMI cable that physically connects the phone to an HDMI monitor. *Then* you can plug your phone into a humongous screen and watch things Really Big.

When attached to a standard monitor or TV, the Droid X2 immediately asserts its orientation to landscape, to match the monitor. This is the only instance I know when the phone uses that orientation for the Home screen, as shown in Figure 20-4.

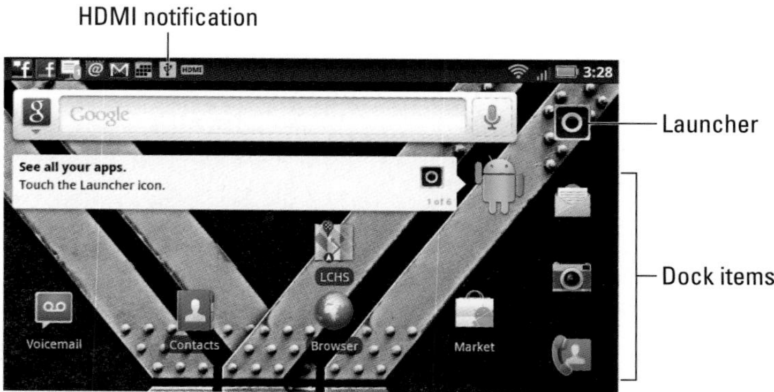

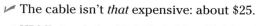

Figure 20-4: HDMI horizontal Home screen orientation.

Put your face really close to the book to see what Figure 20-4 looks like on a large-screen TV.

- The cable isn't *that* expensive: about $25.
- HDMI stands for High Definition Multimedia Interface. (It actually does. I just guessed that's what it meant, and I guessed correctly. Gold star for the author.)

Doing the DLNA thing

Wandering into the land of mysterious acronyms comes DLNA. It stands for the Digital Living Networking Alliance. Your Droid X2 is a DLNA device, which means that it can easily share information — specifically, media files such as pictures, videos, and music — with other DLNA gizmos. The connection can be direct or wirelessly.

The easiest way (if there is such a way) to do the DLNA thing is to configure your networked Windows computer for media sharing. Further, that Windows computer must have access to a wireless network before it can connect with the phone.

To play media from a computer on your phone, follow these steps:

1. **Ensure that the phone's Wi-Fi is turned on, and further that the phone is plugged into a power source.**
2. **Start the DLNA app, found on the Apps screen.**

   The first time you run the app, you'll have to dismiss a few warnings or accept a few conditions.
3. **Touch the huge Play Media button.**
4. **Choose the Windows PC from the list displayed.**

   If you don't see the Windows PC listed, either you haven't configured it for media sharing or it is unavailable on the wireless network.
5. **Choose the type of media you want to play.**

   On my screen I see folders for Music, Pictures, Playlists, and Videos.
6. **Browse to find the media; continue opening folders as necessary.**
7. **Touch a media item to watch, listen, or both.**

   At this point, the phone plays the media, which you can enjoy on the touchscreen.

Press the Back button to back out of a folder or category, or just keep pressing the Back button to return to the main DLNA screen.

- You can use the Share Media option to make the Droid X2's pictures, videos, and music accessible from a DLNA-enabled PC. You can use the PC to browse for the Droid X2, which it finds as a media server.
- The Copy Media options on the DLNA app's screen can be used to copy music, pictures, or video between your phone and a Windows PC. That operation works only when the computer has been properly configured to send and receive files.
- I cover turning on Media Sharing for a Windows computer in my book *PCs For Dummies*. Buy several copies to ensure that you properly understand the information.

21

The Droid X2 on the Road

In This Chapter

- Understanding roaming
- Disabling data-roaming features
- Entering airplane mode
- Contacting friends abroad
- Using Skype Mobile
- Using the Droid X2 overseas

I remember buying myself a very, very long cord for my house phone. It was awesome: I could walk anywhere in the house — even out on the deck — and still talk on the phone. Such freedom was amazing, but yet my travels were limited by the length of the phone cord. That limitation is no longer a problem with the Droid X2: You can take the phone anywhere you go — even overseas. And if you can't go there, you can call someone who is there. It's all possible, no long cord needed.

Where the Droid X2 Roams

The word *roam* takes on an entirely new meaning when applied to a cell phone. It means that your phone receives a cell signal whenever you're outside your service provider's operating area. In that case, your phone is *roaming*.

Roaming sounds handy, but there's a catch: It almost always involves a surcharge for using another cellular service — an *unpleasant* surcharge.

The Droid X2 alerts you whenever you're roaming. You see a Roaming icon at the top of the screen, in the status area. That icon tells you that you're outside the regular signal area, possibly using another cellular provider's network.

There's little you can do to avoid incurring roaming surcharges when making or receiving phone calls. Well, yes: You can wait until you're back in an area serviced by your primary cellular provider. You can, however, altogether avoid using the other network's data services while roaming. Follow these steps:

1. **At the Home screen, press the Menu soft button.**
2. **Choose Settings, then choose Battery & Data Manager.**
3. **Choose Data Delivery.**
4. **If you see a warning, dismiss it.**
5. **Ensure that the Data Roaming option isn't selected.**

   Remove the green check mark by the Data Roaming option.

The phone can still access the Internet over the Wi-Fi connection when you're roaming. Setting up a Wi-Fi connection doesn't make you incur extra charges, unless you have to pay to get on the wireless network. See Chapter 19 for more information about Wi-Fi.

Another network service you might want to disable while roaming has to do with MMS (Multimedia Messaging Service), more commonly known as text messages. To avoid surcharges from another cellular network for downloading an MMS message, follow these steps:

1. **Open the Text Messaging app.**
2. **If the screen shows a specific conversation, press the Back soft button to return to the main messaging screen.**

   (The messaging screen is the one that lists all your conversations.)
3. **Touch the Menu soft button.**
4. **Choose Messaging Settings.**
5. **Remove the green check mark by Auto-Retrieve.**

   Or, if the item isn't selected, you're good to go — literally.

For more information about multimedia text messages, refer to Chapter 9.

When the phone is roaming, you may see the text *Emergency Calls Only* on the locked screen.

Airplane Mode

As anyone knows who has been flying recently, using a cellular phone while on an airborne plane is strictly forbidden. If you did use the phone, the navigation system would completely screw up, the plane would invert, and everyone onboard would die in a spectacular crash on the ground, in a massive fireball suitable for the 5 o'clock Eyewitness News. It would be breathtaking.

Seriously, you're not supposed to use a cell phone when flying. Specifically, you're not allowed to make calls in the air. You can, however, use your Droid X2 to listen to music, play games, or do anything else that doesn't require a cellular connection. The secret is to place the phone in *airplane mode*.

Droid X2 air travel tips

I don't consider myself a frequent flyer, but I travel several times a year. I do it often enough that I wish the airports had separate lines for security: one for seasoned travelers, one for families, and one, of course, for frickin' idiots. The last category would have to be disguised by placing a Bonus Coupons sign or Free Snacks banner over the metal detector. That would weed 'em out.

Here are some of my cell phone and airline travel tips:

- **Charge your phone before you leave.** This tip probably goes without saying, but you'll be happier with a full cell phone charge to start your journey.
- **Take a cell phone charger with you.** Many airports feature USB chargers, so you might need just a USB-to-micro-USB cable. Still, why risk it? Bring the entire charger with you.
- **At the security checkpoint, place your phone in a bin.** Add to the bin any of your other electronic devices, keys, knives, and plutonium. I know from experience that keeping your cell phone in your pocket most definitely sets off airport metal detectors.
- **When the flight attendant asks you to *turn off* your cell phone for take-off and landing, obey the command.** That's *turn off,* as in power off the phone or shut it down. It doesn't mean placing the phone in airplane mode. Turn it off.
- **Use the phone's Calendar app to keep track of flights.** The event title serves as the airline and flight number. For the event time, I insert the take-off and landing schedules. For the location, I add the origin and destination airport codes. Referencing the phone from your airplane seat or in a busy terminal is much handier than fussing with travel papers. See Chapter 17 for more information on the Calendar app.
- **Remember that some airlines may eventually feature Android apps you can use while traveling.** Rather than hang on to a boarding pass printed by your computer, you just present your phone to the scanner.
- **Some apps you can use to organize your travel details are similar to, but more sophisticated than, using the Calendar app.** Visit the Android Market and search for *travel* or *airlines* to find a host of apps.

The most convenient way to put the Droid X2 in airplane mode is to press and hold the Power Lock button. From the menu, choose Airplane Mode. You don't even need to unlock the phone to perform this operation.

The most inconvenient way to put the Droid X2 into airplane mode is to follow these steps:

1. **From the Apps screen, choose the Settings icon.**
2. **Choose Wireless & Networks.**
3. **Touch the square by Airplane Mode to set the green check mark.**

   When the green check mark is visible, Airplane mode is active.

When the phone is in airplane mode, a special icon appears in the status area, as shown in the margin. You might also see the text *No Service* on the phone's locked screen.

To exit airplane mode, repeat the steps in this section but remove the green check mark by touching the square next to Airplane Mode. You can also press and hold the Power Lock button and choose Airplane Mode. The Power Management Widget has an Airplane Mode button as well.

- Officially, the Droid X2 should be powered *off* when the plane is taking off or landing. See Chapter 2 for information on turning off the phone.
- You can place the original Droid X into sleep mode for the duration of a flight. It's faster for the phone to wake up from sleep mode than it is to turn it on. See Chapter 2.
- Bluetooth networking is disabled when you activate the Droid X2 airplane mode. See Chapter 19 for more information on Bluetooth.
- You can compose email while the phone is in airplane mode. The messages aren't sent, however, until you disable airplane mode and connect again with a data network. Unless:

- Many airlines now feature wireless networking onboard. You can turn on wireless networking for the Droid X2 and use a wireless network in the air. Simply activate the Droid X2 Wi-Fi, per the directions in Chapter 19, after placing the phone in airplane mode — well, after the flight attendant tells you that it's okay to do so.

International Calling

Not only can you use your cell phone to dial folks who live in other countries, but you can also take your cell phone overseas and use it in another country. Neither task is as difficult as properly posing for a passport photo, but overseas dialing can become frustrating and expensive when you don't know your way around.

Dialing an international number

A phone is a bell that anyone in the world can ring. To prove it, all you need is the phone number of anyone in the world. Dial that number using your Droid X2 and, as long as you both speak the same language, you're talking! Or, if you're not talking, you're the United Nations!

To make an international call with the Droid X2, you merely need to know the foreign phone number. That number includes the international country-code prefix, followed by the number.

Before dialing the international country-code prefix, you must dial a plus sign (+) on the Droid X2. The + is the *country exit code,* which must be dialed to exit the national phone system and access the international phone system. For example, to dial Finland on your Droid X2, you dial `+358` and then the number in Finland. The `+358` is the exit code plus the international code for Finland, `358`.

To produce the + code in an international phone number, press and hold the 0 key on the Droid X2 dialpad. Then input the country prefix and the phone number. Touch the Dial button (the green phone icon) to complete the call.

- In most cases, dialing an international number involves a time zone difference. Before you dial, be aware of what time it is in the country or location you're calling.
- Dialing internationally also involves surcharges, unless your cell phone plan already provides for international dialing.
- The + character is used on the Droid X2 to represent the country exit code, which must be dialed before you can access an international number. In the United States, the exit code is `011`. (In the United Kingdom, it's `00`.) So, if you're using a landline to dial Russia from the United States, you dial `011` to escape from the United States and then `7`, the country code for Russia. Then dial the rest of the number. You don't have to do that on the Droid X2, because + is always the country exit code, and it replaces the `011` for U.S. users.

- The + character isn't a number separator. When you see an international number listed as `011+20+???????`, do not insert the + character in the number. Instead, dial `+20` and then the rest of the number.
- International calls fail for a number of reasons. One of the most common is that the recipient's phone company or service blocks incoming international calls.
- Another reason that international calls fail is the zero reason: Often times, you must leave out any zero in the phone number that follows the country code. So, if the country code is `254` for Kenya and the phone number starts with `012`, you dial `+254` for Kenya and then `12` and the rest of the number. Omit the leading zero.
- You can also send text messages to international cell phones. The process is the same as making a traditional phone call: Input the international number into the Messaging app. See Chapter 9 for more information on text messaging.
- Know which type of phone you're calling internationally: cell phone or landline. An international call to a cell phone often involves a surcharge that doesn't apply to a landline.

Making international calls with Skype Mobile

Your Droid X2 comes with the Skype Mobile app, which can be used to make inexpensive international calls. It's an excellent option, especially when your cellular contract doesn't provide for international calling.

If you don't yet have a Skype account, use your computer to create one. You need that account to use Skype Mobile. Set up the account by first obtaining the Skype program for your computer: Visit `www.skype.com` to get started. Further, you must have Skype Credit to make the international call. That credit can be purchased from within the Skype program on your computer.

The Skype Mobile app is found on the Apps screen. After starting it, log in with your Skype ID and password.

You can't make an international call unless you've created a contact with an international number. The contact must be a Skype Mobile contact, shown on the Contacts tab on the Skype Mobile Screen, illustrated in Figure 21-1.

To make an international call, touch the Call Phones tab at the top of the screen. Punch in the number, including the + sign for international access as described in this chapter and as shown in Figure 21-1. Touch the Call button to make the call.

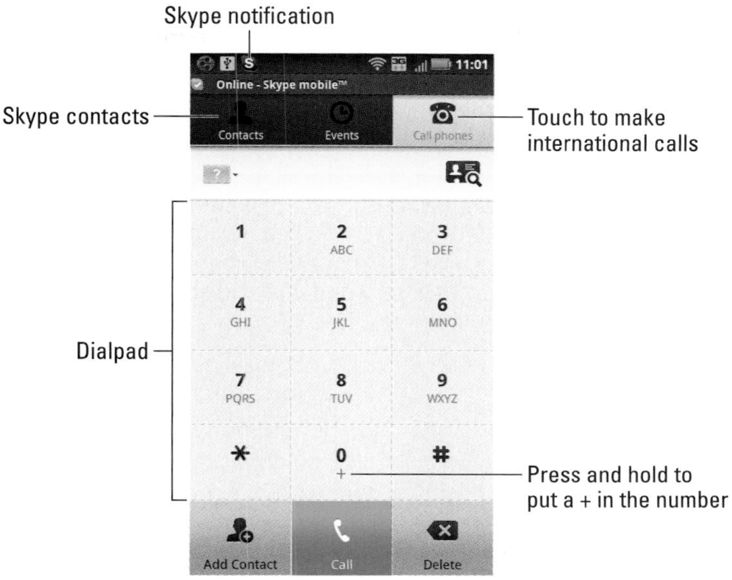

Figure 21-1: Calling internationally with Skype Mobile.

After the call is connected with Skype Mobile, the Droid X2 touchscreen looks similar to the way it looks when you regularly place calls. You can use the phone dialpad, if necessary, mute the call, put it on speaker, and so on.

When you're finished with the call, touch the End button.

- You're always signed into Skype Mobile unless you sign out. Pressing the Home button to switch away from the app doesn't log you out of Skype.
- To log out of Skype Mobile, press the Menu soft button and choose Sign Out. Sometimes the Sign Out command is accessed by first choosing the More command. Touch the Sign Out button to confirm.
- Check with your cellular provider to see whether you're charged connection minutes for using Skype Mobile. Even though the international call is free, you might still be dinged for the minutes you use on Skype to make the call.

Taking your Droid X2 abroad

The easiest way to use a cell phone abroad is to rent or buy a cell phone in the country where you plan to stay. I'm serious: Often, international roaming charges are so high that it's just cheaper to get a throwaway cell phone wherever you go, especially if you plan to stay there for a while.

When you opt to use your Droid X2 rather than buy a local phone, things should run smoothly — *if* a compatible cellular service is in your location. (The Droid X2 uses the CDMA cellular network.) The foreign carrier accepts incoming and outgoing calls from your phone and cheerfully charges you the international roaming rate.

The key to determining whether your Droid X2 is usable in a foreign country is to turn it on. The name of that country's compatible cellular service should show up at the top of the phone, where Verizon Wireless (or whatever your carrier is) appears on the Droid X2 main screen. (See Figure 2-1, in Chapter 2.)

- You receive calls on your cell phone internationally as long as the Droid X2 can access the network. Your friends need only dial your cell phone number as they normally do; the phone system automatically forwards your calls to wherever you are in the world.
- The person calling you doesn't pay extra when you're off romping the globe with your Droid X2. Nope — *you* pay extra for the call.

22

Customize Your Phone

In This Chapter

- Changing the Home screen background
- Working with icons and widgets on the Home screen
- Adding security
- Silencing the phone's noise
- Enabling automatic answer and redial
- Modifying phone settings
- Setting accessibility options

Most people never bother to customize things, despite how easy and potentially enjoyable it can be. I suppose those folks could be afraid that they'll break something, but most people in my travels who refuse to customize anything simply profess contentment with the boring status quo. (Okay, they don't use the word *boring*.) Or maybe they don't know how easily they can customize something technical, such as the Droid X2 phone.

The key to understanding customization is to accept that the Droid X2 is *your* phone. You can change the way it looks, how it works, and where it finds apps, plus a bunch of other interesting tasks, all designed to make the phone your own.

It's Your Home Screen

The Droid X2 sports a roomy Home screen. It's really *seven* Home screens. Of course, the phone comes preconfigured with lots of icons and widgets adorning all seven of the Home screen panels. You can customize them by removing those widgets and icons, especially the ones you seldom use, and replacing them with icons and widgets you do use. You can also change the background, or wallpaper, and even create a slate of custom Home screen panels by setting up a profile.

For the most part, the key to changing the Home screen is the *long-press:* Press and hold your finger on a blank part of the Home screen (not on an icon). You see a pop-up menu, as shown in Figure 22-1. From that menu, you can begin your Home screen customization adventure, as discussed in this section.

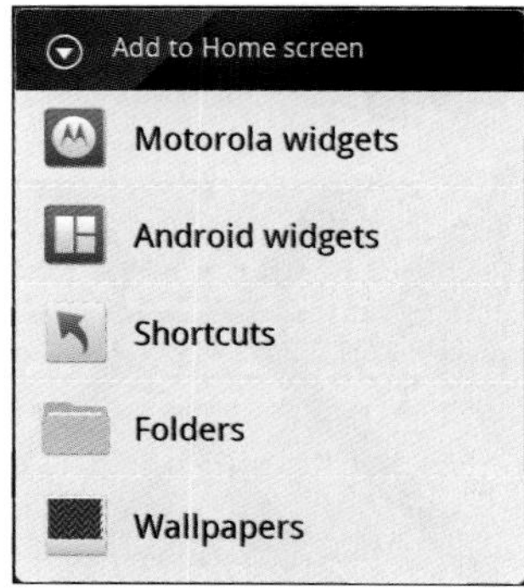

Figure 22-1: The Add to Home Screen menu.

Changing wallpaper

The Home screen has two types of backgrounds, or wallpapers: traditional and live. Live wallpapers are the animated ones. A not-so-live wallpaper can be any image, such as a picture from the Gallery.

To set a new wallpaper for the Home screen, obey these steps:

1. **Long-press the Home screen.**

   Ensure that you're long-pressing on a blank part of the Home screen.

   The Add to Home Screen menu appears (refer to Figure 22-1).

2. **Choose Wallpapers.**
3. **From the Select Wallpaper From menu, select an option based on the type of wallpaper:**

   Gallery: Choose a still image stored in the Gallery app.

   Live Wallpapers: Choose an animated or interactive wallpaper from a list.

   Wallpapers: Choose a wallpaper from a range of stunning images (no nudity).

4. **Choose the wallpaper you want from the list.**

   For the Gallery option, you see a preview of the wallpaper where you can select and crop part of the image.

   For certain Live Wallpapers, a Settings button may appear. The settings let you customize certain aspects of the interactive wallpaper.

5. **Touch the Save or Set Wallpaper button to confirm your selection.**

   The new wallpaper takes over the Home screen.

Live wallpaper is interactive, usually featuring some form of animation. Otherwise, the wallpaper image scrolls slightly as you swipe from one Home screen panel to another.

- You cannot long-press on a Home screen that is already full of icons and widgets. The reason? There is nothing else you can add to that screen.

- The Zedge app has some interesting wallpaper features. Check it out at the Android Market; see Chapter 18.
- See Chapter 15 for more information about the Gallery, including information on how to crop an image.

Adding apps to the Home screen

You need not live with the unbearable proposition that you're stuck with only the apps supplied on the Home screen. Nope — you're free to add your own apps. Just follow these steps:

1. **Navigate to the Home screen panel where you want to place the app icon.**

   The panel must have room for the icon; otherwise, the operation will fail.

2. **Touch the Launcher button to hunt down the app you want to add to the Home screen.**
3. **Long-press the app icon and choose the command Add to Home.**

   The app icon appears on the Home screen, looking like a postage stamp — but one that's not quite stuck yet.

4. **Drag the icon to the desired position.**

   The icon must be placed on a blank part of the Home screen.

5. **Release your finger.**

   A copy of the app's icon is placed on the Home screen. There's no need to clean your fingertip after completing these steps.

The app hasn't moved: What you see is a copy. You can still find the app on the Apps screen, but now the app is — more conveniently — available also on the Home screen.

- Keep your favorite apps, those you use most often, on the Home screen.
- You cannot drop an app in a spot where the Home screen is already full of apps or widgets. Try using a blank part of the Home screen.
- It's also possible to organize apps into groups on the Apps screen. See Chapter 18 for details.

Slapping down widgets

Just as you can add apps to the Home screen, you can add widgets. A *widget* works like a tiny interactive or informative application, often providing a gateway into another app on the Droid X2.

The Droid X2 comes with a several thousand widgets already affixed to the Home screen. You can place even more widgets on the Home screen by following these steps:

1. **Long-press the Home screen where you want to place a widget.**
2. **Choose Motorola Widgets or Android Widgets from the Add to Home Screen menu.**
3. **From the list, choose the widget you want to add.**

   The widget is plopped on the Home screen.

The variety of available widgets depends on the applications you have installed. Some applications come with widgets, some don't.

- The Motorola Widget category contains widgets customized for your Verizon Droid X2 phone. The Android Widget category contains widgets available to users of any Android phone. If you can't find the widget you want in one category, repeat Steps 1 and 2 to look in the other.
- You cannot install a widget when the Home screen has no room for it. Choose another Home screen, or remove icons or widgets from the current Home screen.
- To remove a widget, see the later section "Rearranging and removing icons and widgets."

Creating shortcuts

A shortcut is a doodad you can place on the Home screen that's neither an app nor a widget. Instead, a *shortcut* is a handy way to get at a feature or an informational tidbit stored in the phone without having to endure complex gyrations.

For example, I have a shortcut on my Home screen that uses the Maps app Navigation feature to help me return to my house. I don't use the app when I'm running from the police, either.

To add a shortcut, long-press the Home screen and choose the Shortcuts command from the Add to Home Screen menu (refer to Figure 22-1). What happens next depends on which shortcut you choose.

For example, when you choose a bookmark, you add a web page bookmark to the Home screen. Touch that shortcut to open the Browser app and visit that web page.

Choose a Contact shortcut to display contact information for a specific person. The Droid X2 has shortcuts for Music and the Maps app (Direction & Navigation), for various other apps, and to common phone settings such as battery use and Wi-Fi.

Rearranging and removing icons and widgets

Icons and widgets aren't fastened to the Home screen. If they are, it's day-old chewing gum that binds them, considering how easily you can rearrange and remove unwanted items from the Home screen.

Press and hold an icon on the Home screen to move it. Eventually, the icon seems to lift and break free, as shown in Figure 22-2.

You can drag an icon to another position on the Home screen or to another Home screen panel, or you can drag it to the Trash icon that appears at the top of the Home screen, which deletes the icon (refer to Figure 22-2).

Widgets can also be moved around or removed in the same manner as icons.

When you drag an icon to the bottom of the screen, where the dock is shown in Figure 22-2, the icon replaces one of the three dock items. The dock items appear on all the Home screen panels. (You cannot replace the Launcher icon on the dock.)

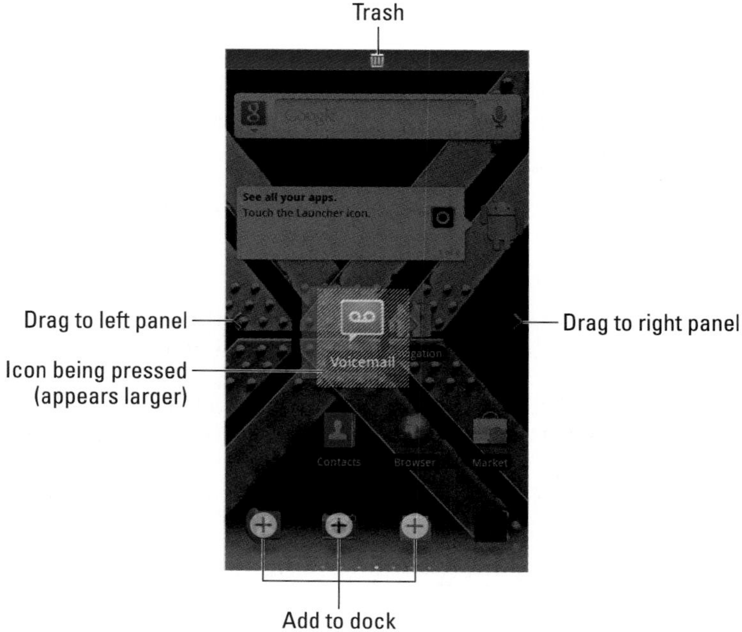

Figure 22-2: Moving an icon about.

- Dragging a Home screen icon or widget to the trash removes the icon or widget from the Home screen. It doesn't uninstall the application or widget; the app can still be found on the Apps screen, and the widget can once again be added to the Home screen.
- You cannot drag an icon off the dock. You can only replace a dock icon with a new icon.
- When an icon hovers over the trash, ready to be deleted, its color changes to red.
- See Chapter 18 for information on uninstalling applications.

Switching profiles

Welcome to Home Screen Trivia. In the seldom-known and little-used category comes the concept of profiles. A *profile* is basically another Home screen configuration, complete with seven panels, each of which can be adorned with apps, icons, widgets, and shortcuts.

So, yes, in a way, there are really 21 Home screen panels. It boggles the mind.

To switch profiles, follow these steps:

1. **Press the Menu soft button while viewing the Home screen.**
2. **Choose the Profiles command.**

   You'll see the three preset Profiles that come with the Droid X2, as shown in Figure 22-3.
3. **Choose a new profile.**

   The Droid X2 begins using that profile, and the various apps, icons, widgets, and other doodads that are configured on its Home screen panels.

You're free to configure each of the three Home screen panels to suit your mood. You can even rename the profiles. While viewing the Profiles screen (refer to Figure 22-3), press the Menu soft button. Choose the Rename command, select a profile to rename, and slap down a new name for it.

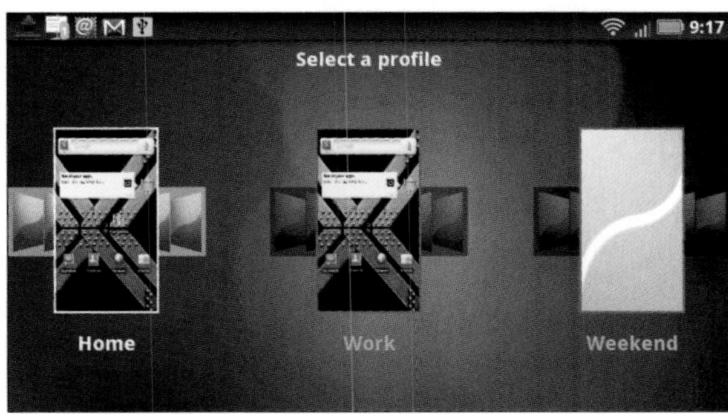

Figure 22-3: Selecting a new profile.

Droid X2 Security

The Droid X2 comes with a simple lock: You slide the touchscreen gizmo to the right to unlock the phone and gain access to its information and features. For most folks, that lock is secure enough. For the rest, the lock is about as effective as using a wet paper bag for armor.

You can add three additional types of security locks to your phone: A pattern lock, a PIN, and a passcode lock. The details are provided in this section.

Finding the screen locks

The Droid X2 keeps its screen locks on the Screen Unlock Security screen. Follow these steps to get to that screen:

1. **From the Home screen, press the Menu soft button.**
2. **Choose Settings.**
3. **Choose Location & Security.**
4. **If no lock is currently set, choose Set Up Screen Lock, otherwise choose Change Screen Lock.**

If a screen lock is already set, you'll have to work the lock to proceed: Trace the pattern or input the PIN or password to continue. You'll then see the Screen Unlock Security screen, which contains four items: None, Pattern, PIN, and Password. Using those items is covered in the sections that follow.

- The security you add affects the way you turn on and wake up your phone. See Chapter 2 for details.
- The locks are not required for answering incoming phone calls. You are, however, required to unlock the phone if you want to use its features while you're on the phone.
- See the sidebar "The lock doesn't show up" for information on setting the Security Lock Timer, which affects when the locks appear after sleeping the phone.

The lock doesn't show up!

The screen locks show up whenever you turn on the phone, or when you wake it up from sleep mode. Whether the locks appear after waking up the phone depends on how long the phone has been sleeping. If you wake up the phone right away, for example, the lock may not show up. It all depends on the Security Lock Timer setting.

The Security Lock Timer determines how long the phone waits after being put to sleep to enable the extra security locks. Initially, the timer is set to 20 minutes. If you like, you can set it to a shorter interval, which is more secure. From the Home screen, press the Menu soft button and choose Settings. Choose Location & Security, then choose Security Lock Timer. Choose a new timeout value from the list.

Removing a lock

To remove the pattern, PIN, or password lock on your Droid X2, choose the None option from the Screen Unlock Security screen, described in the preceding section. When None is chosen, then the phone uses the standard slide lock.

Creating an unlock pattern

The most popular screen lock, and perhaps the most unconventional, is the *unlock pattern.* This pattern must be traced on the touchscreen to unlock the phone.

To set an unlock pattern, follow these steps:

1. **Summon the Screen Unlock Security screen.**

   Refer to the section "Finding the screen locks."

2. **Choose Pattern.**

   If you've not yet set a pattern lock, you may see a text screen describing the process; touch the Next button to skip merrily through the dreary directions.

3. **Trace an unlock pattern.**

   Use Figure 22-4 as your guide. You can trace over the dots in any order, but you can trace over a dot only once. The pattern must cover at least four dots.

4. **Touch the Continue button and redraw the pattern again, just to prove to the doubtful phone that you know the pattern.**

5. **Touch the Confirm button and the pattern lock is set.**

Ensure that a check mark appears by Use Visible Pattern on the Security screen. That way, the pattern shows up when you need to unlock the phone. For more security, you can disable the option, though you have to be sure to remember how — and where — to trace the pattern.

- To remove the pattern lock, set None as the type of lock, as described in the preceding section.
- The pattern lock can start at any dot, not necessarily the upper-right dot as shown in Figure 22-4.
- The unlock pattern can be as simple or complex as you like. I'm a big fan of simple.
- Wash your hands! Smudge marks on the display can betray your pattern.

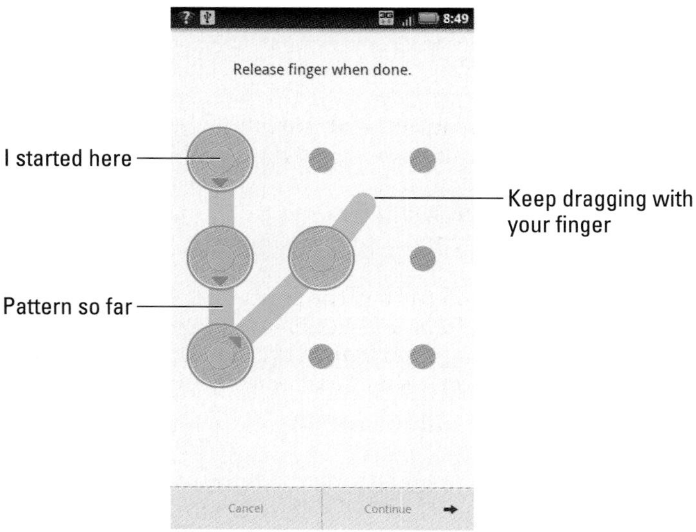

Figure 22-4: Setting an unlock pattern.

Setting a PIN

I suppose that using a PIN, or personal identification number, is more left-brained than using a pattern lock. What's yet another number to memorize?

A *PIN lock* is a code between 4 and 16 numbers long. It contains only numbers, 0 through 9. To set a PIN lock for your Droid X22, follow the directions in the earlier section "Finding the screen locks" to reach the Screen Unlock Security screen. Choose PIN from the list of locks.

Type your PIN twice to confirm that you know it. The next time you need to unlock your phone, type your PIN on the keypad and then touch the Enter button (shown in the margin) to proceed.

Refer to Chapter 2, Figure 2-3 for an image of what the PIN lock screen looks like when you unlock your phone.

Applying a password

The most secure way to lock the Droid X2 is to apply a full-on password. Unlike a PIN (refer to the preceding section), a *password* can contain numbers, symbols, and both uppercase and lowercase letters.

Set a password by choosing Password from the Screen Unlock Security screen; refer to the earlier section "Finding the screen locks" for information on getting to that screen.

The password you create must be at least four characters long. Longer passwords are more secure but easier to mistype.

You'll need to type the password twice to set things up, which confirms to the doubting phone that you know and will, you hope, remember the password.

The Droid X2 prompts you to type the password whenever you unlock the phone, as discussed in Chapter 2. You'll also need to type the password whenever you try to change or remove the screen lock, as discussed in the section "Finding the screen locks," earlier in this chapter.

Various Phone Adjustments

The Droid X2 has many options and settings for you to adjust. You can fix things that annoy you or make things better to please you. The idea is to make the phone more usable.

Stopping the noise!

The Droid X2 features a bag of tricks designed to silence the phone. These techniques can come in very handy, especially when a cell phone's digital noise can be outright annoying.

You can make the phone vibrate for all incoming calls, which works in addition to any ringtone you've set (and still works when you've silenced the phone). To activate vibration mode, follow these steps:

1. **Press the Menu soft button while viewing the Home screen.**
2. **Choose Settings.**
3. **Choose Sound.**
4. **Choose Vibrate.**
5. **Choose Always to ensure that the phone always vibrates.**

Silent mode disables all sounds from the phone, except for music, YouTube, and other types of media, as well as alarms that have been set by the Alarm & Timer and Calendar apps.

To enter Silent mode, follow Steps 1–3 in the preceding set of steps, and then place a check mark by the item Silent Mode.

Performing automatic phone tricks

Two phone settings on the Droid X2 might come in handy: Auto Answer and Auto Retry. Both options are found on the Call Settings screen. Start the Settings icon from the Apps screen and choose the Call Settings item.

By placing a check mark by Auto Retry, you direct the phone to automatically redial a number when the call doesn't go through. Obviously, this feature is ideal for radio show call-in contests.

The Auto Answer option directs the Droid X2 to automatically answer the phone whenever the headset is attached. The three time settings — 2, 5, and 10 seconds — specify how long to wait before the call is answered. The fourth setting, Off, disables the Auto Answer feature.

Changing various settings

Here are a smattering of adjustable phone settings — all made from, logically, the Settings screen. To get there from the Home screen, press the Menu soft button and choose the Settings command.

You can view the Settings screen also by choosing the Settings app on the Apps screen.

- **Screen brightness:** Choose Display and then choose Brightness. The Automatic Brightness setting uses the phone's magical light sensors to determine how bright it is where you are. If you disable that setting, you can move a slider on the screen to specify how bright the display appears.
- **Screen timeout:** Choose Display and then choose Screen Timeout. Select a timeout value from the list. This duration specifies when the phone goes into snooze mode.
- **Ringer volume:** Choose Sound and then choose Volume. Use the sliders to specify how loud the phone rings for incoming calls (Ringtone), Media, and Alarms. If you place a check mark by the Notifications item, the Ringtone setting applies also to notifications. Touch OK when you're done.
- **Keep the phone awake when plugged in:** Choose Applications and then choose Development. Place a check mark by the option Stay Awake.
- **Adjust the onscreen keyboard:** Choose Language & Keyboard and then choose Multi-Touch Keyboard. A smattering of interesting options appears — options you can set when they please you or deactivate when they annoy you.

Setting the Home soft button double-tap function

As master of your Droid X2, you can determine what happens when you press the Home soft button twice. It's called the Double Tap Home Launch function. As the Droid X2 comes out of the box (as least, my Droid X2), pressing the Home soft button twice quickly summons the Voice Commands app. You can change that behavior, so that pressing the Home button twice does a variety of interesting or useful things.

To modify the Double Tap Home Launch function, heed these steps:

1. **From the Apps screen, open the Settings app.**
2. **Choose Applications.**
3. **Choose Double Tap Home Launch.**
4. **Select a new function from the pop-up list.**

   For example, you can choose Dialer to summon the Phone app whenever you press the Home button twice. Choose None to disable the Double Tap Home Launch feature.

A handy option to choose for Double Tap Home Launch is the Camera app. I find that setting extremely useful, even more so than having the Camera app's shortcut on the Home screen dock.

Using accessibility settings

If you find the Droid X2 not meeting your needs or you notice that some features don't work well for you, consider taking advantage of some of the phone's accessibility features. Follow these steps:

1. **While at the Home screen, press the Menu soft button.**
2. **Choose Settings.**
3. **Choose Accessibility.**
4. **Place a check mark by the Accessibility option.**

   Four options become available when Accessibility is on.

5. **Choose an option.**

   Zoom Mode: A magnification window appears on the touchscreen, allowing you to better see teensy information.

   SoundBack: Touching items on the screen generates a tone.

   TalkBack: Touching items on the screen directs the phone to read that text.

   KickBack: Touching items on the screen causes the phone to vibrate slightly.

6. **Touch the OK button after reading the scary warning.**

   The accessibility feature is active.

7. **Repeat Steps 5 and 6 to activate other features.**

To disable any accessibility settings, repeat these steps and remove check marks in Step 5. Or, just uncheck the Accessibility setting to disable them all. Touch OK to confirm.

When TalkBack is activated, you double-tap items on the touchscreen to activate them.

23

Maintenance, Troubleshooting, and Help

In This Chapter

- Checking the phone's battery usage
- Making the battery last
- Cleaning the phone
- Keeping the system up-to-date
- Dealing with problems
- Finding support
- Getting answers to common questions

As one of the few people I know who bothers to read lawn equipment manuals, you could say that I'm a stickler for maintenance. I also confess to properly winterizing every year. In fact, I felt dirty when I put away the lawn mower without properly draining the oil and removing the spark plug. It was the winter of 2007.

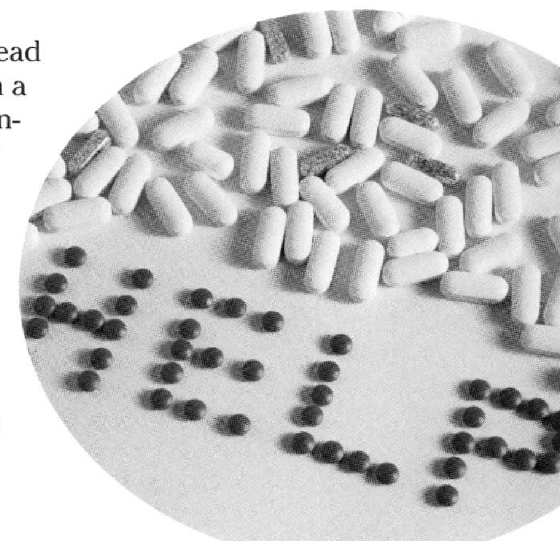

The Droid X2 doesn't require that you change its oil, and you probably don't need to winterize your phone. You do, however, have a few maintenance duties to consider, as well as some troubleshooting advice I have to offer for times of cell phone woe. It's all wrapped up in this chapter.

Battery Care and Feeding

Perhaps the most important item you can monitor and maintain on your cell phone is its battery. The battery supplies the necessary electrical juice by which the phone operates. Without battery power, your Droid X2 is about as useful as a tin can and string for communications. Keep an eye on the battery.

Monitoring the battery

The Droid X2 displays the current battery status at the top of the screen, in the status area, next to the time. The icons used to display battery status are shown in Figure 23-1.

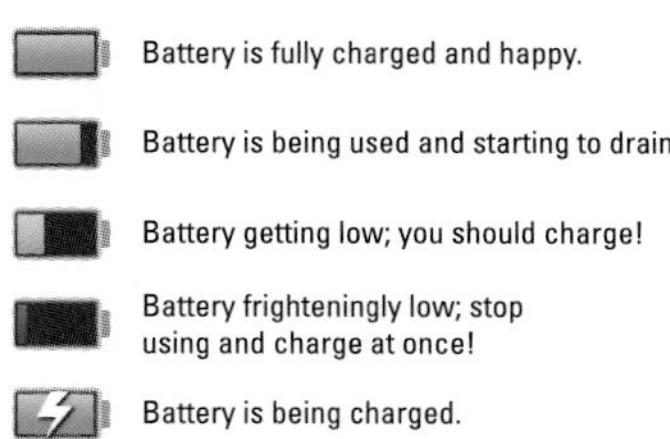
Battery is fully charged and happy.
Battery is being used and starting to drain.
Battery getting low; you should charge!
Battery frighteningly low; stop using and charge at once!
Battery is being charged.

Figure 23-1: Battery status icons.

You might also see an icon for a dead or missing battery, but for some reason I can't get my phone to turn on and display that icon.

You can check the specific battery level by following these steps:

1. **From the Home screen, touch the Menu button.**
2. **Choose Settings.**
3. **Choose About Phone.**
4. **Choose Status.**

The top two items on the Status screen offer information about the battery:

- **Battery Status:** This setting explains what's going on with the battery. It might say *Full* when the battery is full or *Charging* when the battery is being charged, or you might see other text, depending on how desperate the phone is for power.
- **Battery Level:** This setting reveals a percentage value, describing how much of the battery is charged. A value of 100 percent indicates a fully charged battery. A value of 110 percent means that someone can't do math.

Later sections in this chapter describe activities that consume battery power and how to deal with battery issues.

- Heed those low-battery warnings! The phone sounds a notification whenever the battery gets low. (See the orange battery icon shown in Figure 23-1). The phone sounds another notification when the battery gets *very* low. (See the red battery icon in Figure 23-1).
- When the battery gets very low, you see a pop-up message on the screen, urging you to plug the phone in *at once!*
- When the battery is too low, the phone shuts itself off.
- In addition to the status icons, the Droid X2 notification light turns a scary shade of red when battery juice is dreadfully low.
- The notification light glows green when the battery is full or yellow-orange when the battery is charging.
- The best way to deal with a low battery is to connect the phone to a power source: Either plug the phone into a wall socket or connect the phone to a computer by using a USB cable. The phone charges itself immediately; plus, you can use the phone while it's charging.
- The phone charges more efficiently when plugged into a wall socket as opposed to a computer.
- You don't have to fully charge the phone to use it. If you have only 20 minutes to charge and the phone goes back up to only a 70 percent battery level, that's great. Well, it's not great, but it's far better than a 20 percent battery level.

- Battery percentage values are best-guess estimates. Just because you talked for two hours and the battery shows 50 percent doesn't mean that you're guaranteed two more hours of talking. Odds are good that you have much less than two hours. In fact, as the percentage value gets low, the battery appears to drain faster.

Determining what is sucking up power

A nifty screen on the Droid X2 reviews which activities have been consuming power when the phone is operating from its battery. The informative screen is shown in Figure 23-2. To get to that screen, follow these steps:

1. **From the Home screen, touch the Menu soft button.**
2. **Choose Settings.**
3. **Choose Battery & Data Manager.**
4. **Choose Battery Usage.**

   You see a screen similar to the one shown in Figure 23-2.

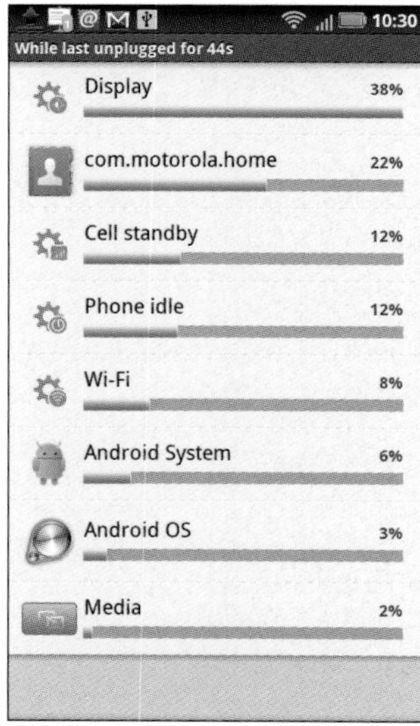

Figure 23-2: Things that drain the battery.

The number and variety of items listed on the Battery Use screen depend on what you've been doing with your phone between charges and how many different programs you're using.

Managing battery performance

The Droid X2 features power modes to help you manage the phone's power consumption. Similar to managing power on a computer, you can configure your phone to use one of these power modes:

- **Maximum battery saver:** In this most restrictive mode, the phone dims the display and disables automatic synchronization after 15 minutes of inactivity.
- **Nighttime saver:** This mode is the same as performance mode during the day, but switches to maximum battery saver mode between 10:00 PM and 5:00 AM.
- **Performance mode:** In this mode, nothing is held back; no timeouts are set. It is, essentially, *no* power management.
- **Custom battery saver:** This mode allows you to configure timeout, brightness, and peak usage times yourself.

To set a power mode on your Droid X2, follow these steps:

1. **From the Home screen, touch the Menu soft button.**
2. **Choose Settings.**
3. **Choose Battery & Data Manager.**
4. **Choose Battery Mode.**
5. **Choose a battery profile from the list.**

To configure the custom battery saver mode, touch the icon (shown in the margin) to the right of that option. You can then use the screen that appears, shown in Figure 23-3, to configure the options, timeouts, and other settings.

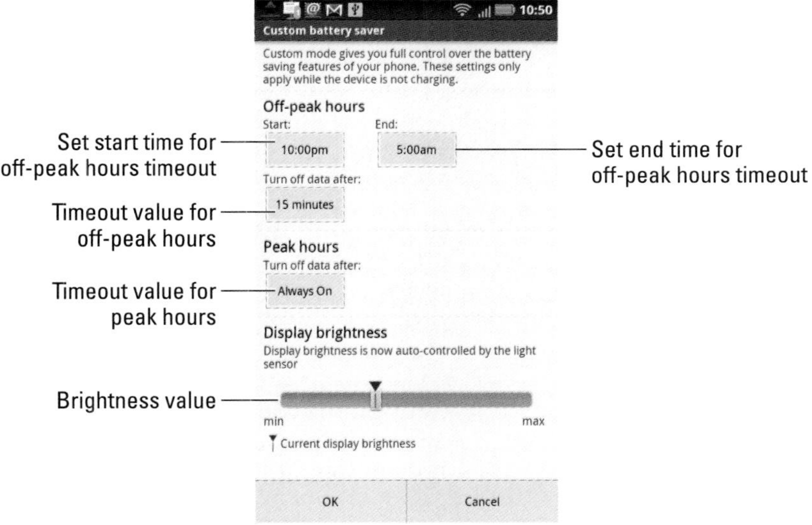

Figure 23-3: Battery settings for the custom battery saver mode.

Saving battery life

Here's a smattering of things you can do to help prolong battery life in your Droid X2.

Turn off vibration options. The phone's vibration is caused by a teensy motor. Although you don't see much battery savings by disabling the vibration options, it's better than no savings. To turn off vibration, follow these steps:

1. **From the Home screen, touch the Menu soft button.**
2. **Choose Settings, then choose Sound.**
3. **Choose Vibrate.**
4. **Choose Never from the Vibrate menu.**
5. **Scroll the Sound Settings screen down a tad.**
6. **Remove the check mark by Haptic Feedback.**

   The Haptic Feedback option is what causes the phone to vibrate when you touch the soft buttons.

Additionally, consider lowering the volume of notifications, which also saves a modicum of battery life, though in my travels I've missed important notifications by setting the volume too low.

Dim the screen. If you look at Figure 23-2 (earlier in this chapter), you see that the display sucks down quite a lot of battery power. Although a dim screen can be more difficult to see, especially outdoors, it definitely saves on battery life.

You set the screen brightness from the Settings app: Choose Display, and then choose Brightness.

Turn off Bluetooth. When you're not using Bluetooth, turn it off. Or when you *really* need that cyborg Bluetooth ear thing, try to keep your phone plugged in. See Chapter 19 for information on turning off Bluetooth. (You can turn it off quickly from the Power Control widget.)

Turn off Wi-Fi. Wi-Fi networking on the Droid X2 keeps you on the Internet at top speeds but drains the battery. Because I tend to use Wi-Fi when I'm in one place, I keep my phone plugged in. Otherwise, the battery drains like my bank account at Christmas. Refer to Chapter 19 for information on turning off the phone's Wi-Fi.

Disable automatic syncing. The Droid X2 syncs quite often. In fact, it surprises me when I update something on the Internet and find the phone updated almost instantly. When you need to save battery power and frequent updates aren't urgent (such as when you're spending a day traveling), disable automatic syncing by following these steps:

1. **From the Home screen, touch the Menu soft button.**
2. **Choose Settings.**
3. **Choose Accounts.**

4. **Choose your Google account.**
5. **Remove the green check mark by each item.**

When saving battery juice isn't important, remember to repeat these steps to reenable background and automatic synchronization.

Regular Phone Maintenance

The Droid X2 gives you only two tasks that you can do for regular maintenance on the phone: Keep it clean, which is probably something you're doing already, and keep important information backed up.

Keeping it clean

You probably already keep your phone clean. I must use my sleeve to wipe the touchscreen at least a dozen times a day. Of course, better than your sleeve is something called a microfiber cloth. This item can be found at any computer- or office-supply store.

- Never clean the touchscreen using any liquid — especially ammonia or alcohol. Those substances damage the touchscreen.
- If the screen keeps getting dirty, consider adding a screen protector. This specially designed cover prevents the screen from getting scratched or dirty but also lets you use your finger on the touchscreen. Be sure that the screen protector is designed for use with the Droid X2.
- You can also find customized Droid X2 cell phone cases, belt clips, and protectors, though I've found that those add-on items are purely for decorative or fashion purposes and don't even prevent serious damage if you drop the phone.

Backing up your phone

A *backup* is a safety copy of the information on your Droid X2. That information includes contact information, music, photos, video, and apps you've installed, plus any settings you've made to customize your phone. Copying that information to another source is one way to keep the information safe, in case anything happens to the phone.

Google account information on your phone — including your Contacts list, Gmail, and Calendar app appointments is backed up automatically. Because the Droid X2 automatically syncs that information with the Internet, a backup is always present.

Where to find phone information

Who knows what evil lurks inside the heart of your phone? Well, the phone itself knows. You can view information about the battery, the phone number, the mobile network, and uptime, plus other information. To see that trivia, summon the Settings app and choose About Phone and then Status.

For specific information about your account, such as minutes used and data transmitted, you have to visit the cellular service's web site. In the United States, the Droid X2 is supported by the Verizon Wireless network at the time this book goes to press. The web site is `www.verizonwireless.com`. You need to set up or access your account, which then leads you to information about your phone usage and billing and other trivia.

To confirm that your Google account information is being backed up, heed these steps:

1. **From the Home screen, touch the Launcher button.**
2. **Choose My Accounts.**
3. **Choose your Google account.**
4. **Ensure that a green check mark appears by every option.**

   When no check mark is there, touch the gray square to add one.

If you have more than one Google account synchronized with the Droid X2, repeat these steps for each account.

I'm required by my Verizon cellular contract to mention the Verizon app Backup Assistant. Let me say this: You don't have to use Backup Assistant. It really doesn't do anything necessary and is a pain in the butt to set up. There. I've completed my contractual obligation.

Updating the system

Every so often, a new version of your phone's operating system becomes available. It's an *Android update* because Android is the name of the Droid X2 operating system, not because your phone is some type of robot.

When an automatic update occurs, you see an alert or a message on the phone, indicating that a system upgrade is available. You have three choices:

- Install Now
- Install Later
- More Info

My advice is to choose Install Now and get it over with — unless you have something (a call, a message, or another urgent item) pending on the phone, in which case you can choose Install Later and be bothered by the message again.

You can manually check for updates: From the Settings screen, choose About Phone and then choose System Updates. When your system is up-to-date, the screen tells you so. Otherwise, you find directions for updating the system.

Help and Troubleshooting

Things aren't as bad as they were in the old days. Back then, you could try two sources for help: the atrocious manual that came with your electronic device or a phone call to the guy who wrote the atrocious manual. Doing either was unpleasant. Today, things are better. You have many resources for solving issues with your gizmos, including the Droid X2.

Getting help

The Droid X2 comes with a modicum of assistance for your weary times of woe. Granted, its advice and delivery method aren't as informative or entertaining as the book you hold in your hands. But it's something!

To get help, open the Help Center app, found on the Apps screen. You see four categories:

- **Guided Tours:** Videos to help you use your phone
- **Tips and Tricks:** Suggestions for doing things you may not know about
- **User Guide:** Documentation for the Droid X2
- **FAQs:** Frequently asked questions and their answers

Choosing some of the items displays information stored on your phone. For other categories, you're whisked off to the Internet for details.

Some of the information presented is pretty good but also pretty basic. It's also, at its core, simply what would have once been printed and bundled with the Droid X2: the dratted manual.

Fixing random and annoying problems

Aren't all problems annoying? Such a thing as a welcome problem doesn't really exist, unless the problem is welcome because it diverts attention from another, preexisting problem. And random problems? If problems were predictable, they would serve in office. Or maybe they already are?

Here are some typical problems and my suggestions for a solution.

General trouble: For just about any problem or minor quirk, consider restarting the phone: Turn off the phone, and then turn it on again. That procedure will most likely fix a majority of the annoying and quirky problems you encounter with the Droid X2.

When restarting doesn't work, consider turning off the Droid X2 and removing its battery. Wait about 15 seconds, and then return the battery to the phone and turn on the phone again.

The data connection drops: Sometimes, the data connection drops but the phone connection stays active. Check the status bar. If you see bars, you have a phone signal. When you don't see the 3G, 1X, or Wi-Fi icon, the phone has no data signal.

Sometimes, the data signal just drops for a minute or two. Wait around and it comes back. If it doesn't, the cellular data network might be down, or you may just be in an area with lousy service. Consider changing your location.

For wireless connections, you have to ensure that the Wi-Fi is set up properly and working. That usually involves pestering the person who configured the Wi-Fi signal or made it available, such as the cheerful person in the green apron who serves you coffee.

Music begins to play while you're on the phone: I find this quirk most annoying. For some reason, you start to hear music playing while you're in a conversation on the phone. I actually wonder why the phone's software doesn't disable music from even being able to play while the phone is in use.

Anyway, it might seem like stopping the music is impossible. It's not: Press the Home soft button to go to the Home screen. (You might have to unlock the phone.) Pull down the notifications and choose the Music Playing notification. Press the Pause button to pause the music.

The phone's storage is busy: Most often, the storage — internal or microSD card — is busy because you've connected the Droid X2 to a computer and the computer is accessing the phone's storage system. To unbusy the storage, unmount the phone or stop the USB storage. See Chapter 20.

When the phone's storage remains busy, consider restarting the phone, as described earlier in this section.

An app has run amok: Sometimes, apps that misbehave let you know. You see a warning on the screen announcing the app's stubborn disposition. Touch the Force Close button to shut down the errant app.

When you don't see a warning or when an app appears to be unduly obstinate, you can shut 'er down the manual way, by following these steps:

1. **From the Apps screen, choose the Settings icon.**
2. **Choose Applications, then choose Manage Applications.**
3. **Touch the Running tab at the top of the Manage Applications screen.**
4. **Choose the application that's causing you distress.**

   For example, a program doesn't start or says that it's busy or has some other issue.
5. **Touch the Force Stop button.**

   The program stops.

After stopping the program, try opening it again to see whether it works. If the program continues to run amok, contact its developer. Open the Market app and choose My Apps. Open the app you're having trouble with and choose the option Send Email to Developer. Send the developer a message describing the problem.

Reset the phone's software (a drastic measure): When all else fails, you can do the drastic thing and reset all the phone's software, essentially returning it to the state it was in when it first popped out of the box. Obviously, you should not perform this step lightly. In fact, consider finding support (see the next section) before you start:

1. **From the Home screen, touch the Menu soft button.**
2. **Choose Settings.**
3. **Choose Privacy.**
4. **Choose Factory Data Reset.**

   A check mark button titled either Erase Internal Storage (Media Area) or Erase SD Card is available. Leave that item blank.

5. **Touch the Reset Phone button.**

   You'll see a final, scary warning.

6. **Touch the Erase Everything button.**

   All the information you've set or stored on the phone is purged.

Again, *do not* follow these steps unless you're certain that they will fix the problem or you're under orders to do so from someone in tech support.

The option to erase the phone's storage *totally* zaps your stuff — videos, music, contacts. I recommend using that option only if you plan on selling or surrendering the phone.

Getting support

The easiest way to find support for the Droid X2 is to dial 611. You're greeted by a cheerful Verizon employee, or an automated robot system, who will gladly help you with various phone issues.

On the Internet, you can find support at these web sites:

- `www.motorola.com/mydroidx2`
- `market.android.com/support`
- `http://support.vzw.com/clc`

Droid X2 Q&A

I love Q&A! Not only is Q&A an effective way to express certain problems and solutions, but some of the questions might also cover things I've been wanting to ask.

"The touchscreen doesn't work!"

A touchscreen, such as the one used on the Droid X2, requires a human finger for proper interaction. The phone interprets a slight static charge between the human finger and the phone to determine where the touchscreen is being touched.

You cannot use the touchscreen when you're wearing gloves, unless they're specially designed, static-carrying gloves that claim to work on touchscreens. Batman wears this type of glove, so it probably exists in real life.

The touchscreen might also fail when the battery power is low or when the phone has been physically damaged.

"The keyboard is too small!"

It's not that the keyboard is too small — it's that you're a human being, not a marsupial. Your fingers are too big!

You can rotate the phone to landscape orientation to see a larger onscreen keyboard. Not every app may feature a landscape orientation keyboard. When one does, you'll find typing on the wider onscreen keyboard much easier than normal.

I've tried, but there is no way to connect an external keyboard to the Droid X2, using either the USB cable or Bluetooth. In the future, some clever manufacturer may develop an add-on keyboard, but it's just not there yet.

"The battery doesn't charge"

Start from the source: Is the wall socket providing power? Is the cord plugged in? The cable may be damaged, so try another cable.

When charging from a USB port on a computer, ensure that the computer is turned on. Computers generally don't provide USB power when they're turned off.

"The phone gets so hot that it turns itself off!"

Yikes! An overheating phone can be a nasty problem. Judge how hot the phone is by seeing whether you can hold it in your hand: When the phone is too hot to hold, it's too hot. If you're using the phone to warm up your coffee, the phone is too hot.

The Droid X2 itself can recognize when it's too hot: You'll see a Cool Down message screen. The phone then goes into a special "chill" mode, where you can make only emergency calls.

If the overheating problem continues, have the phone looked at for potential repair. The battery might need to be replaced.

"The phone doesn't do landscape mode!"

Not every app takes advantage of the Droid X2's capability to orient itself in landscape mode. For example, some games display in one orientation only.

One program that definitely does landscape mode is Browser, described in Chapter 11. So, just because an app doesn't enter landscape mode doesn't mean that it *can't* enter landscape mode.

The Droid X2 has a setting you can check to confirm that landscape orientation is active: From the Apps screen, choose Settings and then choose Display. Ensure that a check mark appears by the item Auto-Rotate Screen. No check mark? Touch the square to put one there.

Part VI
The Part of Tens

In this part . . .

It was agreed that the *For Dummies* books all have one final part that contained lists of helpful items. What wasn't agreed upon was how many items would be in each chapter.

The authors wanted only three items in each chapter. That's because anyone can think of two items, and the third item can merely be a rephrasing of the first item. That trick always works. The publisher, however, insisted on twenty items. A compromise of nine items was suggested by the author of *Scissors For Dummies,* who has only nine fingers. Eventually, ten items was settled upon, ten being a nice round number.

In this part of the book, you'll find chapters that contain ten items each. There are tips, tricks, suggestions, things to remember, and recommendations.

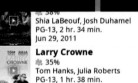

DOW	12,582.77	+168.43	(1.36%)
S&P 500	1,339.67	+19.03	(1.44%)
Nasdaq	2,816.03	+42.51	(1.53%)

Some quotes may be delayed
See disclaimer

Shia LaBeouf, Josh Duhamel
PG-13, 2 hr. 34 min.
Jun 29, 2011

Larry Crowne
35%
Tom Hanks, Julia Roberts
PG-13, 1 hr. 38 min.
Jul 1, 2011

Monte Carlo
40%
Leighton Meester, Katie Cassidy
PG, 1 hr. 49 min.
Jul 1, 2011

Top Box Office

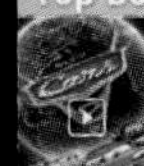

Cars 2
35%
Owen Wilson, Larry The Cable Guy
G, 1 hr. 53 min.
$66.1M

24

Ten Tips, Tricks, and Shortcuts

In This Chapter

- Finding useful places quickly
- Using the Task Manager
- Making the keyboard more usable
- Unlocking dirty words on voice input
- Adding words to the dictionary
- Getting the Amazon Appstore
- Adding direct dial and direct messaging widgets
- Finding a lost phone

I must have been about three when my Grandpa wanted to show me how he could pull a quarter out of my ear. Grandma had already told me how filthy my ears were, so I knew you could pull potatoes out of there. Money, on the other hand, would certainly be a worthy experience. After Grandpa deftly showed me the quarter, I said, "Again!"

A trick truly isn't worthy unless you can do it again. (And, sorry Grandpa, but I wanted to see more quarters, not the same one recycled.) A tip isn't really a tip unless it's something you didn't already know. So with great effort, and clean ears, I present you a chapter full of tricks you can do over and over and tips worthy of being tips.

Your Rich Locations

The Rich Locations app has little to with finding money. It's more to do with creating a customized map experience for worthy things near you. Basically, it's a way to search for things you want to find frequently, without having to mess with the Maps app.

Start Rich Locations from the Apps screen. It's main screen is shown in Figure 24-1. It's kind of deceptive in that the interface makes it look like you can customize things. You really can't; you can only add or subscribe to preset items. My hopes of adding "haberdashery" to the list were summarily dashed.

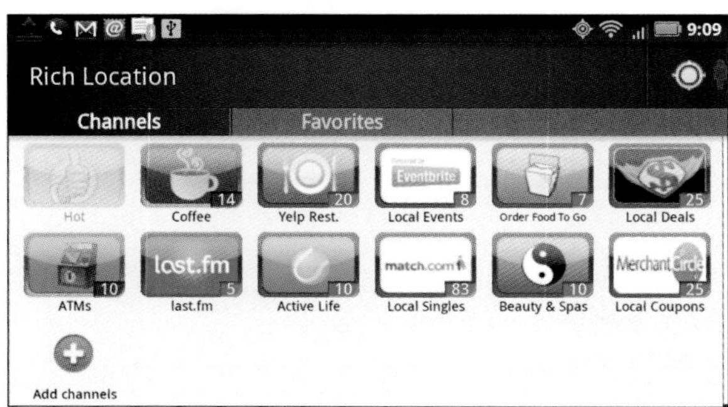

Figure 24-1: Interesting places near you.

Touch a category to instantly see a list of places near you that match that description. It's a far easier thing to do than using the Maps app to search, especially for your present location.

Task Manager

If you want to get your hands dirty with some behind-the-scenes stuff on your Droid X2, Task Manager is the app for you. It's not for everyone, so feel free to skip this section if you just want to use your phone without acquiring any computer nerd sickness that you have otherwise successfully avoided.

The Task Manager app is found on the Apps screen. Its main interface is shown in Figure 24-2. You see all the phone's currently running apps, along with trivial information about each app: The CPU item shows how much processor power the app is consuming, and the RAM item shows how much storage the app occupies.

You can use Task Manager to kill off tasks that are hogging up too much CPU time or memory, or just bug the stuffing from your couch. As illustrated in Figure 24-2, touch items you want to kill, then touch the End Apps button. The apps are silently snuffed out.

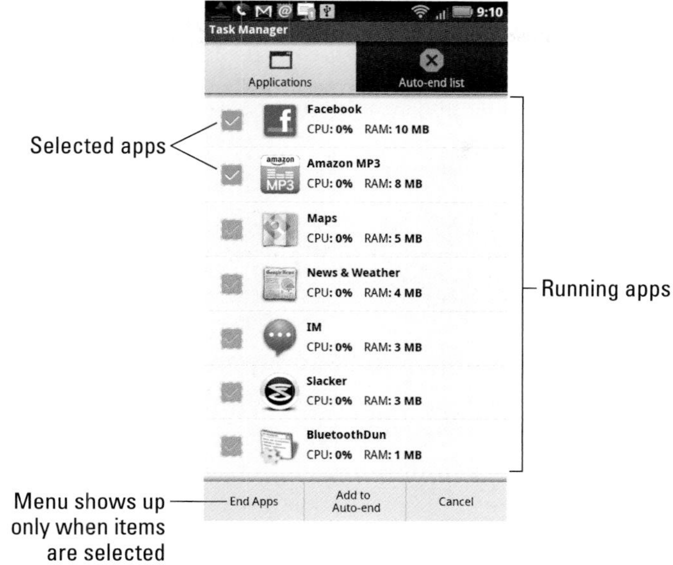

Figure 24-2: Managing your tasks.

A nifty feature in Task Manager is the Auto-End List. When apps have been assigned to that list, they automatically exit two minutes after the display times out. To add apps to that list, select them on the main screen (refer to Figure 24-2) and choose the command Add to Auto-End from the bottom of the screen.

- There is no need to kill off an app flagged as "not running."
- Task Manager doesn't delete apps; it merely stops them from running. To delete an app, use the Android Market as discussed in Chapter 18.
- Also see Chapter 23 on using the Force Stop button to kill an app run amok.

- The Android operating system does an excellent job managing apps. If resources are needed for another app, Android automatically closes any currently open apps as needed. So you really have no need to futz with Task Manager, unless you just enjoy messing with such a thing.

Set Keyboard Feedback

Typing on a touchscreen keyboard isn't easy. Along with the screen being tiny (or your fingers being big), it's difficult to tell what you're typing. You can add some feedback to the typing process. Heed these steps:

1. **While at the Home screen, press the Menu soft button.**
2. **Choose Settings.**
3. **Choose Language & Keyboard.**
4. **Choose Multi-Touch Keyboard or Swype.**
5. **Put a check mark by the option Vibrate on Keypress.**

   This option causes physical feedback when you press a "key" on the onscreen keyboard.
6. **If you chose the Multi-Touch Keyboard option, put a check mark by Sound on Keypress.**

   The Droid X2 makes a sound when you type on the onscreen keyboard. Clackity-clack-clack.

Of the two options, I prefer Sound on Keypress. The phone makes a different sound for the character keys and the space key, which reminds me of my ancient typewriter.

- Yeah, *keypress* is two words: key press.
- Obviously, the Sound on Keypress option doesn't apply to using Swype. See Chapter 4 for information on using the Swype keyboard.

Add Spice to Dictation

I feel that too few people use dictation, despite how handy it can be — especially for text messaging. Anyway, if you've used dictation, you might have noticed that it occasionally censors some of the words you utter. Perhaps you're the kind of person who won't put up with that kind of s***.

Relax. You can lift the vocal censorship ban by following these steps:

1. **At the Home screen, press the Menu soft button.**
2. **Choose Settings.**
3. **Choose Voice Input and Output.**
4. **Choose Voice Recognizer Settings.**
5. **Remove the check mark by the option Block Offensive Words.**

And just what are offensive words? I would think that *censorship* would be an offensive word. But no; apparently only a few choice words fall into that category. I won't print them here, as the Droid X2 censor retains the initial letter and generally makes the foul language easy to guess. D***.

Add a Word to the Dictionary

Betcha didn't know that the Droid X2 has a dictionary. The dictionary is used to keep track of words you type using the multitouch keyboard — words that may not be recognized as being spelled properly.

To add a word to the Droid X2 dictionary, long-press the word after you type it. From the menu that appears, choose the Add *Word* to Dictionary command, where *Word* is the word you want to add.

When using the onscreen keyboard, you can choose the word when it appears in the list of suggestions, as shown in Figure 24-3. Long-press the word, as shown in the figure, to add it to the dictionary. The confirmation that appears is your clue that the word has been added.

To review the contents of the dictionary, open the Settings app and choose Language & Keyboard and then User Dictionary. You see a list of words you've added. Touch a word to edit it or to delete it from the dictionary.

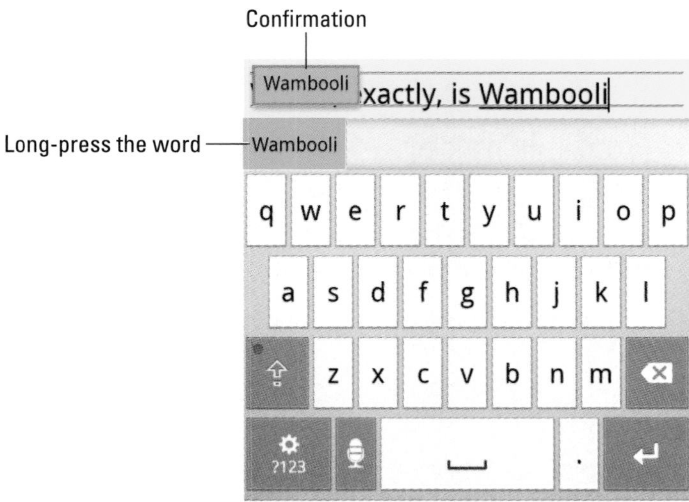

Figure 24-3: Adding a word to the dictionary.

Amazon Appstore

The Android Market isn't the only store in the Droid X2 mall. Amazon launched its own app store a while back, and you can use it to locate and purchase apps for your phone. As an enticement, every day the Amazon Appstore offers a paid app at no cost. You can keep and use that paid app — always at no cost — as long as you keep the Amazon Appstore app installed. Such a deal.

It really helps to have an account at Amazon to best use the Amazon Appstore app.

You need two things to get apps at the Amazon Appstore. First, you need to allow apps to be downloaded from "unknown sources" to your Droid X2. That's not scary; an unknown source is simply an app that doesn't come from the Android Market. Follow these steps:

1. **At the Home screen, press the Menu soft button.**
2. **Choose Settings, then choose Applications.**
3. **Place a check mark by the item Unknown Sources.**
4. **Touch the OK button to confirm.**

The second thing you need is the Amazon Appstore app, which you're not going to find in the Android Market. Instead, visit this web site on your Droid X2 to get the app: `www.amazon.com`. On that page, touch the link `Get Amazon Apps for Android`, then follow the directions on the screen to download the Amazon Appstore.

Downloading apps from the Amazon Appstore works as you would expect: Open the Amazon Appstore, browse for apps, then touch one to get more information and optionally download it into your Droid X2.

Remember to check into the Amazon Appstore every day to see which app that would otherwise cost you money is available free.

Create a Direct-Dial Screen Widget

For the numbers you dial most frequently, use the Favorites list, as described in Chapter 8. For your überfavorites, you use Home screen widgets. Here's how to create a direct-dial contact widget on the Home screen for the people you call frequently:

1. **Long-press the Home screen.**
2. **Choose Motorola Widgets, then choose Quick Contact Tasks.**
3. **Choose the contact you want to direct-dial.**
4. **Choose the phone number, if the contact has multiple phones.**

   Choose the number from the top portion of the contact's information, in the Call category.
5. **Touch the Done button.**

The contact's phone number, and picture (if the contact has one) appears on the Home screen as a widget. Touching the phone icon on the widget summons a dialing menu; if you touch the check box, you enable one-touch dialing for that contact.

The Quick Contact widget can be resized. Long-press it and then drag the corners around with your finger to resize. You can make the Quick Contact widget as large or as small as you like. I prefer smaller, especially when the contact has an ugly picture attached.

Create a Direct Text-Message Widget

Just as you can create a direct-dial shortcut (shown in the preceding section), you can create an icon to directly text-message a contact. The difference is that you choose a phone number from the Text Message list in Step 4 rather than from the Call category.

The widget that appears on the Home screen can be used to instantly send that contact a text message. Simply touch the icon and start typing with your thumbs.

See Chapter 9 for more information about text messaging.

Contact Quick Actions

You may have noticed that a contact's picture contains three dots below the image. Those three dots are there whether the image is a photo or the stock Android icon. They hold significance in that they can be used to summon the Quick Actions menu for that contact, as shown in Figure 24-4.

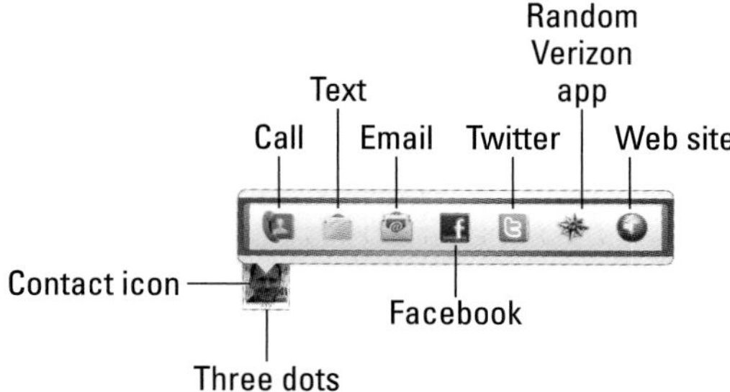

Figure 24-4: Quick Actions for a contact.

Summon the Quick Actions menu by long-pressing the contact's image or icon, whichever appears above the three dots, as illustrated in Figure 24-4.

The number and variety of icons on the Quick Actions menu depends on how much information is available for the contact. But no matter where the contact's icon is found, as long as you see those three dots, you'll see the Quick Actions menu.

Find Your Lost Cell Phone

Someday, you may lose your Droid X2 — for a few panic-filled seconds or forever. The hardware solution is to weld a heavy object to the phone, such as an anvil or a school bus, yet that kind of defeats the entire mobile/wireless paradigm. The software solution is to use a cell phone locator service.

Cell phone locator services employ apps that use the cellular signal as well as the phone's GPS to help locate a missing gizmo. Those types of apps are available on the Android Market. I've not tried them all, and many of them require a subscription service or registration at a web site to complete the process.

Here are some suggestions for cell phone locator apps:

- Lookout Mobile Security
- LocService
- Mobile Phone Locator

25

Ten Things to Remember

In This Chapter

- Locking the phone
- Using landscape orientation
- Taking advantage of text magnification
- Saving typing time
- Minding things that consume battery power
- Check for when the phone roams
- Using the + key to dial international calls
- Mounting and unmounting phone storage
- Taking a picture of your contacts
- Using the Search command

Which is better: To remember something or not to forget something? I would say that it's better to remember something. That implies that you're thoughtful. When you have to "not forget" something that implies a history of forgetting things. So I prefer to remember things and not forget them.

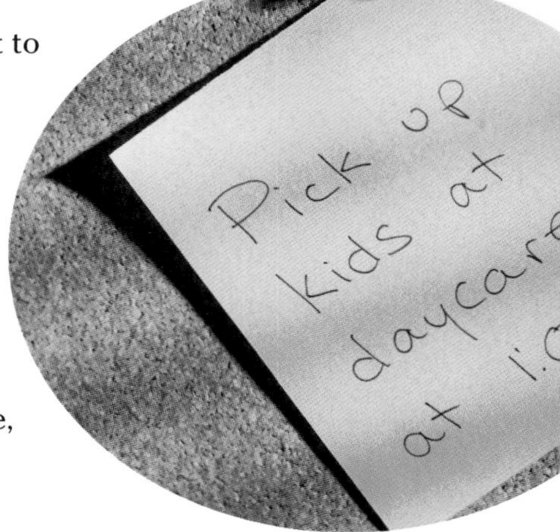

Meanwhile, back in this book, probably more than ten things are worth remembering when it comes to your Droid X2. Even so, I've narrowed the list down to ten great things that neatly fit into this chapter. Any more things you can find on my web site, `www.wambooli.com`. For now, here are ten gems.

Lock the Phone on a Call

Whether you dialed out or someone dialed in, after you start talking, lock the phone: Press the Power Lock button atop the Droid X2. By doing so, you ensure that the touchscreen is disabled and the call isn't unintentionally disconnected.

Of course, the call can still be disconnected by a dropped signal or the other party getting all huffy and hanging up on you, but by locking the phone, you should prevent a stray finger or your cheek from disconnecting (or muting) the phone.

Landscape Orientation

Too many times I find myself using the phone and cursing my stubby fingers. Then I slap myself in the forehead and tilt the phone to the side. Yes sir, landscape orientation comes to the rescue. Some applications give you a wider screen view, larger keyboard, and more room to touch buttons in landscape orientation.

Not every app supports landscape orientation.

Use Text Magnification

When you need to pinpoint where to place the cursor in text, use the little target icon shown in the margin. When that target icon appears, you can press and hold the touchscreen to see a wee li'l magnification window. Use that window to help you position the cursor.

The magnification trick comes in especially handy when editing text. See Chapter 4 for additional information.

Sadly, this trick isn't available on the original Droid X phone.

Use the Keyboard Suggestions

Don't forget to take advantage of the suggestions that appear above the multitouch keyboard when you're typing text. In fact, you don't even need to touch a suggestion; to replace your text with the highlighted suggestion, simply touch the onscreen keyboard's space key. Zap! The word appears.

- The setting that directs the keyboard to make suggestions work is Show Suggestions. To ensure that the setting is active, open the Settings app and choose Language & Keyboard and then Multi-Touch Keyboard.
- Refer to Figure 4-5 (from Chapter 4) to see how the onscreen keyboard suggestions work.

Things That Consume Lots of Battery Juice

Three items on the Droid X2 suck down battery power faster than a teenage wannabe-vampire consumes Clamato juice:

- Wi-Fi networking
- Bluetooth
- Navigation

Both Wi-Fi networking and Bluetooth require extra power for their wireless networking. When you need that speed or connectivity, they're great! I try to plug my phone into a power source when I'm accessing Wi-Fi or using Bluetooth. Otherwise, I disconnect from those networks as soon as I'm done, to save power.

Navigation is certainly handy, but because the phone's touchscreen is on the entire time and dictating text to you, the battery drains rapidly. If possible, try to plug the phone into the car's power socket when you're navigating. If you can't, keep an eye on the battery meter.

See Chapter 23 for more information on managing the Droid X2 battery.

Check for Roaming

Roaming can be expensive. The last non-smartphone (dumbphone?) I owned racked up $180 in roaming charges the month before I switched to a better cellular plan. Even though you too may have a good cell plan, keep an eye on the phone's status bar. Ensure that when you're making a call, you don't see the Roaming icon on the status bar atop the touchscreen.

Well, yes, it's okay to make a call when you're roaming. My advice is to remember to *check* for the icon, not to avoid it. If possible, try to make your phone calls when you're back in your cellular service's coverage area. If you can't, make the phone call but keep in mind that you will be charged roaming fees. They ain't cheap.

Use + When Dialing Internationally

I suppose most folks are careful when dialing an international number. On the Droid X2, you can use the + key to replace the country's exit code. In the United States, that code is `011`. So, whenever you see an international number listed as `011-xxx-xxxxxxx`, you can instead dial `+xxx-xxxxxx`, where the `x` characters represent the number to dial.

See Chapter 21 for more information on international dialing.

Properly Access Phone Storage

To access the Droid X2 storage area using your computer, you must properly mount the phone's storage for use by the computer. For the Droid X2, you mount both the phone's internal storage as well as the microSD card; for the original Droid X, only the microSD card is mounted.

After the storage is mounted, you can use your computer to access files — music, videos, still pictures, contacts, and other types of information — stored on your phone.

When the phone's storage is mounted on a computer storage system, you cannot access phone's storage by using the phone. If you try, you see a message explaining that the storage is busy.

When you're done accessing the phone's storage from your computer, be sure to stop USB storage: Pull down the USB notification and choose Charge Only. Touch the OK button. (See Chapter 20 for more details.)

Do not simply unplug the phone from the USB cable when the computer is accessing the phone's storage. If you do, you can damage the phone's storage and lose all information stored there.

Snap a Pic of That Contact

Here's something I always forget: Whenever you're near one of your contacts, take the person's picture. Sure, some people are bashful, but most folks are flattered. The idea is to build up your Contacts list so that all contacts have photos. That makes receiving a call much more interesting, especially when you see a silly or embarrassing picture of the caller.

When taking the picture, be sure to show it to the person before you assign it to the contact. Let them decide whether it's good enough. Or, if you just want to be rude, assign a crummy looking picture. Heck, you don't even have to do that: Just take a random picture of anything and assign it to a contact. But, seriously, keep in mind that the phone can take a contact's picture the next time you meet up with that person.

See Chapter 14 for more information on using the Droid X2 camera and assigning a picture to a contact.

The Search Command

Google is known worldwide for its searching capabilities. By gum, the word *Google* is now synonymous for searching. So, please don't forget that the Droid X2, which uses the Google Android operating system, has a powerful Search command.

The search command is not only powerful but also available all over. The Search soft button can be pressed at any time, in just about any program, to search for information, locations, people — you name it. It's handy. It's everywhere. Use it.

26

Ten Worthy Apps

In This Chapter

- AK Notepad
- CardStar
- Dolphin Browser
- Gesture Search
- Google Finance
- Google Sky Map
- Movies
- SportsTap
- Voice Recorder
- Zedge

Welcome to the most controversial chapter of this book! It's an almost impossible task to narrow the list of more than 150,000 Android apps for the Droid X2 into the 10 most worthy. I know for certain that I haven't tried all the apps. Still, I feel I should pass along some suggestions and ideas for what I've found to be my favorites. The only restriction I had in my decision-making process is that these apps be free. You can find them at the Android Market. See Chapter 18.

AK Notepad

One program that the Droid X2 is missing out of the box is a notepad. A good choice for an app to fill that void is AK Notepad: You can type or dictate short messages and memos, which I find handy.

Get thee a barcode scanner app

Many apps from the Android Market can be quickly accessed by scanning their barcode information. Scanning with what? Why, your Droid X2, of course!

By using a barcode scanner app, you can instantly read in and translate barcodes to product descriptions, web page links, or links directly to apps in the Android Market.

Plenty of barcode apps are out there; I use one called Barcode Scanner. It's pretty easy. Run the app. Point the phone's camera at a barcode and, in a few moments, you see a link or an option for what to do next. For getting an app, choose the Open Browser option, which opens the Android Market on your phone.

You can use the Barcode Scanner app to take advantage of the various QR code icons that appear in this chapter, as well as throughout this book. To install an app, choose the option Open Browser.

For example, before a recent visit to the hardware store, I made (dictated) a list of what I needed by using AK Notepad. I also keep some important items as notes, things that I often forget or don't care to remember, such as frequent flyer numbers, my dress shirt and suit size (like I ever need that info), and other important notes I might need handy but not cluttering my brain.

Perhaps the most important note you can make is one containing your contact information. A note labeled *In Case You Find This Phone* on my Droid X2 contains information about me in case I ever lose my phone and someone is decent enough to search it for my information. (Also see Chapter 24 for information on finding lost phones.)

CardStar

CardStar is a handy app that answers the question, "Why do I have all these store rewards cards?" They're not credit cards; they're marketing cards designed for customer loyalty programs. Rather than tote those cards around in your wallet or on your keychain, you can scan a card's barcode using your Droid X2 and save the "card" on the phone.

After you've stored your loyalty cards in the Droid X2, you simply run the CardStar app to summon the appropriate merchant. Show the checkout person your phone or scan the barcode yourself. CardStar makes it easy.

Dolphin Browser

Although I don't mind the Browser app that comes with the Droid X2, it's universally despised by many Android phone owners. A better and more popular alternative is Dolphin Browser.

Like many popular computer browsers, Dolphin Browser features a tabbed interface, which works much better than the silly multiple window interface of the standard Browser app on the Droid X2.

The Dolphin Browser also sports many handy tools, which you can access by pressing the Menu soft button. Unlike other Android apps, the tools pop up on a menu you can see on the screen.

Gesture Search

The Gesture Search app provides a new way to find information on your Droid X2. Rather than use a keyboard or dictate, you simply draw on the touchscreen the first letter of whatever you're searching for.

Start the Google Search app to begin a search. Use your finger to draw a big letter on the screen. After you draw a letter, search results appear on the screen. You can continue drawing more letters to refine the search or touch a search result.

Gesture Search can find contacts, music, apps, and bookmarks in the Broswer app.

Google Finance

The Google Finance app is an excellent market-tracking tool for folks who are obsessed with the stock market or want to keep an eye on their portfolios. The app offers you an overview of the market and updates to your stocks, as well as links to financial news.

To get the most from this app, configure Google Finance on the web, using your computer. You can create lists of stocks to watch, which are then instantly synchronized with your Droid X2. You can visit Google Finance on the web at `www.google.com/finance`.

As with other Google services, Google Finance is provided to you for free, as part of your Google account.

Google Sky Map

Ever look up into the sky and say, "What the heck is that?" Unless it's a bird, an airplane, a satellite, a UFO, or a superhero, the Google Sky Map will help you find what it is. You may learn that a particularly bright star in the sky is, in fact, the planet Jupiter.

The Google Sky Map app is elegant. It basically turns the Droid X2 into a window you can look through to identify things in the night sky. Just start the app and hold the phone up to the sky. Pan the phone to identify planets, stars, and constellations.

Google Sky Map promotes using the Droid X2 without touching the screen. For this reason, the screen goes blank after a spell, which is merely the phone's power-saving mode. If you plan extensive stargazing with the Google Sky Map, consider resetting the screen timeout. Refer to Chapter 2 for details.

Movies

The Movies app is the Droid X2 gateway to Hollywood. It lists currently running films and films that are opening, and it has links to your local theaters with showtimes and other information. It's also tied into the popular Rotten Tomatoes web site for reviews and feedback. If you enjoy going to the movies, you'll find the Movies app a valuable addition to your Droid X2.

SportsTap

I admit to not being a sports nut, so it's difficult for me to identify with the craving to have the latest scores, news, and schedules. The sports nuts in my life, however, tell me that the very best app for that purpose is a handy thing named SportsTap.

Rather than blather on about something I'm not into, just take my advice and obtain SportsTap. I believe you'll be thrilled.

Voice Recorder

The Droid X2 can record your voice or other sounds, and the Voice Recorder is a good app for performing that task. It has an elegant and simple interface: Touch the big Record button to start recording. Make a note for yourself or record a friend doing his Daffy Duck impression.

Previous recordings are stored in a list on the Voice Recorder's main screen. Each recording is shown with its title, the date and time of the recording, and the recording duration.

Zedge

The Zedge app is a helpful resource for finding wallpapers and ringtones for the Droid X2. It's a sharing app, so you can access wallpapers and ringtones created by other Android phone users as well as share your own.

Zedge features an easy-to-use interface, plus lots of helpful information on what it does and how it works.

Index

• A •

• B •

• C •

• E •

• F •

• M •

• S •

• U •

• V •

• W •

• Z •

Notes

Notes

Notes

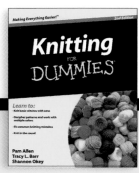

Internet

Blogging For Dummies, 3rd Edition
978-0-470-61996-4

eBay For Dummies, 6th Edition
978-0-470-49741-8

Facebook For Dummies, 3rd Edition
978-0-470-87804-0

Web Marketing For Dummies, 2nd Edition
978-0-470-37181-7

WordPress For Dummies, 3rd Edition
978-0-470-59274-8

Language & Foreign Language

French For Dummies
978-0-7645-5193-2

Italian Phrases For Dummies
978-0-7645-7203-6

Spanish For Dummies, 2nd Edition
978-0-470-87855-2

Spanish For Dummies, Audio Set
978-0-470-09585-0

Math & Science

Algebra I For Dummies, 2nd Edition
978-0-470-55964-2

Biology For Dummies, 2nd Edition
978-0-470-59875-7

Calculus For Dummies
978-0-7645-2498-1

Chemistry For Dummies
978-0-7645-5430-8

Microsoft Office

Excel 2010 For Dummies
978-0-470-48953-6

Office 2010 All-in-One For Dummies
978-0-470-49748-7

Office 2010 For Dummies, Book + DVD Bundle
978-0-470-62698-6

Word 2010 For Dummies
978-0-470-48772-3

Music

Guitar For Dummies, 2nd Edition
978-0-7645-9904-0

iPod & iTunes For Dummies, 8th Edition
978-0-470-87871-2

Piano Exercises For Dummies
978-0-470-38765-8

Parenting & Education

Parenting For Dummies, 2nd Edition
978-0-7645-5418-6

Type 1 Diabetes For Dummies
978-0-470-17811-9

Pets

Cats For Dummies, 2nd Edition
978-0-7645-5275-5

Dog Training For Dummies, 3rd Edition
978-0-470-60029-0

Puppies For Dummies, 2nd Edition
978-0-470-03717-1

Religion & Inspiration

The Bible For Dummies
978-0-7645-5296-0

Catholicism For Dummies
978-0-7645-5391-2

Women in the Bible For Dummies
978-0-7645-8475-6

Self-Help & Relationship

Anger Management For Dummies
978-0-470-03715-7

Overcoming Anxiety For Dummies, 2nd Edition
978-0-470-57441-6

Sports

Baseball For Dummies, 3rd Edition
978-0-7645-7537-2

Basketball For Dummies, 2nd Edition
978-0-7645-5248-9

Golf For Dummies, 3rd Edition
978-0-471-76871-5

Web Development

Web Design All-in-One For Dummies
978-0-470-41796-6

Web Sites Do-It-Yourself For Dummies, 2nd Edition
978-0-470-56520-9

Windows 7

Windows 7 For Dummies
978-0-470-49743-2

Windows 7 For Dummies, Book + DVD Bundle
978-0-470-52398-8

Windows 7 All-in-One For Dummies
978-0-470-48763-1

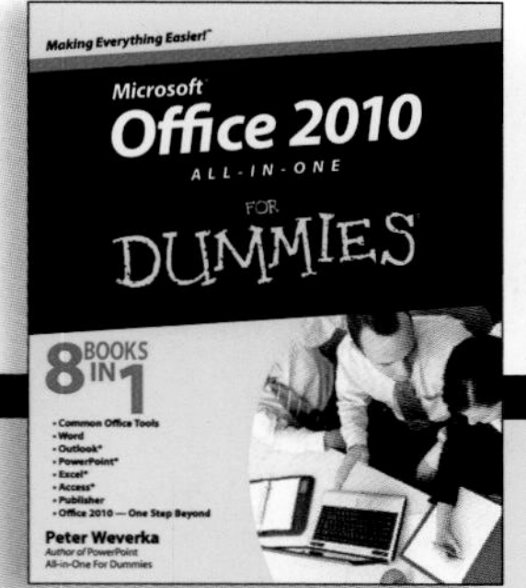

Available wherever books are sold. For more information or to order direct: U.S. customers visit www.dummies.com or call 1-877-762-2974. U.K. customers visit www.wileyeurope.com or call (0) 1243 843291. Canadian customers visit www.wiley.ca or call 1-800-567-4797.